Global Networks

Global
NETWORKS

The Vodafone–Ericsson Journey to Globalization and the Inception of a Requisite Organization

Christopher J. Ibbott

First published in 2007 by
PALGRAVE MACMILLAN
Houndmills, Basingstoke, Hampshire RG21 6XS and
175 Fifth Avenue, New York, N.Y. 10010
Companies and representatives throughout the world.

PALGRAVE MACMILLAN is the global academic imprint of the Palgrave
Macmillan division of St. Martin's Press, LLC and of Palgrave Macmillan Ltd.
Macmillan® is a registered trademark in the United States, United Kingdom
and other countries. Palgrave is a registered trademark in the European
Union and other countries.

ISBN-13: 978–0–230–55117–6
ISBN-10: 0–230–55117–3

This book is printed on paper suitable for recycling and made from fully
managed and sustained forest sources. Logging, pulping and manufacturing
processes are expected to conform to the environmental regulations of
the country of origin.

A catalogue record for this book is available from the British Library.

A catalog record for this book is available from the Library of Congress.

10 9 8 7 6 5 4 3 2 1
16 15 14 13 12 11 10 09 08 07

Printed and bound in China

To my wife Trudie and daughters Lucy and Katie

Contents

List of Figures

Abbreviations

Allocentric	means one's interest and attention centered on other persons (Webster's Third New International Dictionary), the importance of focusing on others being the insight of game theory
AMPS	Advanced Mobile Phone System, the US analogue standard specification developed by Bell Labs [AT&T]
ARPU	Average Revenue Per User
BSC	Base Station Controller
BT	British Telecom
CFO	chief financial officer
CMO	chief marketing officer
CTO	chief technology officer
eAuctions	reverse (web-based) electronic auctions
ECB	English Cricket Board
Emptoris	refers to the company Emptoris, Inc. of 200 Wheeler Road, Burlington, MA 01803, USA
ERA	Ericsson Radio Systems AB
F1	Formula One
FCC	Federal Communications Commission
GA	Global Agreement
G-NW	Global Network Technology
G-NW-SCM	Global Network Supply Chain Management
GPA	Global Purchasing Agreement
GPB	Global Price Book
GPRS	General Packet Radio Service
GRM	global review meeting
GSCM	global supply chain management
GSM	Global System for Mobile Service, digital
GT&Cs	Global Terms and Conditions
HQ	headquarters
HR	human resources
HSPA	high-speed packet access
ICT	Information and Communications Technologies
INTP	Integrated Network and Technology Plan
ION	interorganizational network
IOS	interorganizational system
IS	information system

ITTM Council	IT and Technology Management Council
KPI	Key Performance Indicator
Lead OpCos	Lead Operating Companies
LEOS	Low Earth Orbiting Satellite
LOI	Letter Of Intent
MHz	megahertz
MSC	Mobile Switching Center
NMT	Nordic Mobile Telephone network, the standard developed by the Nordic Telecom Administration
OpCos	operating companies
RAN	Radio Access Network
RFI	Request for Information
RFQ	Request for Quotation
SCM Council	Supply Chain Management Council
SRA	Svenska Radio Aktiebolaget
TACS	Total Access Communication System, the British analogue mobile telephone standard, based on the US AMPS system
Terminals	telecom industry language for mobile devices or phones
TOA	transnational organizational architectures
UMTS (3G)	Universal Mobile Telecommunications System
UTRAN	UMTS Terrestrial Radio Access Network
VO	virtual organization
WAP	Wireless Access Protocol

Acknowledgements

I would like to acknowledge and thank Vodafone Group Plc for their sponsorship and support of my continued pursuits in learning and development. The unique experiential learning experience of a formative transformational business on its intra- and interorganizational journey to globalization presented herein is an outcome of such learning and development, and is now presented as a learning contribution for others in business practice and academia. A special thanks to those many former colleagues and those friends from the Vodafone world with whom my team and I had the privilege to interact for about eight years. Without their personal involvement, goodwill, innovation, and their collective commitment to success, the positive globalizing economic synergy outcomes for Vodafone and its mobile network infrastructure supplier partners would not have been possible.

A special note of thanks too to Telefonaktiebolaget LM Ericsson, their management, and all those whose foresight and complementary contributions added formative value to this unique and telecom-industry-led globalization project; many of them also remain personal friends today.

With the early formative learning of the Vodafone–Ericsson globalization experience, the ensuing development similarly engaged many additional committed contributors in each of the companies, namely, Nokia, Nortel, and Siemens, as they were then known. Owing to industry consolidation we now have the formation of Nokia Siemens Networks, and the UMTS business of Nortel becoming a part of Alcatel Lucent.

Professor Bob O'Keefe, Head of the School of Management at the University of Surrey in the United Kingdom, has spent many hours guiding me with the content and creating a rational structure through which to communicate the experience and the ensuing messages for learning. Bob was the first supervisor for my original doctoral research and remains a valued friend.

Finally, to my family, my wife Trudie and our daughters Lucy and Katie, a special note of thanks for their support and tolerance of my continued pursuits in learning and excellence.

1 Introduction

Globalization

In the 1990s a business could find itself transacting with multiple local entities within a national or international organization, and all on different terms. Thus, doing business with, say, a global manufacturer of paper across ten nations might mean doing business with ten separate business units. Intra-unit communication and transparency were not encouraged. Today, business consolidation, the transparency of the Internet, and competitive market pressure make such business practice less possible, if not impossible, for businesses that transcend national boundaries. The pursuit of so-called globalization abounds, not just in global brands and cross-border transactions but also in business practices and the supply chain.

The questions then arise, What actually is "globalization"? When is a firm truly global? Suppliers of products talk as if they are global, yet often act internationally. An international business is one that has either a direct or indirect presence in multiple geographies and operates in the image of its home market; this situation can be very prevalent in American and German companies, for example. A global company is one that permits its local operations to act in the image of the market locally, and yet can act in a truly homogeneous way with respect to the supply and/or provision of its core products and services. Many companies claiming to be global are in fact international, with operations located in several countries but the seat of control and the definition of the corporate culture entirely in the "head office."

Microsoft and Apple, for example, are not global by this definition. No airline company, as an extreme example, is. They are all international. Vodafone, however, is global: its sourcing and supply-chain activities were transformed to be entirely global for the major part of its investments, while services remain local.

This book provides an insight into a substantive globalization experience that offers an empirically based alternative organizational model for the transformation to global. Initially, this book centers on the strategy to globalize the business relationship between two otherwise international organizations in the mobile telecommunications sector, namely, Vodafone and Ericsson, whose business links were seated in multiple in-country arrangements. The trigger for this relationship was the Vodafone requirement to remove costs in the acquisition and deployment of mobile network infrastructure across its national equity interests and to therefore demonstrate aggregation synergies arising in anticipation and as a consequence of a merger (AirTouch Communications, Inc., of California) and later an acquisition (Mannesmann AG of Germany).

We will subsequently consider how Vodafone further enhanced this outcome to similarly globalize its interorganizational business relationships with Nokia, Nortel, and Siemens. The final phase in this book discusses the Vodafone move from the informal and center-led approach that delivered substantial aggregation cost benefits to Vodafone, to the center-controlled organization under the initiative of One Vodafone that was implemented in April 2005.

This book, however, is not just a story and not simply a single organizational model. The experience presented leads to some strong messages that are articulated at the end of this chapter and further developed in later chapters. The story and the messages are concerned with these aspects of organization:

▶ Globalization: what it is and what it can mean
▶ Transformation: how we get to globalization
▶ Horizontal and vertical relationships: how we organize and integrate within and across organizations
▶ Virtual global organizing
▶ Strategic organization relationships
▶ Global leadership

The intention is to display an example of what Jaques calls the requisite organization: "doing business with efficiency and competitiveness and the release of human imagination, trust and satisfaction in work."[1] (page pair 2)

Globalization and Organization

Global boundaries between companies, markets, and people have become irrevocably blurred.[2] A multinational structure is one that creates a federation of national entities stemming from a single parent. A global organization is one in which the world is treated as an integrated whole organized around a strong headquarters that focuses on scale. A transnational organization is neither centralized nor decentralized but contains aspects of each strategy (global/international).[3]

In a transnational structure, the parent organization may centralize certain core processes and/or activities. Henry Wendt, when CEO of SmithKline Beecham, described the differences between transnational and multinational organizations:

> The difference in outlook between transnationals and multinationals is the difference between a globe and a map. The surface of a globe has neither a beginning nor an end, neither a centre nor a periphery; it is a continued integrated whole. A map has a definite centre, peripheral places, and remote corners; it is a discontinuous, hierarchical fragment. And for the traditional multinational, the home market and the headquarters

*stand at the centre of the map and send out expectations to progressively less
important provinces. In sum, the transnational corporations view the world as one vast,
essentially seamless market in which all decisions are grounded solely in the desire to
gain a global competitive advantage.*[4] (pp. 275–276)

The evolving boundaryless solution, founded in the transnational format, might best be described as *glocal*, because it aims to merge a global strategy with respect for local presence.[5] The glocal company utilizes local control but also calls for central integration and economies of scale. For in-country, services-based business on a global scale, the role of the center function should include the lead in setting a vision and establishing and espousing a strategy and governance structure that are consistent both globally and locally. The in-country role of a services business, such as a mobile phone network operator, is compliant execution of the vision and strategy to the optimum benefit of the business interests in the given local market conditions. What is referred to as global in this book owes much to the concept of glocal.

According to Daft, a transnational model can perhaps be viewed as the learning organization extended to the international arena, where a large multinational company with subsidiaries (and/or equity interests) exploits both global and local advantages and represents the most current thinking about the kind of structure needed by complex global organizations.[6] In achieving coordination, a sense of participation and involvement by subsidiaries and a sharing of information, new technologies, and customers require a multidimensional form of structure, thereby making the transnational model more than just an organizational model, but a state of mind, a set of values, and a shared desire to make a worldwide learning system work. Daft goes on to suggest that "each part of the (transnational) organisation can serve as an independent catalyst, bringing together unique elements with synergistic potential, perhaps other firms (for example, suppliers) or subsidiaries (and/or affiliates) from different countries to improve performance" (p. 501).

Transformation

Intra- and interorganizational transformation necessarily must comprise at least a vision (where), a strategy (what), and a how. This book demonstrates that when the people are involved whose status quo is potentially at variance with the individual or departmental roles of the future, then positive, sustainable outcomes prevail. Further, the scope of what is intended in the new definition of the organizational role of their team may go beyond the current boundaries and into unfamiliar territory. The "organization" discussed in this book was an informal and nonvisible, global, virtual social network that had no organization chart or budget presence, yet it seriously contributed to Vodafone's economic position through aggregation cost synergies.

The transformational approach taken in this book is based upon the "process-oriented" journey metaphor[7]—a metaphor, or to quote Morgan,[8] "a way of thinking and a way of seeing."(Grant and Oswick, 1996, p. 1)[9] As an example, the European and Trukese journey approaches are contrasted.[10] The European approach begins with a plan and tries throughout the "voyage" to remain "on course." Dealing with the unexpected requires first an alteration to the plan and then an appropriate response. Reference is made to Lewin's three-stage change model of "unfreezing," "change," and "refreezing."[11] Bevan's thesis makes reference to the interpretation by Inns (1996) of this characterization as a "destination-oriented" journey, this process being viewed as a "rational, structured and linear journey" (p. 24)[12]

On the other hand, the Trukese begin with an objective rather than a plan, set off toward the objective, and respond to conditions in an ad hoc fashion. In utilizing information provided by the wind, the waves, the tide, and so on, they steer accordingly with all effort directed toward whatever is necessary to reach the objective. Bevan expands on the work of Inns by stating that the "process-oriented" journey is essentially an explorative process where clear outcomes are not known in advance and change is cyclical, with no arrival or final "homecoming," namely:

> Change is not as programmable and predictable as Lewin-type models imply, since repercussions on different parts cannot always be accurately forecast. The development of the journey metaphor in relation to organisational change from a destination-oriented model allows important, but previously hidden elements of the journey to come to the fore: uncertainty, circularity, exploration, and unpredictability. (p. 55)

The emergent aspect of the planned approach to the management of change includes processual and contextual perspectives that share the view that change cannot and should not be "frozen," nor should it be viewed as a linear sequence of events within a linear time period. Instead, it should be viewed as a continuous process[13]—which is consistent with the views of Inns. Macredie and Sandom indicate that different supporters of this perspective view change as a continuous process aimed at aligning an organization with its environment and is best achieved through many small-scale incremental changes that, over time, can amount to a major organizational transformation.[14]

Horizontal and Virtual Organizational Relationships

With increasingly large global customers, global competitors, and the need to control costs, an organizational structure containing a small set of independent affiliate companies will no longer do the job.[15] Today's organizational structures demand intensive communication, and without information technology it is highly doubtful that many of these organizational changes under way could exist. The exact forms that organizational structures will eventually take remains uncertain, but they will be more interdependent both internally and externally and will be coordination intensive and, therefore, more information technology (or systems) intensive.

Galbraith commented that along with the lateral (or horizontal) organization, the vertical hierarchical organization also requires some discussion.[16] He asserts that the cross-functional capability when fully implemented is a lateral organizational capability, in which the different functions are coordinated, but without communicating through the vertical hierarchy. The lateral organization is a mechanism for decentralizing general management decisions and creates an ability to be multidimensional and flexible. There are three types of lateral organization: across functions, across business units, and coordination across countries referenced, with no reference made to interorganizational aspects in the global context. Galbraith also discusses three basic types of relationships in such organizations: informal and voluntary, formal groups, and integrators. All three levels are relevant in this book.

Individuals must share information or expertise that was once a major source of power, accept responsibility for issues over which they have only limited control, and propose initiatives and action in an environment in which measures and metrics are unclear or in transition.[17] Shared confidence (and trust) among those who work across organizational boundaries frame the environment for interunit support.

Separate functional companies in a network are coordinated through mutual interests or by a focal company, which plays the role of network integrator.[18] Network integrators create governed networks rather than loosely coupled, informal networks. First, the integrator usually performs the dominant function in the value-added chain of the business and buys key items for the network. Second, in general the integrator builds a power base but works in the mutual interest of the network, having built trust and relationships among the members.

According to Burn and Barnett, virtual organizations are electronically networked and transcend conventional organizational boundaries by using linkages that may exist within and between organizations.[19] A virtual organization culture consists of those members of a (virtual) community that have common shared values and beliefs.[20] Organizational cultures that are accepting of technology, highly decentralized, and change oriented are more likely to embrace virtuality and proactively seek these opportunities within and without the organization.[21] Burn and Barnett conclude that a virtual culture is a perception of the entire virtual organization held by its stakeholder community and operationalized in choices and actions that result in a feeling of *globalness* with respect to value sharing and time-space arrangement. They also conclude that the virtual organization is recognized as a dynamic system and hence one wherein traditional hierarchical forms of management control may not apply, about which little has been written.[22]

Since it is a relatively new idea, virtual organization lacks a universally accepted definition.[23] Mowshowitz sketches a theory of virtual organization expressed as a set of principles for meta-managing goal-oriented activity based on a categorical split between task requirements and their satisfiers. In this formulation the essence of virtual organization is the systematic ability to switch satisfiers in a decision environment of bounded rationality. Collaboration is implicit in the practice of meta-management, or the management of management.[24] In a case study, Faucheux finds that this collaboration may be considered supportive of the global (interorganizational and intercompany) virtual team concept formed within and between the customer and supplier organizations. Mowshowitz, however, does not state whether his concepts are interorganizational, only that a virtual team is an instance of a social organization, which designates an abstract requirement for a group of individuals that collectively possess certain skills.

Faucheux says that the dynamics of virtual organizing are closely tied to self-organizing, in making sense of one's action through elucidation of the experience of the actors themselves—who are best situated for doing so. The very logic of virtual organizing drives toward the longer term and toward more responsible relations with the environment. Further, virtual organizing detaches the core of the enterprise (or enterprises, in this case) from its concrete operations, conceiving it now in more abstract terms in dealing with a wide range of possible appropriate responses the firm might take to business (or interorganizational) opportunities in the global economy. The collaborative dimension of human activity emphasizes the necessarily collective cooperative nature of human activity and is therefore characteristic of a community of individuals communicating with one another through critical dialogue. Concluding, Faucheux makes the following points relevant to the Vodafone-Ericsson situation and the horizontal or meta-relationships that arose through the global and virtual community or variant social networks:

▶ Actions become more public and transparent, contributing to a deflation of power games, or covert manipulations, in favor of more worthwhile mutual influences like recognition and trust.
▶ Actors are induced to make more use of dialogue-based and dialectic models of thinking, since critical reflection requires a collective, collaborative effort for avoiding personal biases.
▶ Actors achieve a better appreciation of the broader contexts—social, cultural, biological, and cosmic—in which their lives are embedded. They therefore respond to real needs rather than egocentric fantasies.
▶ Actors make progress in recognizing their creative nature, letting it express itself more spontaneously in behavior sufficiently balanced by self-reflection.

Vodafone in the Wireless Telecommunication Industry

In advance of the Vodafone merger with AirTouch, the notion of cross-entities or equity holdings acting in a homogeneous way globally was not current practice in the telecom industry, be it brand, supply chain, or, indeed, organization. Even within the Vodafone Group at that time, although there was to some degree a coordinated approach to its major network infrastructure suppliers, each national entity nevertheless had its own contract and therefore commercial and local relationship. There was no notion of a global brand, and organizationally the various properties were managed on an arms-length basis through the participation of Vodafone executives on the local operating company board of directors.

In the early days, new investment companies, for example, in Holland, Greece, and Australia, were supported by specialist expatriate employees dispatched from Vodafone in the UK; it follows that all such operations were therefore in the image of the UK operation even though Vodafone had less than a 100% equity holding. The operations were, however, carried out in the interests of services to the local markets, all of which were in the early stages of development.

The joint impact of the merger of Vodafone and AirTouch was a combined geographic footprint that made the consideration of economic cost synergies, hitherto not taken into account, an attractive proposition and certainly material to the attributed value of the combined enterprises. The principal synergy considered at that time was the potential associated with the acquisition of the mobile network infrastructure; although no public targets were announced, internal targets were established. Later, with the Mannesmann AG acquisition by Vodafone, publicly declared cost synergy benefits were announced.

In 1998 we at Vodafone resolved mutually with Ericsson that "globalization" was the path to joint success. The intent was absent of definition, save the economic aggregation synergy ambitions of the Vodafone side and the expressed willingness of Ericsson to pledge its support for the endeavor, and certainly no organization preexisted through which the task could be undertaken. I, then a director in the Vodafone UK mobile network operator, was assigned the task by the executive to explore and develop the realization of the cost synergy ambitions of Vodafone (interestingly, in addition to rather instead of normal duties, which at that time included IT, procurement moving to supply-chain management, and project management). This experiential journey engages the period through to October 2005, when the author retired from Vodafone to establish himself in private practice. In this context "experiential" may take on a double meaning; namely, a derivative of prior and developed experience and/or the willingness to experiment and to act on one's judgment and intuition (or indeed counterintuition) conditioned by the results achieved in the context of the vision and strategy.

The initial countries that were party to this interorganizational collaborative endeavor in addition to the two center-functional leaders and their teams were the UK, the Netherlands, Greece, and Australia/Fiji. Ericsson was the mobile network infrastructure supplier to each of these companies or equity interests; at that time Vodafone held a 100% equity position only in the UK company, and Ericsson owned 100% of each of its in-country operations involved.

The inaugural meeting of the participating parties in this collaborative endeavor was held in the UK on February 25–26, 1999. The vision and strategy were outlined to the team, with some initial nervous anticipation on the part of some. However, there was a mutuality of readiness to engage in this new industry-leading endeavor; this was to be the formative virtual team.

Agreed actions from that meeting were the initiation of a number of virtual workstreams. These were tasks or initiatives assigned jointly to the Vodafone-Ericsson in-country teams on behalf of the participating companies of both organizations.

The obligation of these teams was to assure the collective interests of all parties and to engage such other resources from either organization as and when required. All countries took away such assignments, interestingly with no discussion about budgets and no question of the authority of the meeting or forum in which they were participating. At this stage the virtual workstreams were focused principally in the areas of creating improvements in the supply chain between the two globally dispersed organizations; however, one virtual workstream focused on creating an interorganizational system (IOS) that was subsequently operationalized by Ericsson under the guidance of a virtual workstream leadership; again, with no budget discussion.

My de facto role as leader (not announced internally) was not questioned in either organization. This role involved the creation of a new and formative social network that was to later expand (the merger with AirTouch and acquisition of Mannesmann AG). From this network a number of cross-cultural personal friendships developed, some of which, at least for the author, have survived to the present day. In summary, the nexus of a global virtual community had been founded; there was no formal recognition of this community, yet it existed; no budget was discussed in Vodafone save within the small (UK operator based) center team of the author, yet there were uniform engagement and active participation, virtual workstreams beneficial to the Vodafone interests and one assumes to those of Ericsson as they engaged, and emergent cost synergy benefits soon attributed to the Vodafone interests arising from their participation. The social network would eventually emerge to be the rich source of mutually beneficial social capital that often achieved results in the occasional face of adversity and performed repeatedly in the later governance structure for Vodafone. This founding catalyst expanded over time as the Vodafone-Ericsson community participation increased in the years to come.

The global reach of this initiative was to expand following the Vodafone merger and acquisition, which included at one stage thirteen operating company subsidiary and affiliate interests participating with Vodafone in the globalization endeavor with Ericsson. Such operating company engagement in this collaborative endeavor was voluntary. This voluntary aspect created a sustainability to and for the collective or operator cluster, with the focus being on making the joint endeavor work rather than, as is often the case, working on a local level in a contrary way to center-led (or center-controlled) initiatives; in this case what was global or collective is what the group directly or indirectly contributed to and/or participated in.

One of the most forthright collective achievements was the realization and continuing development of Global Terms and Conditions (GT&Cs) and Global Price Books (GPB) governing the interorganizational relationship, as they together formed in effect a "global constitution" following their adoption locally by each of the Vodafone operating interests. Preexisting local agreements with the supplier were extinguished save by exception and agreement of the team that certain local preexisting conditions should not be sacrificed. This, in effect, created a single but globally dispersed interface between Vodafone and Ericsson, variously embracing 60% and more of the Vodafone expenditure globally with Ericsson, leading to effective cost synergy yield for all parties through, for example, simplified administration and commercial relationship management; reduced diversity of sourced equipment and software configurations; convergence on the alignment of common testing once for the group, thereby leaving the local focus on the fulfillment of operational excellence and a positive customer service experience.

There was no preexisting or formal introduction to this globally dispersed virtual organization or community that had evolved in Vodafone, no budget, and no organization chart in which its existence was visible; yet it existed, functioned well, and throughout its existence yielded substantial aggregation cash synergies. I traveled frequently to meet the participating in-country management teams of the Vodafone organization to assure their understanding and positive engagement with this globalization initiative and to solicit their unqualified support. The same approach was taken by me with the executive management of the Ericsson team, notwithstanding the asymmetry of such a relationship.

Subsequently my initiative was in the same way embraced by others as the Vodafone and supplier community and activities expanded. The impact was to develop a social network inclusive of many key stakeholders. In all, this approach was extended to a community of up to twenty-three Vodafone operating company interests that collectively formed four multi-operator clusters towards the major mobile network infrastructure suppliers (Ericsson, Nokia, Nortel, and Siemens). Collectively, across eighteen operators in the Vodafone fiscal year 2005–2006 this network accounted for capital and operating expenditures totaling approximately €8 billion; certain operators participated in two or more of these supplier-based clusters.

Virtual Global Organization Models

For sustainable success and the positive engagement of the key stakeholders, I resolved that the center function would be an inclusive multicultural team for which candidate applications would be invited from the Vodafone operators. With the support of their management, the candidates were selected to join the center team on a temporary or secondment basis, normally for no longer than two years; this had the progressive benefit of developing an effective global knowledge transfer borne in this experience back to the in-country operations. A requirement for the candidates was that their management saw the assignment as a part of the candidate's personal development and career plan, thereby assuring the reentry path at the end of the period; the candidates also necessarily had to be highflyers and, arising from the selection process, accepted by the serving center team and the served Vodafone operator community prior to appointment.

A phenomenon emerged in this experiential journey, namely, that although the actual organization of the virtual community did not evidence itself on any chart, notwithstanding the financial aggregation synergy yields that certainly were visible, in effect what had been created was a nonhierarchical, global virtual and horizontal organization that spanned the vertical in-country operations over which it had a (controlling) meta-influence. More precisely, those in the virtual community were in fact acting outside their usual role in the normal hierarchy. The role of individuals in this virtual community was solely and only resolved by the individuals' capacity to produce or lead and the acceptance of the assignment by those over whom they were to have impact. This may sound very counterintuitive, but as one who experienced this journey, I can confirm what was achieved was vested in the actors engaged—a period of high and unbounded innovation wherein we were setting the course, not following those of others.

Lipnack and Stamps coined a term, "TeamNet," to describe networks of teams that cross conventional boundaries to improve horizontal organizational relationships while complementing or coexisting with the traditional prescriptions of vertical hierarchy;[25] they cross boundaries and have fewer bosses and more leaders. Brown quotes Mohrman and Porter, stating that managers need to be both effective vertical (organizational) strategists and horizontal (organizational) strategists (p. 421).[26] TeamNets combine two organizational ideas: teams (where small groups of people work with focus, motivation, and skill to achieve shared goals) and networks (where disparate groups of people and groups "link" to work together on a common purpose).

Analyzing a virtual organization (VO) on the strategic or operational level draws a relevant distinction.[27] The strategic level is concerned with the co-operation between all the partners of the VO, whereas the operational level is concerned with the way individual partners carry out their own business processes. In the initial context of this case, the partners make up two levels: first, the interorganizational level between the global organizations of Vodafone and Ericsson, and second, the level within and between the companies of those two global organizations. Bultje and van Wijk's research is focused on the strategic level, which is consistent with the domain in the Vodafone-Ericsson case. The author's experience, as with Bultje and van Wijk, was focused on the cooperation between different organizations, not specifically on the internal cooperation of one organization.

Bultje and van Wijk's extensive literature review discovered twenty-seven characteristics of VOs. To attempt to determine the relevance and priorities of the characteristics, they undertook six case studies on firms that differed on three points: being small versus large, Dutch versus international, and Information and Communications Technologies (ICT) based versus non-ICT based. All the twenty-seven characteristics were mapped on the six companies. Bultje and van Wijk conclude two working definitions derived from a shortened list of twelve characteristics.

The first working definition is that "A virtual organization is primarily characterised as being a network of independent, geographically dispersed organisations with partial mission overlap. Within the network, all partners provide their own core competencies and the co-operation is based upon semi-stable relations. The products and services provided by a Virtual Organisation are dependent on innovation and are strongly customer-based" (p. 16). The second is that "A virtual organisation is secondarily characterised by a single identity with loyalty being shared among the partners and the co-operation based on trust and information technology. In addition, there is also a clear distinction between a strategic and an operational level" (p. 16). They conclude that the characteristic present in a VO is determined from one of these typologies: internal VO, stable VO, dynamic VO, and Web company.

The best fit to the situation discussed in this book is a "Stable VO", defined as a VO based on the cooperation between different organizations that aims at contracting out noncore competencies by a "main" organization (often a core partner). These noncore competencies are contracted out to several committed suppliers, which are closely related to the main organization. The two different globally dispersed organizations are Vodafone and Ericsson; they jointly form the "main" organization for the realization of aggregation cost synergies. Actors from the in-country operating companies of both organizations with contributors from their center functions collectively, at the execution level, comprise the committed suppliers in this definition. An outcome of such a network is the ad hoc establishment of social networks within and between what was a geographically dispersed network of individuals (nodes) and within which were also formed virtual teams from both organizations. Social capital, on the other hand, focuses on those social networks that exist and the character of those networks, the strength of the ties, and the extent to which those networks foster trust and reciprocity.[28]

In the virtual organizational environment in which there exists interdependence between organizations, for the organization to be successful, trust at an organizational level must exist within a two-way, "no blame" culture. In interdependent organizations the synergy of knowledge may be the principal benefit of the interdependence. Unlike conventional teams, a virtual team works across space, time, and organizational boundaries (to include interorganizational) with links strengthened by webs of communication technologies.[29] The intuitive rationale for successful virtual teamwork is to involve the right people from the internal and external organizations, carefully define the purpose, and establish excellent communication links (a media mix, including e-mail, conference calls, and face-to-face meetings to support interactions and relationships). As important as positive relationships and high trust are in all teams, they are even more important in virtual teams; in the background research, people interviewed stressed the importance of face-to-face meetings to solidify virtual teams.

Lipnack and Stamps posit that it takes more than one leader to lead a successful virtual team; many authors assume without discussion that a team needs a single leader. Although ranking members of the team may be confusing, specialization abounds in virtual teams; one's area of expertise most often defines one's role in task-oriented virtual teams (discussed later in relation to the approach taken toward the organizational contribution). Also important is investing in face-to-face meetings for the start-up and launch phases (of the virtual team), reserving time for meetings to assess team progress, creating breakpoints where the team converges and realigns its work, and celebrating success. Lipnack and Stamps quote John Case and John Schuster, "Open-book management that advocates providing essential information to everyone in the organisation is one way to contribute trust to the environment" (p. 228) and James Coleman, "Social capital is the 'structure of relations between and among actors,' individual or organisation"(S98).[30]

Lipnack and Stamps claim that TeamNets are dynamically balanced between the decentralizing forces of independence and the integrating forces of cooperative interdependence; however, it is relationships that are essential to bind the team together. Also, in networks, leaders appear at the nexus of purpose and commitment, where responsibility is taken and shared work gets done. To be effective in an interorganizational and intercompany relationship transformation involves sometimes either accepting the leading global virtual team's initiatives or following the lead of others as a contributor or being an observer. Such relative roles may from time to time change by agreement. Additionally, one of the worst mistakes a TeamNet can make is to ignore existing boundary crossings (within and/or between organizations), hence the author's focus on the social network. TeamNets are multileveled forms of organization, this cross-level, and multiple-role feature of networks being one of its sources of power. In another context concerning research on communication patterns, De Meyer discusses the importance of the role of "boundary spanning" individuals, persons who have the capability of monitoring what is going on in the outside environment and translating the external information into messages comprehensible to the group to which they belong;[31] this is a likely attribute of the role of the author.

Strategic Interorganizational Relationships

Lipparini and Fratocchi note that there is an emergence of transnational organizational architectures (TOA) in which value-generating activities are distributed among different countries and actors, then recomposed at the corporate level without losing efficiency.[32] They also discuss the concept of a central actor, an actor of high relational intensity with interfirm architecture management (or boundary crossing) and leveraging functions; this would broadly equate to the role of the author in the Vodafone-Ericsson case. Although the context of this approach (a single organization) is at variance to the discussion in this book, the roles and competencies of the center of the organizational architecture are broadly valid; however, the case context in this book is both interorganizational and intercompany, including two global organizations (that of the supplier and customer) within which each has multiple companies geographically dispersed. The strategic roles proposed by Lipparini and Fratocchi are those of global scanner, relationship builder, competencies combiner, functional coordinator, system integrator, and strategic orchestrator. Finally, they point out that TOAs are characterized as metastructures that embrace the external relationship fabric; TOAs have organizational and geographic boundaries, which can rapidly be redefined, as can focal points and centers or perhaps intergenerational virtual team clusters of excellence, as in the emergent social network in this case.

According to Lewis, within transaction relationships information sharing is limited, whereas in an (interorganizational) alliance one cannot define every detail; the most important dependency is trust (and the open sharing of information).[33] Lewis comments further that in an alliance mutual trust means that you can depend on each other to adapt as necessary, as it may entail changes within which clear outcomes are not known and therefore cannot be planned in advance, somewhat consistent with the "process-oriented" journey metaphor.[34] It is important to recognize that alliances live through people, and when top executives work together, the subordinate teams know that it is safe to cross boundaries; that is, only with joint leadership can you expect joint fellowship. Lewis also suggests that consistent (meaning the same) joint leadership at policy and operating levels from early negotiation through implementation is required for interorganizational alliance success. As will be shown in our case, however, although the substance of what is espoused holds true, the suggested formalities of boundary crossing were not in evidence, as such activities were bound in social networks and the ensuing social capital therein.

The literature does not explore how individual-level knowledge affects the formation and management of an interorganizational relationship or how the individual-level efforts shape the structure of an alliance, even though they play a critical role in the formation process.[35] In the Vodafone-Ericsson and the later case discussions, however, this is particularly relevant given the author's leading role in the transformation of both the interorganizational and intercompany relationships. It is relevant as well for the other actors representing either a global organization or any of the involved companies in the globalization initiative.

Larsen notes that a very important concept in the area of interorganizational cooperation is the "network." Given the sometimes contradictory use of the term in the literature, the term "global social network" (consists of an almost infinite number of connections between actors or nodes or various interdependent, independent or linked clusters, many of which have a purpose) is used to denote the underlying social relationships, wherein each person is seen as a node connected to a number of other nodes.[36] Superimposed on the global social network are a number of purposeful arrangements whereby organizations or the individuals in them cooperate across organizational boundaries. Larsen states further that when interorganizational arrangements are created, new relationships appear between existing nodes in different organizations. Researchers have analyzed various forms of interorganizational arrangements with respect to temporal rigidity (how long a set of organizations is likely to maintain the relationship) and hierarchy (power vested principally in one organization is regarded as centralized in contrast to distributed or decentralized power sharing). Although the objective was to create a framework to help researchers in the virtual organization field, there is not a category as defined that fits the contexts espoused in this book, which in the terms of the analysis is between a virtual organization (distributed power, short term) and a satellite organization (distributed power, long term).

One motivation for the use of interorganizational networks is to strengthen existing commercial relationships and lock in partners by increasing the costs of switching to new trading partners.[37] In this case the prohibitive costs of switching the supply partner is borne in the complexity and limited interoperability between suppliers of the network infrastructure being acquired, in contrast to any lock-in derived from the mode of networking between the two global organizations. In fact, as will be demonstrated, the value of the business to business networking is related to the sharing of common information about both the interorganizational relationship, within which transactions may also be executed. The costs of creating this virtual space are somewhat immaterial in the overall equation in this case. Contrary to the conclusions of Steinfeld et al., a major value of networking in the virtual environment in this case was to break down organizational hierarchy by creating a horizontal global relationship.

According to Chisholm, a network is a set of autonomous organizations that come together to reach goals that none of them can reach separately.[38] Chisholm states that the formation of interorganizational networks represents a response to the complexity and interdependence arising from the extensive collaboration at different levels in the organizations, the emergent situation in this case study.

Chisholm presents the key features of the socioecological view of interorganizational networks, based on Trist:

> *Interorganisational networks operate as abstract conceptual systems that enable members to perceive and understand large-scale problems in new ways.*
>
> *Networks differ from interorganisational relationships because they improve the ability of the organisations to deal with ill-defined, complex problems or issues that individual members cannot handle alone. Such activity is oriented to the shared vision, purpose, and goals that bind the members together.*
>
> *Loose-coupling and voluntary participation are other features of these systems, which rest on horizontal rather than a hierarchical principle: one organisation or member does not have a superior-subordinate relationship with another.*
>
> *Network organisations are self-regulating wherein the members and not a central source of power are responsible for developing a vision, mission, and goals for initiating and managing work activities. The shared vision provides the context that orients all network activity.[39]*

Chisholm suggests further that a network steering committee should govern the network, guide the network activities and network development, and link the network continuously to member organizations and the larger outside environment. The steering committee should include representatives from all stakeholder organizations and groups involved in the network, and the members should have enough authority to speak for their organizations and commit them to network decisions. Chisholm also discusses task forces and states that having a focal point for communication and coordination is crucial for networks to function. The author demonstrates through the experiential evidence presented there was indeed emergent and variable informal steering functions within and leading in the social network however the appointments were by invitation from within.

The idea of a corporate global village (in this case, simultaneously variant and multiple intra- and interorganizational) wherein a common culture of management unifies the practice of business around the world is more dream than reality.[40] Further, Handy suggests that it is unwise to trust people whom you do not know well, whom you have not observed in action over time, and who are not committed to the same goals.[41] Trust inevitably requires some sense of mutuality, of reciprocal loyalty; virtual organizations, which feed on information, ideas, and intelligence, cannot escape the dilemma. Handy notes that a shared commitment still requires personal contact to make it real. One solution he posits is to turn people into members; the concept of membership, when made real, would replace the sense of belonging to a place with a sense of belonging to a community, even if that community were a largely virtual one.

Organizational Culture and Leadership

In the context of transformation and boundary-crossing individuals, Daft provides a consolidated view that transformation leaders share these characteristics:

> [Transformation leaders are] characterised by the ability to bring about change, innovation, and entrepreneurship. Transformation leaders motivate followers not just to follow them personally but to believe in the vision of corporate transformation, to recognise the need for revitalisation, to sign on for the new vision, and help institutionalise the new organisation process.[42] (p. 507)

Transformational leaders build a coalition to guide the transformation process and work to develop a sense of teamwork among the participating groups. Such a coalition should include people from all levels of the organization who can engage the commitment of others (within their company and/or organization) and successfully guide the transformation process (to the achievement of the realization of the business objectives). The so-called coalition of the author was his own social network and the social capital built up therein, combined with all such other similar networks at all levels built up by all of the other people in the globally dispersed virtual community.

A real team is a small number of people with complementary skills who are committed to a common purpose, performance goals, and an approach for which they hold themselves mutually accountable.[43] When this criterion cannot be met, then they will rely on individual leadership skills that they have developed over the years. However, with trust as a foundation, companies— or groups within companies—can share their know-how to achieve results that exceed the sum of the parts.[44] The author, being more mature in years, saw the opportunity beyond his own experiential learning as one of engendering a global ethos into a group situation that, if left to its own devices, might continue to think "locally." Instead, what was created were virtual communities joined in a mission in common and absent of discrimination either in participation or benefit, somewhat contrary to normal management thinking and practice; often the "law" is determined by the "big guy" or the one with the most political smarts.

All of the aforesaid was experiential learning that emerged from the early endeavors in the Vodafone-Ericsson relationship, and all was industry leading and formative through which an organizational model for the management of transition to globalization was created.[45] The merger with AirTouch and the acquisition of Mannesmann AG introduced additional new Vodafone operating interests, several of which had established principal supplier relationships with companies other than Ericsson for provision of mobile network infrastructure.

Schein embarks on an alternative perspective, arguing that although leadership is often discussed as a critical variable in defining success or failure of organizations, one needs also to examine the complement of how leaders create culture and how culture defines and creates leaders.[46] Of relevance to this case and its emergent social network is the notion that culture is to a group what personality or character is to an individual, phenomena that are below the surface and powerful in their impact but invisible and to a considerable degree unconscious. Culture is the result of a complex group learning process that is only partially influenced by leader behavior (p. 11). Schein's formal definition of culture is "a pattern of shared basic assumptions that was learned by a group as it solved its problems of external adaptation and internal integration, that has worked well enough to be considered valid and, therefore, to be taught to new members as the correct way to perceive, think, and feel in relation to those problems" (p. 17).[47]

Schein differentiates between leadership and management, stating that leadership creates and changes cultures, whereas management and administration act within a culture. His discussion that a critical issue in any new group, such as the virtual and global social network formed in this case study, is how influence, power, and authority will be allocated has hierarchical connotations that were not present in this case. The nonhierarchical horizontal community formed in this case, being informal and yet a powerful learning organization that delivered significant economic results, was not subject to the traditional management and leadership styles, yet it had its own persuasive culture for those engaged therein.

Although the author had a leadership role in this case, the view taken was that the cultural strength was vested in the collective power, expressed in influence to bring about the desired and sustainable outcome, and not in the hierarchical position of the actors in the group. This was evident in the author's approach in global meetings of progressively moving over time to the rear of the room in group meetings to allow others in the extended group to take on leadership roles. Of importance to note is that in this case the "group" was formed within and between the different global organizations, which perhaps extends the dimension of what Schein may have had in mind, which is more aligned to an organization or company or combination thereof.

Another defining factor to be considered in the success or failure of a group is the conduct dynamic of the participating actors. In the initial forum between Vodafone and Ericsson, a Swedish company, there was simultaneously a high level of group engagement and an absence of individuals seeking to dominate proceedings; from a Schein perspective, a factor defining the culture in what was otherwise a multicultural (in beliefs and origin) gathering of actors from around the world. Although the high-performing outcome of the group was not compromised, there are two Swedish words that perhaps describe the ethos of the group in its moderate but nevertheless industry-progressive endeavor, *Lagom* and *Jantelagen*.[48]

Lagom is translated as "everything in moderation" or the "middle way," that which is "just right." *Jantelagen*, on the other hand, is a Scandinavian concept with the underlying theme of societally enforced humility and restraint; essentially, self-promotion is not permitted regardless of one's accomplishments or talents—the idea that being different, particularly if it means being *better than others*, is not something to boast about. Although *Jantelagen* is observed by some as a threat to Sweden's global competitiveness, such moderate conduct in the proceedings of this case seemed to have served it well and not compromised a successful outcome. The requirement for a sustainable outcome imposed a degree of federalism in that the forward path necessarily had to merge the interests of the participating parties or entities for a compounded and positive benefit in globalization.

The Messages

This book develops some key messages that are stated here and developed further within the book.

Going global is a transformational journey. It cannot be planned or programmed. It requires improvisation and experimentation within a space that is constructive and collaborative but strongly led. Real sustainable outcomes stem from innovation, adaptation, and variously collective and self-motivation within the organizational social network. Transformation of an organization itself is an experiment with an uncertain outcome, although the endeavor should be underpinned by a vision and supporting strategy. There must necessarily be objective leadership with delegated executive support to see the task through, absent of unnecessary bureaucratic or limiting restraint or constraints. Although not envisaged at the time, the Vodafone-Ericsson project was to become a "pilot" for future globalization, thereby establishing a catalyst for radical and transformational change with sustainable impact.

"The art of the good society and of the good (requisite) organisation is to ensure opportunity for the use of their full potential by its entire people" (page pair 30).[49] Although there is a notion of formality and preordained structure in the words of Jaques, it would be reasonable, however, to conclude that exactly such conditions prevailed or were available for those who sought to take advantage of what was essentially a "greenfield" opportunity, albeit within and between international organizations.

Going global means going beyond international. Simple structures are not appropriate—the complexity of equity interests and varying structures across partners (multi- and transnational; highly centralized versus decentralized control) dictates more complex solutions. But direct control over resources is not always essential. The organizational models and modes of operation developed were about the seeding of ideas and the culmination thereafter of the globalization of the preexisting multiplicity of in-country relationships.

Structure does not need to be visible and formalized to achieve effective business results. Many organizations that proclaim to be global are in fact international with a multiple-country footprint, at best often operating in the image of and subordinated to the control and culture of the organization's corporate offices. In other words, the in-country operations have a "slave" role to the "master" on all aspects of policy, process, and practice. In this book, the emergent models and approaches for true globalization had a high level of informality and were inclusive in operation and practice in satisfying the ambitions of the business. A collective culture and high levels of goodwill toward the acclaimed successes developed from this approach. Further, this book introduces two new counterintuitive stereotype organizational options for consideration in globalization or cross-entity and cultural initiatives.

Most such endeavors are steeped in formalization and prescriptive and perceptive inclusion and do not consider the actual needs versus the ambition nor, least of all, seriously consider securing the knowledge of individuals not in management roles. In a services-based business it is inappropriate for the center to be presumptuous about the customer-facing activities. True globalization operates in general as a homogeneous whole while accommodating local variations for success, absent compromising the strategic endeavor.

Going global means working together. Data and knowledge must be shared, and virtual collaboration must occur—across nations, within firms, and across firms. But firms that collaborate must also compete, and ultimately costs are driven down. It is often declared that "knowledge is power"; it is perhaps more appropriate to declare that "shared knowledge is power" or even that the "sharing of knowledge creates power." The systemized base of knowledge is limited to what individuals are willing or motivated to share; however, people make the difference and create the hurdles to compliance with a rigid IT approach that leaves much tacit knowledge outside the reach of the community. Such knowledge is more likely to be shared only in situations in which there is mutual trust. Corporate knowledge management roles as posited only serve as a deterrent to knowledge sharing unless the corporate culture is open and shares information and is not solely acquisitive for its own corporate purposes that are absent or delinquent in serving the tacit needs of the user community; compliance or conformance in the former case contrast with being flexible, open, and dynamic, supporting a productive organisational outcome in the latter case.

Going global involves getting people going. The success of any venture depends upon the actors involved and their behavior. People must take responsibility for success and act in creative ways without authority. Persuasion, inclusive engagement, and motivation can be more powerful than direction. In transformational organizational settings, the leadership should pay attention to the needs of the individual on the team to ensure that the aspirations of each for achievement and growth are satisfied by the leadership acting as a coach and mentor. Accept that leadership is not a derivative or privilege of rank or of being the boss; instead, the individual situational capacity to contribute to matters in hand is more relevant.

Space within which to innovate, void of the stereotypical process rigor, will lead to personal motivation and recognition through team identity and collective culture that is more powerful than the immediacy of personal economic gratification. Such practices demonstrably lead to the establishment of a requisite organization, as defined at the start of this chapter: "doing business with efficiency and competitiveness and the release of human imagination, trust and satisfaction in work." Formality and compliance to processes and authorities of past practice or to processes that lack relevance to the timeliness of the business situation at hand are surefire ways to demotivate people, something at which companies are good, wherein compliance is more important than progress or results

2 The Birth and Growth of Vodafone and Wireless Telecoms

From Racal to Vodafone

Vodafone was formed in 1984 as a subsidiary of Racal Electronics Plc. Then known as Racal Telecom Limited, approximately 20% of the Company's capital was offered to the public in October 1988. It was fully demerged from Racal Electronics Plc and became an independent company in September 1991, at which time it changed its name to Vodafone Group Plc.

Racal Electronics, the provider of military defense electronics, was awarded the first UK cellular telephone license in December 1982. The UK analogue (TACS) service was launched by Racal Vodafone on January 1, 1985, with the first mobile cellular call made from Trafalgar Square in London to Newbury in Berkshire in the first minutes of the New Year celebrations.

Under the terms of its license to operate, the network company was not permitted (at that time) to sell its services directly to the market, so in 1984 Vodac Limited was formed as its service provider. Later in 1987 Vodata Limited was formed to offer a range of value-added services, such as voice mail, and in October 1987 Vodapage Limited was launched to offer a national paging service.

By 1988 Racal Vodafone was demonstrating market success and had achieved profitability, accounting for one-third of Racal's profits. That year 20% of the Racal Vodafone equity was floated in the financial markets; and a 50:50 joint venture with Ericsson, called Orbitel Mobile Communications Limited in the UK, was established to manufacture GSM products (Global System for Mobile Service, GSM having originally stood for *Groupe Spécial Mobile*). Orbitel was evidence of Racal Vodafone's commitment to providing a globally compatible GSM network; Racal Vodafone was a signatory to the GSM standards negotiations concluded in September 1987. I joined Orbitel as a consultant director on August 15, 1994, to be responsible for the Terminals (GSM and test mobile phones) Business Unit, specifically, their design, manufacture, marketing, and sales worldwide.

In September 1991 Racal and Vodafone were fully demerged (the largest demerger in UK history), and Vodafone Group Plc was listed on the New York and London Stock Exchanges, with Gerry Whent as the first chief executive; in the same year the firm saw its UK cellular market share increase to over 56%. The firm was also recognized with the British Standards Award for Quality, the first ever made to a telephone network for either fixed or mobile services. In October 1991 Vodafone and Telecom Finland made the world's first international GSM (digital) roaming mobile telephone call, and by December that year Vodafone had launched the UK's first commercial GSM mobile phone service.

The world's first international GSM roaming agreement was signed in June 1992 between Vodafone and Telecom Finland, meaning that the customers of either firm could enjoy the services of the other; for example, a Vodafone customer visiting Finland could utilize the services of Telecom Finland, and vice versa. Vodafone opened up the nonbusiness market in the UK with the introduction of "LowCall," a service for the low-usage mobile phone customer offered at a tariff reduction of 40% from the business tariff. In November 1992 the Business Enterprise Awards named Vodafone Group Plc Company of the Year.

The Vodafone Group formed or participated in major new international alliances in 1993. The German mobile phone operator E-Plus, in which Vodafone had an interest, was awarded a cellular operating license; Vodafone joined consortiums to operate the first GSM digital cellular networks in South Africa and Fiji; Vodafone Pty launched its GSM digital service in Australia; and the Panafon GSM digital cellular network was launched in Greece. Vodafone Group International Limited was formed in August 1993 with the role of acquiring operating licenses and supervising the Vodafone Group international investments. In September of that year Vodafone was named the best mobile network in the UK and had connected its one-millionth customer by December.

The Vodafone Group joined the Globalstar consortium in March 1994, which was formed to develop and launch a Low Earth Orbiting Satellite (LEOS) celestial mobile phone service to complement the GSM land-based cellular services. In November of this year Vodafone also launched its digital data fax and short message service (SMS) in the UK.

As a result of the overwhelming nonbusiness customer demand in the UK, Vodacall Limited was set up in April 1995 to provide the specialist service this market demanded. At the end of the year Vodafone also agreed to sell its 50% interest in Orbitel to Ericsson, making it a 100% Ericsson subsidiary. By the end of the year over five hundred specialist retail outlets and seven High Street retail chains distributed mobile phones connecting to the Vodafone UK network.

Following the decision to sell the interest in Orbitel, I was invited to join Vodafone Group Services Limited as the director of project management reporting to Sir Gerald Whent, the group chief executive; I joined Vodafone Group on May 1, 1996. My principal sponsors for this move were E. John Peett CBE, a Vodafone main board director since 1985 (he retired in

October 1997) who was also a non-executive director in Orbitel, and Phil Williams, the Vodafone Group HR director. My responsibilities included leading the relationship between Vodafone and Ericsson, including the commercial arrangements with/for Vodafone Limited (the UK mobile network operator) and Chris Gent, who was and had been the managing director since January 1985 and was a member of the main board of directors.

Sir Gerald retired from the company in December 1996 and was succeeded in January 1997 by Chris Gent. As part of the Queen's Birthday Honours in June 2001, Chris was awarded a knighthood for his services to the telecommunications industry. Chris retired from Vodafone July 31, 2003, and was succeeded by Arun Sarin. Chris then became an honorary life president of the company, a specially created unpaid role, from which he resigned in March 2006, stating that "when I was an executive at Vodafone, we were mercifully free of company politics and blame culture." Chris became the non-executive chairman of GlaxoSmithKline (GSK) in January 2005.

On the appointment of Chris Gent to the Vodafone Plc Group CEO position in January 1997, David Channing Williams became the managing director of Vodafone Limited; he had been with Vodafone Group Plc since 1985 and had been appointed to the board in 1996. On February 14, 1997, David announced my appointment as director, IT and project management, under the more general banner of "Change for the Future." I was to retain project management (which included Ericsson for mobile network infrastructure), add purchasing (for which I led the transformation to supply chain), and given the consolidation task of merging the disparate IT departments of Engineering Software Development, Engineering Computing Operations, and Commercial (Software) Services. This eventually became a consolidated organization of about eight hundred people.

New GSM digital tariffs incorporating per-second billing and including "bundled" minutes became operational in April 1996, and by June Vodafone had become the first UK network to reach two million customers. In September Vodafone became the first UK operator to offer PrePay service, meaning a service with no contractual obligations.

By March 1997 Vodafone in the UK acquired a 100% interest in a number of service providers, namely, Talkland, Peoples Phone, and Astec Communications. In July the company reorganized its approach to distribution by aligning service provision with the markets being served, forming Vodafone Corporate, Vodafone Connect, and Vodafone Retail. The one-hundredth network operator roaming agreement was announced in July, and by October the UK network had reached its three-millionth customer, two million of which were on the GSM network. In December Vodafone Group reached an equity adjusted worldwide customer total of five million customers.

In late 1997 I was invited to brief Chris Gent and David Channing Williams on the status and issues concerning the Vodafone-Ericsson business relationship with which they might assist me; this briefing was in advance of their visit to Stockholm to meet with Dr. Lars Ramqvist, the CEO of Ericsson. Although I had a technical background, I had been experienced in business since 1974. During this time the IT industry traversed a few periods of recession and changes in the commercial paradigm that arose.

In the Ericsson and Vodafone cases in late 1997, the notion of price or customer cost stability over an extended period was alien to me, particularly when the competitive landscape of the operators of the day sought to advance their propositions to their end-customers; in short, the operator required, in my opinion, a declining cost profile both to stay competitive and deliver shareholder satisfaction. The challenge, however, both then (moving ahead with GSM or 2G second generation) and now (moving ahead with 3G [third generation]), was or is that the choice of supplier for the radio network was a cul-de-sac choice. That is, once the selection had been made, the switching costs are prohibitive and thwart with risk should one contemplate such a move. This gives rise to an interesting conundrum: how do you negotiate and/or improve your commercial or business position with a supplier in such circumstances?

It was clear to me that the value of the business relationship to the parties must be at least one of the key attributes, which was certainly the case between Ericsson and Vodafone, given their formative relationship and the positive profile of Vodafone. After their Stockholm meeting, Chris and David told me to contact Nils Grimsmo of Ericsson to advance my business endeavors on behalf of Vodafone. To my surprise, Nils was the Ericsson managing director and their most senior person in the UK, yet I had not come across him in London or Stockholm. Accordingly, I arranged to meet with Nils. He was instrumental in collaborating with me in the industry-leading globalization journey, from which emerged a new counterintuitive requisite organization and a novel interorganizational system relationship. Nils, along with another key operation person on his team, Kaj Snellman (both of whom have now retired), and I remain friends today.

I also learned quickly from this experience that while being respectful of the organizational hierarchy, be it that of Vodafone or the supplier, I needed to forge ahead and essentially create an asymmetry in my business relationships against which I found no resistance; this required me to be connected to the key top management of the main suppliers. This was to be my practice across my endeavors within and between Vodafone and other organizations with which Vodafone worked and for which I was responsible. I was to develop in the ensuing journey a cross-industry and substantive social network, which I would venture to say, is no longer achievable in the industry. Even at this stage of the journey, nothing in what I sought to do commercially or in the business relationship was bounded (save being legal), nor was I subject to any stated roles or responsibilities or preset methodologies or approaches; in reflection I would conclude that I had the authority and trust of management to pursue my instincts and intuition in the interests of Vodafone, a status of innovative privilege that was to last until the onset of a new organizational form in April 2005, as discussed later.

Vodafone announced the sale of its 35% equity holding in Pacific Link in Hong Kong in January 1998, and in the same month announced that its equity position in Libertel, a network operator in Holland, had increased from 26.5% to 61.5%, thereby creating a new subsidiary. The company later announced an increased equity position in the Dutch operator Libertel to 70%. The company announced in March that the Misrfone consortium in Egypt, in which Vodafone had a 30% interest, had been awarded a license to build the country's second mobile phone network. In July Sir Ernest Harrison, who had been Vodafone Group's chairman since the flotation in 1988, announced his retirement; and Lord MacLaurin, the former chairman of Tesco Plc in the UK, succeeded him. In the final quarter of 1998 Vodafone in the UK announced a record number of new customers—933,000 (of which 755,000 were Pay as You Talk, formerly PrePay), more than three times the previously quarterly record—taking the total customer base to 4,874,000, of which 1,175,000 were Pay as You Talk customers.

Shortly after the strong end to 1998, Vodafone in the UK announced on January 15, 1999, that it had connected the five-millionth customer.

Telefonaktiebolaget LM Ericsson

ASEA, AGA, and LM Ericsson formed Svenska Radio Aktiebolaget (SRA) in 1919, but shortly after its formation Marconi of the UK became a partner and ASEA and AGA sold out their interests. Åke Lundqvist, who features throughout the Ericsson history, joined SRA in the mid-1960s with a degree in electrical engineering and became the managing director in 1977.[1]

In 1977 Ericsson of Sweden and Philips of the Netherlands formed a consortium to bid to build a complete new fixed network for the Kingdom of Saudi Arabia. They won the contract and in 1979 won a second contract to expand the network. Almost as an afterthought, money was allocated to build a mobile telephone network, the afterthought having been inspired and marketed by Åke Lundqvist and the then chairman of Ericsson, Björn Lundvall, during a visit to Sweden by the Saudi minister of communications. By this time Ericsson had won contracts to supply switches (MTXs, or the Ericsson product known as an AXE switch) to the Nordic NMT (cellular) networks; luckily, the frequencies (450 MHz band) for which the NMT was specified were available in Saudi Arabia. As the specifications were in the public domain, operators were free to define their networks in accordance with them, and manufacturers were free to design and manufacture equipment to them. Ericsson was the first to begin to exploit this "gift" in a systematic way.[2]

In 1978 SRA acquired Sonab and its land mobile terminal product that had the potential for further development into a mobile telephone terminal. Åke Lundqvist, however, felt that something should be done to consolidate resources in the phone development area, but the issue was where to locate such an operation. By the autumn of 1983 the Ericsson Mobile Telephone Laboratory was inaugurated in Lund, Sweden, which today is still the center of such development.[3]

In late 1981 the top management of Ericsson decided to assign the responsibility for mobile telephone systems to a single body, SRA; on January 1, 1983, this division became a wholly owned company within Ericsson and was renamed Ericsson Radio Systems AB (ERA).[4] However, in 1980 talks had commenced with the Dutch PTT regarding construction of an NMT 450 cellular system. This time Åke Lundqvist realized that if Ericsson were to win the deal in face of strong competition from Motorola, SRA needed to build a cell planning capability of its own, that is, to offer a complete network deployment capability. Åke recruited the expertise of Chandos Rypinski from the United States, who was also familiar with Motorola business practices. In the autumn of 1981 SRA, with a system package of three parts—radio base stations, the AXE switch for the MTX, and a highly advanced cell-planning service—won the Dutch contract and had joined the traditional divisions of Ericsson by becoming a systems house. This was to be a turning point for SRA.[5]

In early 1982 Åke Lundqvist assigned Mats Ljunggren (who joined SRA directly from university in 1968) to prepare material for a possible attack on the U.S. market; on March 3, 1982, the Federal Communications Commission (FCC) announced the date for filing applications for cellular operating licenses (June 7, 1982). Many of the entrepreneurs who filed for applications specified Ericsson equipment; of 130 applications for the first 30 markets, 40 had specified Ericsson. This was a surprise for Motorola, as they had anticipated with their strong market position that they would yield a market share over 90%. Eventually, 194 applications were submitted. The second-round filings for markets 31–60 were being prepared for submission to the FCC on November 8, 1982, and third-round filings on March 8, 1983. Ericsson achieved its first contract success from a joint venture formed by Graphic Scanning and MetroMedia in November 1983, with a service launch date of January 3, 1985, in Chicago. Ericsson went on to win a number of other contracts.[6]

In the UK British Telecom (BT) had been awarded a cellular operating license as a private-sector competitor in December 1982, one year prior to Vodafone's award, and therefore had a head start. It was crucial to Vodafone that contract dates for their network launch were met; Åke Lundqvist together with Duncan McDougal was yet again involved in the contract closure with Vodafone, in favor of Ericsson, for the supply of the TACS (or analogue) network with a contracted in-service date of March 15, 1985. At the time of the applications for the award of the operating license, the expectation was that by 1990 each of the two networks would achieve 100,000 customers; the number was closer to 500,000–600,000 each. This contractual achievement was important to Ericsson, because they had now become suppliers of all three standards, NMT (Nordic Mobile Telephone network, the standard developed by the Nordic Telecom Administrations), AMPS (Advanced Mobile Phone System, the US analogue standard specification developed by Bell Labs (AT&T)), and TACS (Total Access Communication System, the British analogue mobile telephone standard, based on the US AMPS system) Gerry Whent, the CEO of Vodafone, had become aware of the intent of Cellnet, their competitor in the UK, to start up commercial service on January 1, 1985, and requested that Ericsson also advance their in-service date to January 1, 1985.

Ericsson was successful in meeting this objective. BT had chosen Motorola as their supplier at launch.[7]

Merger and Acquisitions

Vodafone Group Plc announced the completion of the merger with AirTouch Communications, Inc., on June 30, 1999. The resulting company, Vodafone AirTouch Plc, had a market capitalization of $110 billion (£67 billion) and operations in 23 countries and on four continents. At that time Vodafone owned interests in operations in the UK, Australia, Egypt, France, Germany, Greece, Malta, the Netherlands, New Zealand, Fiji, South Africa, Sweden, and Uganda and an interest in the Globalstar satellite system. AirTouch owned interests in the United States, Belgium, Egypt, Germany, India, Japan, Poland, Portugal, Romania, South Korea, Spain, and Sweden and also an interest in the Globalstar satellite system.

In 1998 and in anticipation of the aforesaid merger, I had been invited by Julian Horn-Smith (appointed to the Vodafone Group Plc board in June 1996 and managing director of Vodafone Group International Limited) on behalf of the executive to consider and pursue cost synergy opportunities, given that at that time Ericsson GSM mobile network infrastructure was deployed in the UK, the Netherlands, Greece, and Australia/Fiji. (Julian became Sir Julian in the Queen's Birthday Honours list in June 2004.) It had been the practice of Vodafone in start-up activities to initially embed an expatriate team from the UK; essentially such networks were established and operated in the image of the UK, which meant the use of Ericsson mobile network infrastructure. Each of these operators in which Vodafone had equity interest (100% in the UK) also had its own contract with the supplier, and the offshore (to the UK) activities were run essentially as a portfolio with Vodafone representatives on each of the board of directors.

Although there had been commercial comparison exercises between operators having Ericsson as a common supplier for mobile network infrastructure, the idea of positively collaborating to pursue aggregation synergies had not previously been undertaken, nor was it established practice to do so in the telecom industry at that time. Such synergy benefits became focal in all subsequent acquisitions, none more so publicly expressed than that of Mannesmann AG; thereafter, my opinion would be sought since such anticipated synergies were generally financially relevant. I therefore was on the threshold of a challenge for which the objective was clear although absent of instructions on what and how to achieve it; this was consistent with the innovative spirit and opportunities in the company at that time.

This task was to expand rapidly with the onset of the merger with AirTouch and later the acquisition of Mannesmann AG. I recall in an early-day discussion with Julian Horn-Smith, he suggested that I needed to build some bridges for success; in hindsight that advice simultaneously said everything and nothing, yet that simple guidance was sufficient to activate my self-momentum and motivation and, absent management constraints, left ample space for individual innovation and leadership. Julian personally provided support for and recognition of the financial achievements of the virtual team and me through to my retirement in October 2005, for which I am indebted. The journey that ensued after the merger and acquisition is both history and the subject of the case study set forth in this book. Julian retired in July 2006 after more than twenty-two years of service to the company since its birth in 1984; he was appointed non-executive chairman of Sage (UK) Limited effective August 1, 2006.

On March 1, 1999, Vodafone Group Plc announced that its equity adjusted customer base had reached 10 million worldwide, and on April 21 the UK had connected its two-millionth Pay as you Talk customer. With the Vodafone and AirTouch shareholders having voted overwhelmingly in favor of the merger and the EU regulatory bodies consenting to the transaction, the new company, Vodafone AirTouch Plc, came into being on June 30, 1999. By that time Vodafone in the UK had over 6.16 million customers, and the new company had a proportionate customer base of almost 28 million customers.

On September 21, 1999, Bell Atlantic Corporation and Vodafone AirTouch Plc announced that they had reached a definitive agreement to create a new wireless business (which became known as Verizon Wireless) in the United States composed of the wireless assets of both companies; this business was later strengthened by the addition of the cellular and PCS assets of GTE Corporation, a merger completed in early 2000.

Following the exchange of letters without resolution, Vodafone Group Plc sent a letter to the management board of Mannesmann AG in Germany on November 19, 1999. Vodafone declared that because Mannesmann had refused to negotiate on its merger proposal, Vodafone had decided to put a new proposal directly to the Mannesmann shareholders. On the same day Vodafone Group Plc announced the terms of the intended offer for the whole of the issued share capital of Mannesmann. By the end of the year Vodafone UK had 7.94 million customers, and the Vodafone Group had a proportionate global customer base of more than 35.5 million customers. Trevor Merriden offers an external insight into the situational politics and events of this phase of the Vodafone journey under the stewardship of Sir Christopher Gent.[8]

On February 14, 2000, terms were agreed with the supervisory board of Mannesmann AG: Mannesmann shareholders would own 49.5% of the newly enlarged group. The European Commission gave its conditional consent to the acquisition on April 12, 2000. By the end of June the combined group had a proportionate customer base of over 59 million.

Vizzavi was launched in May 2000, which was a 50:50 joint venture company between Vodafone AirTouch Plc and VivendiNet that would deliver a multi-access branded Internet portal for Europe. Verizon Wireless was also launched the same month in the United States, a combination of the cellular, PCS, and paging assets of Vodafone AirTouch Plc and Bell Atlantic Corporation. Further businesses would be added on the completion of the merger between Bell Atlantic Corporation and GTE Corporation, at which point Verizon Wireless ranked as market leader in the U.S. wireless industry, serving more than 23 million customers. As of July 2006 Vodafone had a 45% interest in Verizon Wireless.

At the annual general meeting of Vodafone AirTouch Plc on July 28, 2000, the shareholders approved the change of the company's name back to Vodafone Group Plc.By September 30, 2000 as announced in the release on 14 November 2000, the Vodafone Group Plc global proportionate customer base had risen to over 65.75 million. The regional breakdown of this proportionate customer base was as follows: Continental Europe, over 37.4 million proportionate customers; the United States serving over 26 million customers; Asia, and the Pacific, 4.9 million; the UK over 10.2 million customers, Middle East, and Africa, 1.7 million. The largest network in the Vodafone Group was D2 in Germany with 16.4 million customers. Additionally, and as a point of reference, the market capitalization of the Vodafone Group Plc as reported on October 23, 2000, in the *Daily Telegraph* was £169,846 billion.

Vodafone Limited had been conducting 3G network trials since early 1999, demonstrating successfully 3G multimedia services with partners, including Ericsson, Nortel Networks, and Lucent Technologies. Those trials had enabled Vodafone Limited to gain firsthand, practical experience in the deployment of 3G networks, ensuring that the rollout of high-bandwidth services offered by this next-generation technology could be implemented efficiently. The UK subsidiary of Vodafone announced on April 27, 2000, that it had successfully bid £5.964 billion for License B in the auction conducted by the UK government for licenses to operate 3G mobile telecommunications services. On August 29 the UK Radiocommunications Agency notified Vodafone that as a result of the auction, License B would be granted on September 1, 2000. License B, two blocks of 15 MHz paired spectrum, was the largest available to the existing operators of cellular networks in the UK and would run for a period of twenty years. Subject to the availability of 3G network infrastructure and handsets, Vodafone Limited also announced that it intended to offer customers commercial service on its new 3G network in 2002.

On December 7, 1999, Vodafone announced that it had chosen Ericsson to supply infrastructure for its next-generation network technology, GPRS (General Packet Radio Service) in the UK, the Netherlands, and Greece. Set to bring customers high-speed data services and enhanced Internet capabilities over existing digital GSM mobile networks, Vodafone AirTouch would begin to introduce GPRS from January 2000.

GPRS would provide mobile customers the ability to access services such as train timetables, receive detailed directions and local maps, and realize true home shopping on the move simply using their handheld devices. GPRS, which is particularly suited to WAP (Wireless Access Protocol), would introduce high-speed data to Web-based services, including the Vodafone interactive services.

As of March 25, 2002, Vodafone was the first mobile operator to offer commercial GPRS roaming across Europe. Vodafone customers in twelve countries—Belgium, France, Germany, Greece, Ireland, Italy, the Netherlands, Portugal, Spain, Sweden, Switzerland and the UK—would be able to access their Vodafone services over GPRS in a growing number of destinations when traveling in Europe. Vodafone stated its intention to progressively expand GPRS roaming to cover other networks, including all remaining European Vodafone operators and partner networks by the end of 2002.

Creation of the Global Brand

Another noteworthy and more visible aspect of globalization was the move by Vodafone to a global brand within which existed demonstrable cost synergies in revenue generation and cost savings. The brand identity of operating companies in which Vodafone had an equity interest was very much a local in-market matter, with no global coordination; even with a majority equity interest, operations retained local brand identities, e.g., Libertel in Holland, Panafon in Greece and later Omnitel in Italy, D2 in Germany, Airtel in Spain. Specifically in the UK, the seat of the company's head office, the policy was that sponsorship promoting the brand would not be at a regional level in country, thereby avoiding bias and preferences in seeking to attract customers.

Vodafone's global brand migration plan was introduced in 2000, based on an interim period of dual branding to enable the transfer of brand equity from the valuable and successful operating brands of Vodafone subsidiaries to a single Vodafone brand. By adopting a single brand, Vodafone's European subsidiaries and Vodafone would be able to benefit from cost synergies, such as brand advertising; media buying; global products and services branding and advertising; and associated marketing activities. Revenue synergies would be generated by increased use of Vodafone products and services, promoted by a seamless, consistent Vodafone brand.

Vodafone then embarked upon a plan to move its various in-country brands progressively toward the single, global brand of Vodafone. Vodafone announced on October 29, 2001, that Telecel Vodafone in Portugal and Airtel Vodafone in Spain were moving toward the single brand ahead of the early 2002 timetable following a transitional period of dual branding. Telecel Vodafone had adopted Vodafone as its brand on October 22, 2001, more than three months ahead of schedule. This success was due to a Vodafone brand awareness achieved through introduction of the dual brand logo in all advertising campaigns and sponsorship programs. Airtel Vodafone moved its brand to Vodafone on October 27, 2001. Airtel Vodafone's move to the single brand was preceded by a brief interim of dual branding, with the single brand supported by an extensive multimedia advertising campaign in Spain.

Other dual-branded subsidiaries moved to the single Vodafone brand over the next twelve months. D2 Vodafone (Germany) moved to the Vodafone brand in March 2002; Europolitan Vodafone (Sweden), in April 2002 (Vodafone Sweden was later sold to Telenor of Norway). Omnitel Vodafone

(Italy), Libertel Vodafone (Netherlands), Panafon-Vodafone (Greece), Click Vodafone (Egypt), and Eircell Vodafone (Ireland) all followed a similar route within the next twelve months.

David Haines, Vodafone's global brand director, commented:

> *The initial positive acceptance of the Vodafone brand has meant that we have been able to introduce the single brand ahead of schedule in Portugal and Spain. A seamless, consistent Vodafone brand across Europe initially will help drive our customers' usage of Vodafone products and services when roaming or while in their home country. This will enhance Average Revenue Per Customer [ARPU] as well as creating cost and revenue synergies.* (Vodafone Group Press Release of 29 October 2001)

Finally, on November 10, 2004, Vodafone announced the global launch of Vodafone live! with 3G across an unrivaled thirteen countries. Vodafone live! with 3G would be available in Austria, France, Germany, Greece, Ireland, Italy, Japan, the Netherlands, Portugal, Spain, Sweden, Switzerland, and the UK.

Vodafone had also embarked on a program to attract partner networks, somewhat analogous to a franchise in which the partner network (operator) delivers services in common with those of the Vodafone Group and with rights of use of the brand and relevant logos. A key point is that Vodafone would have no equity or management interests in the partner networks. The company's annual report for fiscal year ending March 31, 2006, noted that Vodafone has "equity interests in 26 countries, through its subsidiary undertakings, joint ventures, associated undertakings and investments. Partner Market arrangements extended the Group's footprint to a further 32 countries."

Manchester United, Cricket, and Ferrari

In February 2000 Vodafone UK announced a commercial alliance with Manchester United wherein Vodafone became the principal sponsor; this four-year agreement started on June 1, 2000. Vodafone also became the telecommunications and equipment services partner to Manchester United, making the relationship more a commercial alliance than just the traditional shirt sponsorship. Although Manchester United was a regionally based team in the UK, I recall the logic being that they were and remain a global brand and that such sponsorship in support of the Vodafone brand promotion would attract customers worldwide.

When the latest £36 million, new four-year deal, was signed in December 2003, Vodafone said it would roll out a wide range of club content, including results, news, still and video images, ring tones, and games, through its services. However, in November 2005 it was announced that this latest deal, worth about £9 million ($15.5 million) a year, would instead end in May 2006. Vodafone then announced, as they described it, the signing of an exciting, exclusive three-year agreement to sponsor the UEFA Champions League commencing on July 1, 2006. As a result of the sponsorship deal, Vodafone would become both an official partner and the official mobile network of the UEFA Champions League. The agreement would be central to Vodafone's global sponsorship strategy and reinforce the company's long-term commitment to football. The new partnership would enable all Vodafone operating companies, partner networks, and affiliates to provide their customers with access to the world's largest and most prestigious club competition. The partnership would enable Vodafone to deliver content, including video highlights packages and goal alerts, from all UEFA Champions League matches to football fans on the Vodafone live! with 3G consumer service.

Previously, however, Vodafone in the UK had established a partnership with English cricket that dated back to the West Indies tour in 1997, when they first signed as official team sponsor. In July 2005 Vodafone announced a new four-year deal with the English Cricket Board (ECB), which extended to the England Women's Team, the England "A" Team, and the ECB National Cricket Academy. The deal will see the partnership continue to develop as the needs of both the team and cricket fans in this country evolve. This sponsorship of the English cricket team has brought great recognition to Vodafone both in the UK and around the cricketing world.

Vodafone's backing of Ferrari's assault on the Formula One (F1) world title started in 2002 with its three-year sponsorship deal with Ferrari—the largest in Vodafone's history. During the spectacular 2002 F1 season, Ferrari F1 won the drivers' and teams' world championships. This collective Vodafone Group sponsorship in the promotion of the Vodafone brand globally was the result of leveraging the global footprint synergy to create affordability not otherwise possible by any one of its operating interests alone. Vodafone believes in backing winners and building on success. Although based in the UK, Vodafone is a global organization that wants its brand to be seen around the world. Working with Ferrari offered the company high-profile exposure in an exciting sport with an enormous global audience. Vodafone would also be able to use their technical know-how to develop innovative services that bring F1 enthusiasts closer to every race. As the world's most glamorous sport tours the world, Vodafone can deliver news and action from the F1 circuit through the Web, Vodafone live! mobile phones, WAP mobiles, and their text alert service.

On December 16, 2004, Vodafone announced that it had resolved to continue its sponsorship of the Ferrari team for the 2005 and 2006 seasons. However, in December 2005 Vodafone announced that it would get the full title sponsorship it wanted from the start of the 2007 season, in a five-year deal worth £160 million; the team would be known as the Vodafone McLaren Mercedes team.

Move to the Next-Generation 3G Technology

In May 1998, the UK government announced its decision to auction licenses for the use of the 3G radio spectrum. On April 27, 2000, following the completion of the auction, the Chancellor of the Exchequer announced that the auction had yielded a total input of £22.48 billion, about four times the initial expectation of £5.0 billion. Vodafone paid £5.96 billion for its 3G license in the UK.

The early but none the less substantive financial synergies arising for Vodafone from the collaborative globalizing endeavors with Ericsson, and progressively the other major mobile network infrastructure suppliers, came principally from the GSM, or 2G capital investments. At the point of initiating the aggregation synergies endeavor in 1998 and as a result of the merger and acquisition, the GSM supplier choices had already been made by the operators. There was not much scope left for discussion of operating costs or, indeed, the normal commercial leverage of being able to, at will, switch suppliers for better commercial terms and/or operational performance. Because of the industry application of GSM standards, the granularity of interoperability and interworking (essentially within the radio access and network there were not any because equipment cannot be mixed-and-matched from various suppliers for the radio access network) meant that operators were faced with cul-de-sac choices. With high switching costs and risk, once the radio network vendor had been chosen, introducing a second vendor was ordinarily suboptimal.

In the 1990s the commercial world was not terribly transparent, thereby allowing the vendors to operate using an approach of "global product, local business," a quote attributed to Dr. Lars Ramqvist, the CEO of Ericsson in the period 1990–1998. The early evidence in the course of the Ericsson aggregation initiative certainly gave credence to the philosophy across the Vodafone operating interests, as it similarly did as we moved toward Nokia, Nortel, and Siemens. This exposure became a rich source of early economic synergy benefits, combined with iterative rounds of "cherry-picking" as the disclosures occurred that the rate of GSM deployment was running strong at the end of the 1990s.

As the world and the telecom industry were moving toward the twenty-first century, however, such industry-leading aggregation initiatives as those in which Vodafone and its key mobile network infrastructure suppliers were engaged rapidly evidenced a transparent, global paradigm. That is, for Vodafone, and I believe for many others who followed, the suppliers could no longer enjoy variable terms and pricing between operators of common equity interest holdings; transparency and a leveling prevailed that forced a new, competitive paradigm. Now a company such as Vodafone, with multi-operator interests, could clearly see sourcing practices and commercial terms because there was a single, multilocation supplier. But cross-supplier transparency also prevailed, as this Vodafone global aggregation activity exemplified, which will be shown later. In the twenty-first century, there is nowhere for the supplier to hide and generate inequitable cost pricing differentials to the operators.

With the onset of 3G, however, the leveraging opportunities for the collective aggregation actions in the interests of Vodafone Group, without compromise to the local operations, were different. Although there may have been an operational or preferential logic to follow past decisions of choice of supplier for 3G mobile (radio and core network) technology, it was neither a mandatory nor a preemptive decision. Vodafone and the industry required all qualifying vendors wishing to supply 3G mobile network infrastructure in the group to evidence collaborative cross-supplier test programs that successfully demonstrated interworking and end-to-end interoperability (which includes the Terminal, or mobile phone). A supplier who failed to meet this compliance requirement would have a very short life in 3G; in the event although somewhat later than expected, the four main vendors to Vodafone (Ericsson, Nokia, Nortel, and Siemens) achieved this requirement.

Certain of the initial supplier choices for 3G were made before achieving a coordinated group collaborative approach. After the AirTouch merger and Mannesmann acquisition, more than twenty operators were now in the Vodafone Group. The key supplier options now included Nokia, Nortel, and Siemens in addition to Ericsson. However, the pre-existing supplier selection decisions by the operators did not compromise the future financial synergy opportunities.

I was appointed to the position of director, global supply chain management effective July 1, 2000, thereby moving me from Vodafone Limited to Vodafone AirTouch International Limited and to the organization of Thomas Geitner. Thomas reported to Julian Horn-Smith and had recently been appointed as COO and a group main board member. The company announced on June 23, 2003, that Thomas was to become the group chief technology officer. I was to report directly to Thomas for the period from about April 2001 until around April 2003, during which period I continued to enjoy innovative and entrepreneurial "freedom." Then Thomas introduced an external recruit, Detlef Schultz, as his new group supply chain director; Detlef's responsibilities embraced IT, Terminals, and mobile network infrastructure (my continuing responsibility).

With this newly created multi-billion-Euro portfolio of Detlef's, this was without question to change my position, at least in the hierarchy, although it did not impact my relationship with my social network, in which there were a number of key stakeholders in the business overall. A subsequent change, however, to the organization dynamic for Detlef was Arun Sarin's announcement at the investor conference in October 2004 that the responsibility for Terminals supply chain management was to be transferred to the group CMO organization. The effect of this change was to make my role, team, and activities a dominant economic part of the surviving group supply chain function, which from my perspective now created a crowded management space. The end of innovation was approaching, with my "wings," or more important, those of the role, being progressively clipped through these and subsequent changes. Nevertheless, I got along well with Detlef, to whom I provided and mutually received excellent support. Our friendship has survived the experience into my retirement from the firm. The issues or circumstantial challenges were never personal matters between us.

Supplier contract awards for the Radio Access Network (RAN) together with the cost of deployment normally represents more than 50% of the network capital expenditure. Early announcements of contract awards were the outcome of the normal Technical Request for Information (RFI), Request for Quotation (RFQ), and final negotiation process, which combined the forces of the global and in-country resources to act as a homogeneous team before the potential suppliers so the commercial terms could be leveraged in the group's interests. This approach was to assure that each Vodafone in-country bid leveraged the diversity of the potential forecasted future expansion requirements of the group collective or community.

The first 3G supplier announcement was in March 2000 when Japan (J-Phone at the time) chose for its 3G mobile network infrastructure Nokia, NEC, and Ericsson in that order of magnitude of market share. Japan carried out two subsequent rounds of RFQs, in which the global virtual team was involved, announcing the supplier market share outcomes in October 2000 and October 2002. This was a strategic award, as the 2G mobile network was the localized Japanese PDC (Pacific Digital Cellular, the Japanese digital standard) standard supplied solely by Ericsson, who were now the benefactor of the smallest 3G market share.

The further market significance of these announcements was that Vodafone had decided to deploy, for the first time in Japan, a mobile network compliant to a global standard, thereby enabling inbound and outbound customer roaming. The technical significance was that although there was interoperability between 2G and 3G network technologies and the Terminals would make such a switch transparent for the user, no such capability existed between 3G and PDC, thereby requiring higher standards of 3G excellence in Japan for service assurance. That is, if 3G coverage dropped, then, unlike other networks that would default to GSM (2G), in Japan the call would be dropped and negatively impact the customer experience.

On December 19, 2001, Vodafone announced that Vodafone (Spain) and J-Phone (Japan) had successfully conducted the world's first 3G roaming call. The call was made between John de Wit, then chief executive of Vodafone, using a single-mode 3G handset, and Darryl Green, then president of J-Phone, using a Japanese single-mode 3G mobile. J-Phone was the first operator in the Vodafone Group to launch its 3G service, which occurred on December 20, 2002.

The dogged industry trail to that point has been well documented elsewhere, spanning issues of technology manifesting itself in both the network and the Terminals for quite some time, which was a main contributor to the supplier meltdown that ensued in the 2001–2003 period. Major layoffs occurred, as much as 50% or more in some cases. The impact of the supplier meltdown was to create a period of financial uncertainty and make doubtful the ability of some to survive. Nevertheless, the four key suppliers to Vodafone found safe passage by various means, notwithstanding the continuing excess of industry production capacity in an otherwise crowded market. Supplier consolidation began in 2005–2006 with the announced Ericsson-Marconi, Alcatel-Lucent-Nortel, and Nokia-Siemens transactions.

In May 2000 Vodafone in the UK announced the selection of Ericsson for its 3G mobile network infrastructure, the same choice as previously made for the GSM network. Vodafone in Spain announced the selection of Nortel for its 3G network infrastructure in September 2000, with its GSM network provided by Ericsson. Vodafone D2 in Germany selected Ericsson and Siemens as its 3G suppliers in November 2000, which represented a continuity of supply for GSM but with a variable balance of market share. Swisscom in Switzerland, although an affiliate in the Vodafone Group, nevertheless also embraced the global collaboration spirit and announced their choice of Ericsson for 3G infrastructure, who were also their vendor of GSM.

Another affiliate to the group, SFR in France, announced their choices of Nokia and Siemens for 3G infrastructure in March 2001, omitting Alcatel in this case. Vodafone in the Netherlands announced the continuity of Ericsson as their 3G network supplier choice in April 2001. Vodafone Omnitel in Italy announced their choices in May–July 2001: Nokia, their GSM supplier, and Nortel; this decision supported a global strategic direction to introduce in Italy a second supplier for 3G. Vodafone in Portugal concluded their outcome and opted for a two-supplier approach in July 2001, somewhat against the global strategy; nevertheless, the newly introduced supplier was Nortel, with which a common understanding was eventually reached. In August 2001, Vodafone Sweden selected Nokia for 3G network infrastructure, who also supplied their GSM, and 3GIS (3G Infrastructure Services) AB also opted for Nokia, as announced later in October. 3G Infrastructure Services AB is a joint venture set up by telecom operators Hi3G Access and Vodafone Sweden in order to share network infrastructure during the build-out of 3G UMTS networks in Sweden. 3G Infrastructure Services AB will build and operate a network that covers 70% of the Swedish population. Hi3G Access and Vodafone Sweden have equal stakes in the joint venture. Each partner in the joint venture has been granted 3G licenses to provide 3G services to almost 100% of the Swedish population.

Proximus in Belgium, also an affiliate to the group (the CTO was actually a Vodafone secondee (a secondee is someone who has moved from one company to work temporarily in another)), worked closely with the global team; they announced in January 2002 that they would continue with Nokia as their 3G supplier. Vodafone in Ireland announced its 3G infrastructure supplier as Nokia in September 2002; Ericsson provided GSM. These decisions created synergy leverage both locally and at the group level, contributed to the publicly quoted cost synergy targets after the Mannesmann AG acquisition, and ended a seriously active period. Essentially, the ethos was to leverage at the global level all local "Buy decisions," as Robert Osborn, a colleague in Japan, proposed naming such an event; that is, any requirement in common with two or more operators would be leveraged up to secure improved commercial terms, especially price.

In 2001 I became the nominated sponsor for eCommerce on what was termed the "Buy-side," with a particular emphasis on the supply chain. The continued evolution of eRelationship, introduced as an interorganizational system (IOS) in the Vodafone-Ericsson global relationship and actually hosted by Ericsson, was ongoing, having been a virtual workstream in the formative stages of the journey. The next dimension to be introduced was eRFI or eRFQ, which led to the option for reverse electronic auctions (eAuctions). We held the first eAuction for a second-source supplier for the UK 3G network infrastructure.

On February 12, 2004, Vodafone announced the commercial launch of its 3G services in Europe. The first service from Vodafone was the Vodafone Mobile Connect 3G/GPRS datacard, Europe's first high-speed laptop datacard. This datacard was available in Germany, Italy, the Netherlands, Portugal, Spain, Sweden, and the UK over the subsequent four weeks. The commercial launch of the 3G datacard followed successful customer trials conducted across Europe with thousands of business customers. As noted earlier, Vodafone live! was launched on November 10, 2004. Initially launched in October 2002, Vodafone live! was the first mobile service to integrate handsets, networks, content, and services to produce an end-to-end, easy to use product. Vodafone live! with 3G became the next generation of Vodafone's multimedia consumer offering. The customer experience was transformed by faster download speeds and improved quality of sound and images, encouraging increasing adoption and usage of Vodafone's services.

As of March 2006, Vodafone had spent a total of £14.7 billion on 3G licenses around the world. At that time the company also announced that it had met its target of 10 million customers who were using its 3G mobile phone services.[9]

The Telecom Industry Introduction of the Reverse eAuction

Toward the end of 2001 a Vodafone Group eCommerce initiative was started in which there three principal segments: Buy-side, In-side, and Sell-side. I was assigned the role of "process sponsor" for the Buy-side activities. In support of this responsibility I recruited into the business Ling Siow Chang as head of e–Supply Chain, who joined the management team in November 2001 to lead the eCommerce activities.

Although the scope of the process sponsor was general to the business, it was nevertheless interesting to resolve a methodology to model a mobile network infrastructure Web-based reverse eAuction, because of the substantial amounts of money involved. The process led to an industry-leading outcome.

In the meantime, at Vodafone-Panafon in Greece, a vendor selection process was under way to award the 3G UMTS (Universal Mobile Telephone System used synonymously with 3G or Third Generation) mobile network infrastructure contracts that needed to be deployed by June 2004, in time for the Olympic Games. The RFI was issued in November 2001. What happened next was to become the conceptual precursor for the industry-leading use of reverse eAuctions for the acquisition of mobile network infrastructure; this became a major shift in the game structure of sourcing, a change being principally advantageous to Vodafone.

The first Web-based mobile network infrastructure eAuction was held to provide a second 3G Radio Access Network (UTRAN) supplier for the UK. The eAuction used the Emptoris application and engaged four vendors (Ericsson, Nokia, Nortel, and Siemens). Using the vendor RFQ responses as the initial input for the eAuction, this event ran from October 28 to October 30, 2003, compressing substantially the several months of multiple RFQ rounds used in Greece to just a few days. This event was to change the industry game for both Vodafone and the vendors, who, of course, much preferred the old-fashioned way of face-to-face negotiations. The key game attributes of the eAuction are that the business is awarded to the vendor with the lowest cash cost and any bids on the Global Price Book (GPB) become binding pricing thereafter, win or lose the eAuction.

Beer reports that the eAuction pilot projects were an immediate success and quotes Chang, my head of e–Supply Chain. Chang comments that eAuction cost reductions were expected to be around 10–15%, but "the actual result was 30–50%."[10] I would posit that an eAuction is a tactical mechanism that advances the pace of price reduction to the "floor," the lowest point at which the vendors are willing to do business; one cannot discount the possibility that vendors may indeed bid below cost on the basis of their assessment of longer-term expectations or forecasts. It remains an open question, at least for mobile network infrastructure, as to whether eAuctions have a continued strategic role absent substantive enhancements to the model used.

In the Vodafone fiscal year 2004–2005 (April 2004 to March 2005), 1,148 eAuctions were held for a gross value of "€1.0 billion of spend" and substantial savings, the magnitude of which is "estimated to be in excess of €300m," with an "average eAuction price reduction (to date) of 26%"; "18 local operators participate in the program."[11] The cross-category momentum had clearly been established in practice across the Vodafone Group.

Chang summarizes: "We spent 2003 on proof of concept, in 2004 we focussed on strategies and we expect e-sourcing to be 'business as usual' throughout Vodafone by the end of this year [2005]."[12] Beer reports that Vodafone has a proposed eAuction spending target of €2 billion for the financial year ending March 2006.[13]

Vodafone to March 31, 2006

As of March 31, 2002, Vodafone had an investment in either the number-one or number-two operator on twenty-five out of the twenty-eight mobile markets in which it operated, based on registered customers. The company reported a revenue turnover of £22,845 million and a free cash flow of £2.4 billion; the company also recorded a proportionate customer base of 101.1 million, having passed the 100-million mark during the year, less than ten years after having achieved 1 million customers.

The position by March 31, 2006, was a revenue turnover of £29.4 billion with a free cash flow, after having paid net taxes of £1.7 billion on revenue of £6.4 billion, and a proportionate customer base of 170.6 million. As the media have well recorded, there has recently been movement in the group executive and non-executive board position.

The following was reported in the *Financial Times* of London on June 6, 2006: "Is Vodafone, the acquisition machine, now itself a takeover candidate? Its market capitalisation of $140-billion ranks ninth in the world. After August's jumbo dividends this falls to $119-billion, and 34th place." Only time will tell.

3 The Journey to a Global Network Starting Positions: How It All Began

Vodafone

It was established in late 1998 that, in order to realize the global cost synergies anticipated by Vodafone as arising from a potential merger (at that time) with AirTouch Communications, Inc., of California, the interorganizational relationships with supply partners needed to be globalized—without actually qualifying what was intended by the term "globalization" or indeed, in the circumstances, how this relationship transformation was to be achieved. What was clear, however, was that "globalization" should not be considered synonymous with "centralization"; in fact, the contrary. As became evident later, it was paramount that this globalization endeavor engage the parties affected by implementation of the chosen strategy, an inclusive process that was to remain the ethos through this and the subsequent phases to a point of inflection introduced in Chapter 5. It was recognized that the mobile network infrastructure cost synergies for Vodafone could only be realized by the in-country operations. The value and effectiveness were demonstrably evident throughout the subsequent achievement of the financial aggregation cost synergies.

The initial supply partner with whom the Vodafone Group Plc interests had the greatest level of expenditure on cellular network infrastructure (and, therefore, potential leverage) was Ericsson Radio, AB of Sweden. This infrastructure included radio network and switching hardware, software, and various services. It was anticipated that this lead supplier status would be unchanged by the forthcoming merger, which was the case, although new suppliers were also chosen. In 1998 I met with Nils Grimsmo, group managing director of Ericsson Telecommunications Limited and a Norwegian based in the UK who was the contact for all matters relating to Ericsson and Vodafone. We resolved that there was a shared interest and common strategy in seeking to globalize the business relationship that would contribute to the aggregated cost synergies now being sought by Vodafone. The operational focus would be the enhancement of all aspects of the interorganizational (end-to-end) supply chain management processes and elimination of replicated functions and processes.

My role initially, as a director in Vodafone Limited, was to lead this globalization program on behalf of Vodafone Group equity interests. I had led management of the business relationship with Ericsson Radio AB since May 1996. This role included managing commercial negotiations, the business relationship, and the development and introduction of supply chain management principles and processes into the firm. Vodafone Limited was the largest and longest-established Ericsson customer in the Vodafone Group Plc equity interests at that time.

There were initially four network operating companies who were customers of Ericsson and in which (at that time) Vodafone Group Plc had the majority equity interest:

▶ Vodafone Limited (UK); 100% equity interest
▶ Libertel (Holland); 70% equity interest
▶ Panafon (Greece); 55% equity interest
▶ Vodafone Australia (to include Fiji); 91% equity interest

The latter three companies had in 1998 explored a Global Purchasing Agreement (GPA) with Ericsson, mediated by Paul Wybrow of Vodafone Group International Limited. I was invited to attend occasional meetings as an adviser (but not negotiator). These Vodafone companies suspected (rightly so) that the UK commercial position with Ericsson was more beneficial than their own. What this exercise accomplished, however, was to begin to get the Vodafone operating companies exchanging information with each other.

It is relevant to recognize that historically these Vodafone equity interests essentially operated under the jurisdiction of the local in-country management. There were, of course, communication between those companies and an overall group management but no particular obligation to engage in supply partnerships and/or practices in common. This globalization program, therefore, was to embark on a journey into areas previously not engaged in or exploited for the common commercial benefit.

The commercial terms and supply chain processes motivated voluntary participation of these companies toward globalization of the interorganizational relationship with Ericsson, as well as created a positive dynamic in the relationships within and between the organizations. Given the commercial sensitivity of much of the detailed information, since this was the first globalization venture in the industry sector, disclosure will be limited throughout due to confidentiality, although the nature of the outcome will be clear.

Ericsson

Within Ericsson, the local companies were (and are) each 100% owned subsidiaries. The initial business relationship between the two global organizations (Ericsson as supplier and Vodafone as customer) was at a local

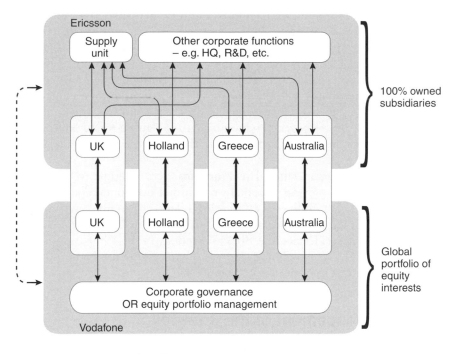

Figure 3.1 **The Vodafone-Ericsson interorganizational relationships prior to globalization project**

Source: Ibbott, C. J. (2001). An IS-Enabled Model for the Transformation and Globalisaiton of Interorganisational and Intercompany Relationships. Doctor of Business Administration (DBA). Brunel University, U.K., p. 131

in-country level as illustrated in Figure 3.1. The Vodafone (*shown at bottom*) and Ericsson (*shown at top*) equity interests transacted separately negotiated commercial agreements. Vodafone equity interests were run and operated by the local management teams. The Vodafone corporate offices in the UK governed the Vodafone interests. The Ericsson local subsidiaries were subject to their own business rules as established through their corporate organization and regional governance. Communication between Ericsson and Vodafone was carried out indirectly through their local equity interests.

Vodafone orders for Ericsson products (equipment, software, etc.) were placed with the Ericsson local country subsidiary, as were any requests for forecasted supply requirements. All communication locally was direct (that is, not mediated) through meetings, letters, e-mails, faxes, and telephone calls. Usually, communication and meetings between the Vodafone and Ericsson corporate units, however, were mediated and arranged by Ericsson's local subsidiary; the local Ericsson representatives generally attended all customer meetings with the Ericsson corporate units. Ericsson viewed the interorganizational relationships as multiple and "owned" by each of their in-country subsidiaries. In this approach, even if equipment supplied was the same to the customer in different countries, the configurations and supply processes varied between countries, giving rise to unnecessary costs, lack of economic scale, and therefore lack of cost synergy yields, for all engaged parties.

The global interorganizational relationships were multiple, vertical, and hierarchical with no particular formal or informal horizontal coordination. The strategies being followed at the local level by both Ericsson and Vodafone were therefore local, not coordinated or driven from a collective corporate perspective. In fact, the Ericsson strategy in the 1990s as espoused by the then CEO, Dr. Lars Ramqvist, was one of global products and local business, in contrast to what prevails today.

The Commencement of the Journey Toward a Global Network

The Vodafone-Ericsson meeting that initiated the journey took place in Newbury, UK, on February 25–26, 1999.[1] In attendance were the participants of the four in-country Vodafone operating interests (in the UK, Holland, Greece, and Australia/Fiji), their Ericsson in-country counterparts together with the team leaders (me and my Ericsson counterpart), and a few members of their teams. My objective in discussing the scope of the actions agreed at this inaugural meeting is to demonstrate the scope of these virtual workstreams, the geographic distribution of the assignments, and the inclusive approach. Although the two organizations shared a common strategy, to globalize the business relationship, there was to be no sharing of information concerning synergy yields; therefore, any asymmetry in the timing or value of such benefits was accepted mutually by the parties. There was, however, transparency of the variable synergy yields among the Vodafone interests, all coordinated by my center or global team. Prior to this inaugural meeting there was no preordained plan or anticipated approach that was to be followed, only a joint Vodafone-Ericsson commitment to globalize the interorganizational business relationship. Vodafone clearly declared its intention to realize its internal global cost synergy objectives arising from the intended merger with AirTouch.

This meeting established virtual workstreams that were assigned jointly to the in-country operations of both Vodafone and Ericsson, with each set up to pursue relevant initiatives on behalf of the collective group. The participants at the meeting also agreed that all progress on the virtual workstreams would be reported to this forum, although detailed project plans and economic objectives were not set.

To open this meeting, I made a presentation on global supply chain management, a concept new to the non-UK companies. I specifically noted that the meeting was the inaugural endeavor to share views and opinions on the new subject of supply chain management. Afterward, we would agree on actions to take in this endeavor. I stated further that although cost of acquisition is key, it cannot be separated from the necessity to change processes, working practices, and even how and what purchases we specify. A supply chain management principle, which includes price, has other attributes for us to consider. Vodafone Limited has agreed on a policy to cover such matters. After explaining Vodafone's required commercial principles, I stated that there must be an acceptance on both sides (Vodafone and Ericsson at both the global and local levels) of the inevitability of changed practices and processes for the overriding cost aggregation objectives to be realized. It shall no longer be a head-bashing session solely based on price. Vodafone Limited, because of its recent eighteen-month experience with Ericsson, can already attest to the value of accepting the propositions of change.

I shared the sourcing philosophy that Vodafone Limited had introduced and agreed to the acquisition of mobile network infrastructure (this presentation had been given April 15, 1997 to Nils Grimsmo, among others). I concluded with a statement of the mutually adopted philosophy: We agreed that our joint philosophy was that at all times Vodafone would be able to state (to any third party) that even though Ericsson may be the dominant supplier of mobile network infrastructure, it has at no time abused its dominant position. This was a crucial philosophical point in the supplier relationship to reinforce for the meeting participants, given that this was a supplier relationship in which there was a high (or even prohibitive) cost to switch to an alternative, as well as service risk to customers.

I explained a difference between global and local thinking with an example: in a local situation, to secure best commercial terms, one often has more than one supplier to assure competition. However, in global thinking, this same debate for competitive commercial terms must be elevated to the global stage. In-country it may be reasonable to have multiple suppliers, but this should only be contemplated if it does not compromise the simplicity of execution within country. For network infrastructure in the GSM standards, overhead and complexity are compromised if multiple mobile network infrastructure supply partners are engaged, especially if the mandate of the operating company is to a homogeneous national network service of consistent quality.

Although all existing trading relationships between the Vodafone and Ericsson organizations were vested in local in-country agreements, it was now a key requirement for the open sharing of all commercially sensitive information. It created transparency (for the first time) to the Vodafone and Ericsson organizations of all transactions and the terms thereof being conducted between the parties in the consenting group; that is, all commercial differentials would become entirely visible to all. Although not stated at this time, this transparency meant that when or if an Ericsson subsidiary was in communication with any one of the Vodafone subsidiaries, it essentially was talking to a part of an otherwise homogeneous single global entity, which was a major step in overcoming the hurdles of globalizing. This was to be the first step toward forming a global virtual community joined through an emergent and co-evolving new culture within and between both organizations.

The actions taken at the inaugural meeting enhanced the focus on global cost synergies arising particularly from the new global scale established with the AirTouch merger and the later Mannesmann AG acquisition. This required the transformation of otherwise local in-country customer-supplier business relationships, their vision, and their practices onto a global stage. New interorganizational and intracompany (within and between either organization) relationships would need to be created. This endeavor was to be a new, formative, direction-setting experience for both the companies involved and the industry as a whole. Vodafone intended to utilize the organizational learning experience from this program as the basis for engaging with other prospective global supply partners emerging from the merger and acquisition.

The construct of this inaugural and subsequent global virtual team meetings was the participation by individuals from both the Vodafone and Ericsson local companies and others from the central or corporate resources. I and my Ericsson counterpart had joint responsibility for the global leadership. This forum was to become a defining event for global virtual team networking and was certainly the most advanced such forum in the Vodafone organization at the time. These meetings were hosted in rotation by the joint in-country operations to avoid the perception of this globalization program as being UK (or head office) centric. This approach had the benefit of reflecting its global inclusion. The participants in this and subsequent such meetings had now de facto agreed to engage in an informal, nonhierarchical, horizontal team structure. Figure 3.2a illustrates the hierarchical composition of participants in the early meetings. The number of total Vodafone and Ericsson participants over time increased because of the increasing number of engaged operating companies following both the Vodafone merger and subsequent acquisition.

Given the differences between the job titles and positions within the Vodafone-Ericsson organizations and the companies therein, I have attempted to standardize the positions of the meeting participants to the prevailing role definitions in the UK and do not believe that any major disparity has been introduced. In the figure my position is categorized as a director, whereas the Ericsson global contact's position, as a managing director. Throughout these meetings I was the senior representative for the Vodafone organization. The figure shows the positions of the participants, the number and types of meetings, and the locations where the meetings were held.

A secondary benefit of operating in an informal way was that the virtual team was obligated to show evidence of progress and/or conclusions at the future global forums. A tertiary benefit was the inclusive virtual progress that arose because the meeting participants had to consult with others in their companies on the assigned actions. Therefore, the process would result in recommendations for implementation that were known beforehand to be executable by the parties. This approach contrasts with a detached centralist approach wherein the impacted parties may not be consulted or included in the decision-making process and decisions may be made without taking their interests into account. Two initial points of agreement from the inaugural

Global Forum meetings							
Positions of participants	Newbury	Maastrict	Athens	Nynashamn	Cairo	Lisbon	Bucharest
Vodafone Org.:							
Managing director	0	0	0	0	0	0	0
Director	3	2	1	2	2	2	2
Executive	1	2	2	3	7	6	6
Senior manager	2	3	3	8	8	8	13
Other actors	1	3	3	4	3	6	3
Total in attendance:	7	10	9	17	20	22	24
Ericsson Org.:							
Managing director	2	2	2	3	2	2	2
Director	0	2	2	1	2	2	2
Executive	3	3	3	7	8	9	5
Senior manager	0	2	2	7	12	12	16
Other actors	1	1	4	2	1	1	1
Total in attendance:	6	10	13	20	25	26	26

Figure 3.2a **Composition of participants in and locations of the global forum meetings**

Note: The Global forum meetings were the core meetings

Source: Ibbott, C. J. (2001). An IS-Enabled Model for the Transformation and Globalisaiton of Interorganisational and Intercompany Relationships. Doctor of Business Administration (DBA). Brunel University, U.K., p. 319

meeting had transformational significance, even at this early stage. The participants representing their in-country operating interests collectively agreed on the outcomes for action. They also agreed that they had de facto informally and voluntarily acceded local "power" to a global governance body of which they had become a part (a matter that was to be formalized later). Most of the participants probably did not fully realize the eventual ramifications of the latter point.

This inaugural meeting also initiated a number of virtual workstreams, for example, the creation, structure, and negotiation of a Global Price Book (GPB) and the commercial terms to be associated therewith for the interorganizational business of the participating Vodafone companies. I considered this a first move toward what would financially motivate and move matters forward, at least on the Vodafone side. The first GPB was accepted and backdated effective April 1, 1999. While simultaneously recognizing there may be some difficulties in its creation, a target completion date of the end of July 1999 was agreed.

The participants also discussed that whatever the going-forward process would become, it would be inclusive of the geographically dispersed Vodafone companies. I do not believe that at this stage the significance of this move had fully registered with the Vodafone-Ericsson team or what was now becoming a global virtual community. This action, however, meant that the UK had the first (virtual) team assignment to both agree to the relevant configurations between the operating companies and to conclude the first global pricing on behalf of the collective. This was to be the first accession of "power" in-country in the transition toward the global leadership and a transformed intra- and interorganizational paradigm. These actions commenced the transformation of local intercompany and interorganizational business relationships. No local negotiations were thereafter permitted on the defined product set in the GPB.

The role of the Ericsson local in-country companies was also changed. This, too, was a visible move, at least for Vodafone, toward deriving global cost (specifically not limited to price) synergies arising from the global scale and coordinated actions, a framework on which to build the Ericsson relationship and later relationships with others. Further, this move provided the basis and mechanism through which to harmonize, standardize, and limit the diversity of equipment being sourced—a true supply chain endeavor. Clearly, such a move leads to scalar volumes for Ericsson, ease of redirection in the event of changed delivery timing requirements, and the prospect of field quality improvements for the mobile operator the more polarized the delivered configurations.

Completion of this action would also yield the first tangible cost synergy benefit to the local Vodafone operating companies resulting from their voluntary participation and motivate (it was hoped) them toward the broader aspects of the global initiative. The contractual structure meant that the operating companies had to voluntarily elect into this program and eventually change their local agreements to incorporate the global proposition. This change progressed by and through new global agreements to a newly formed and collective global constitution that was to eventually discharge all prior local in-country Vodafone-Ericsson business agreements.

Significantly, taking this first step began the process of acceding commercial governance and negotiating authority on their behalf to a third (albeit internal) party, their future input being through the global forum and virtual workstreams. I was the signatory to these agreements and the commercial governance generally associated therewith. However, a governance forum was later introduced to draw up such legal global agreements for the Vodafone Group whose decisions de facto obliged the Vodafone in-country operating company's compliance. The in-country operating company had the responsibility through its governance procedures to adopt the globally agreed matters into local agreements with Ericsson. In concept, the same applies to the onset of significant changes in interorganizational and intercompany practices. I considered the eventual organizational ramifications to be potentially far more significant should it be the desire to embrace fully the aggregation cost synergy opportunities across the end-to-end supply chain.

In anticipation of what I thought requisite for a globalizing proposition to function effectively (and without impact to the engaged participants) over different geographies and time zones, we included an agenda item in the inaugural forum called "Utilization of Intranet and Extranet," the concept being to support the interworkings between organizations and companies. This thought was triggered by my reading of Orlikowski, who discusses a situated change perspective in which the "organisational transformation is seen here [in the situated change context] to be an ongoing improvisation enacted by organisational actors [people] trying to make sense of and act coherently in the world."[2] Such circumstances exactly parallel this program, in that the organizational changes effected here were not planned, a point also challenged by Orlikowski. The timely visibility of all the globalization activities, unencumbered by time and geography, therefore was anticipated to be key factor.

The relevant prompt came from Orlikowski and Hofman, in which they discuss Groupware Technologies.[3] The introduction of this topic unfortunately quickly moved the discussion on to the technology of EDI. I was not, however, seeking a technological debate but one on the eventual need for a global informational coordinating "mechanism," but at that time did not give the idea much further thought. This mechanism eventually took the form of IS-Enablement[4] to the overall process of further changes required in the program. The ensuing concept I introduced in pursuit thereof as the embodiment of the interorganisational global relationship was later operationalized by Ericsson and became known as eRelationship (an assigned virtual workstream action for the Dutch subsidiary).

The other joint Vodafone-Ericsson in-country virtual workstreams initiated in the inaugural meeting were the Global Agreement (undertaken in the UK); optimization and therefore reduced diversity of the available Radio Base Station configurations (UK); the optimization of MSC (Mobile Switching Center) and BSC (Base Station Controller in GSM) switch configurations and expansion options (Greece); common software, audit, testing, and delivery (Australia). All Vodafone and Ericsson in-country operations and their center functions combined and acted in support of all the virtual workstream assignments.

Face-to-face time is an important facet in the development of an effective and cohesive globally dispersed virtual community. To that end it was determined that all such future meetings would be hosted on rotation, thereby enabling cluster-member countries to embrace the cultural diversity and neutralize the impact of the in-country operator size. This decision became quite competitive in a positive way, with clear evidence of national pride in being the host country. This socially interweaving approach was to cement and bond this virtual community. I observed no natural bias or clustering in the manner in which the team came together at such meetings, including between Vodafone and Ericsson; such meetings were initially scheduled quasi quarterly.

In addition to the meetings, many other communications and exchanges occurred between people within and between both organizations. Vodafone held ad hoc virtual team meetings that engaged individuals from the local companies participating in the program, including central resources. These virtual meetings were held to coordinate internal actions and/or establish a Vodafone position with respect to the Ericsson position on any given issue. Such meetings had the supplemental value of virtual team networking and extending the reach of the emergent social network. I had many meetings related to the global negotiations, which included discussions with the purpose of creating momentum to move the process forward, and many relating to Ericsson's local and corporate organizational structure. These communications included e-mails, faxes, telephone calls, conference calls, and such other meetings deemed appropriate.

I made a number of visits to participating companies, both with and independently of an Ericsson executive (Kaj Snellman), to promote the interest and continued support for this interorganizational globalization initiative. I generally focused the presentations on the developing and/or evolving concepts around the globalization paradigm. These presentations, interspersed with the global forum, were made to a local in-country Vodafone or Ericsson audience, or on some occasions to both. There was no strategy to the sequence in which the visits were made other than to extend the reach of and stakeholder engagement in my personal social network. I was also invited by Ericsson to make a number of presentations to their general management aimed at stimulating awareness in a broader audience of the relevance and achievements of the mutual globalization program. I was generally introduced as the voice of what became Ericsson's largest global customer for mobile network infrastructure.

Summary of the Inaugural Global Forum and Outcomes

This forum was not the derivative of a written mandate or a recognized entity in any budget but an informal interorganizational formation of a global virtual team sharing an interest within which a new and diverse cross-organizational culture emerged. It was a voluntary endeavor establishing a unique and truly global social community and culture in pursuit of objectives not otherwise pursued in the mobile telecommunication industry. A further outcome was the development of and accrual of social capital among the parties. Even at this stage, this organization did not exist in any company charts or in any budget. Although it was essentially invisible, it eventually generated substantial aggregation cost synergies for Vodafone.

Another important factor is that all business transactions between Vodafone and Ericsson arising from these initiatives happened in-country. Without their engagement the synergy realization would not have been; nothing was transacted at the global level notwithstanding the leadership role. Given the ensuing financial contributions over the years to follow, this attests to the great influence this global forum and its participants had over the in-country operating units, as well as the influence of my de facto role and the reciprocal influence of and with the key stakeholders, all of whom were in my social network.

It was agreed that progress on all the virtual team (or virtual workstream) activities would be jointly reported at the subsequent global Vodafone-Ericsson meetings. These virtual teams could independently set up whatever meetings they thought necessary with anyone they considered relevant to the achievement of their agreed action point. Other than the meeting discussing the existing UK Price Book, the basis on which the global terms would be initially developed, no commitments on either price or cost savings from either organization were either made or sought as preconditions to engaging in these global workstreams. This is interesting given the variable magnitude of financial benefit and the fact that the interorganizational and intracompany relationships were threshold changes through engagement in this essentially informal program. The immediate initial impact would be on Ericsson through reduced prices, with the volume and/or process economic benefits lagging, whereas the Vodafone organization received, relatively speaking, immediate value—testament to the asymmetry in the incentives arising from the common strategy of globalization. From the Vodafone perspective, the financial cost synergies were the stimulus and business measure of performance of this program. Although there remained many concerns as to how this program would actually evolve and exactly what practices and processes would be required to change that had not been anticipated, all the actions were nevertheless undertaken positively by the parties.

All the participants had positions in hierarchical line operations in either the Vodafone or Ericsson organization. When the teams accepted their assigned tasks, they had to communicate with and gain the cooperation of colleagues within their organizational hierarchy to implement the virtual workstreams identified by the global forum. Therefore, by the time resolution to an action was presented to the global forum, implementation in each of the operating companies was assured through this inclusive approach. Even though a central (or collective) approval must be sought, in reality the approval only confirms what is already known to be viable action—in direct contrast with most centrally driven programs, which essentially hand down decisions, this strategy may have the sense of a federal approach and therefore the slow route, by having a community strategy and the assignment of a team contributions, the virtual workstream teams focused on solutions rather than questioned the merits of the assignment. Perhaps these outcomes attest to the value of a shared interorganisational global culture.

For a number of the Ericsson and Vodafone participants in the inaugural meeting, the rationale and objectives were not clearly understood in advance because no agenda was provided. Many were surprised by and unprepared for the meeting content. It had been a deliberate choice not to brief prior to the meeting so that the message could be conveyed simultaneously to both organizations and immediate responses could be given to feedback. The proposals were very well received. The meeting provided a platform for commercial discussions and discussions on improvement projects in many areas, in addition to improving the overall Vodafone-Ericsson global business relationship.

A Dutch participant commented that the working principles were the most important thing that came out of the meeting; they enabled the team to work together in a professional and amicable way. However, he indicated that Ericsson's local Dutch organization greatly lacked understanding of the principles involved because of their lack of internal communication. The suggestion was that perhaps there should have been a formal approach to the communications. My own observation supports that view, in light of his recalling a prior intermeeting communication among the Vodafone participants, which gave him a better understanding. However, the situational circumstances for this inaugural interorganizational meeting were chosen purposely to avoid premeeting positioning and so achieve spontaneous responses on the proposals for globalization.

Maastricht, Holland

The next global forum, the first test of commitment, was hosted in Maastricht on April 14–15, 1999. The premeeting dinner was held at L'Auberge Neercannes, near Maastricht. It was already evident that the hosting of these meetings was to become in itself a competitive endeavor, perhaps seeking to display an element of national pride. Anecdotally, this restaurant boasted (in the wine cellar, or cave in the hillside) a plaque signed by all the prime ministers who were party to the famed Maastricht Treaty. I am quite sure that nothing should be read into that coincidence in choice of venue, nor should one imply any omen or indeed any parallel in anticipation of the outcome of this series of global meetings. At the predinner cocktail reception, the group was substantially more relaxed than at the meetings, and informal social networking was under way with no evidence of national grouping but rather an effective integration of the cultural mix.

The approach to this and subsequent meetings was for each of the Vodafone and Ericsson participants to have individual premeetings prior to the combined forum. For Vodafone this was the opportunity to align on the relevant global, meaning the multiple in-country operating company, issues to be raised in the joint forum session. The point to note is that the virtual operating company teams (or Ericsson cluster) had already identified that this forum was an opportunity to raise collective global matters to Ericsson, an unintended but nevertheless positive attribute. As the focus of this book is on the leadership, management, and organizational experiential learning, operational details considered at these meetings will not be discussed here. This meeting resolved to invite the Egyptian mobile operator in which Vodafone had an interest to join what had now been labeled the Ericsson "Club." It was interesting that people actually sought to learn more of this "Club," what its benefits were and how to join, perhaps attesting to the fact that good news travels fast. The invitation to Egypt was a preemptive move in anticipation of the Vodafone-AirTouch merger, which would be complete in June 1999.

Athens, Greece

The next meeting on May 26–27, 1999, was hosted in Athens. A Dutch participant from Vodafone commented that during this meeting was the first time the attendees felt as one and part of a truly global company; perhaps there should have been a qualifier that it was the experience of this community to which he referred, not the company in general. The mood of the joint teams over dinner, attended by the president of the Ericsson local company, was very relaxed. It was again evident in the actions of the meeting participants and their vigorous exchanges that the informal network was beginning to work. Following the dinner this time, there was a "breakout group" from both organizations that elected to head for the nightlife, while the more mature or cautious (like me) elected to retire for the night. A Dutch representative also recalls questioning, in his mind, the conflict between the cost of staging these meetings and the objectives of the extensive cost reduction programs; my view was that perhaps the richness of these meetings may have temporarily escaped his attention.

In the meeting Ericsson's Dutch team proposed to initiate a "low-hanging fruit" activity for the mutual economic synergy benefit. They proposed an activity through which the individual Vodafone operating companies could share best practice, and thereby have the potential to realize quick collective (cost synergy) wins. The meeting accepted that this activity should proceed. The observation was that the culture of this community was becoming embedded in a way that stimulated thinking about ways to achieve cost synergy savings. It was also clear that the scope of communication outside this global forum, nonetheless facilitated by it, was establishing a complex and informal social network that essentially got things done. It must be stressed again that this global forum had an informal status; it perhaps was unusually demonstrable innovation seated within a corporate structure. The existence of this community was demonstrated by the financial performance in cost synergy contributions yielded, at least as measured within Vodafone. One may conclude that had all the normal mandate processes been adhered to, the positive financial outcomes and the collaboration realized would not have occurred.

Amsterdam, Holland

I was invited to make a presentation to a meeting on July 26–27, 1999, in Amsterdam. This meeting had already been scheduled for the AirTouch properties prior to the merger of AirTouch with Vodafone. The operating companies at this meeting were trading with Ericsson, already engaged in seeking to achieve the globalization of certain activities. The new countries represented and to whom I was introduced were Germany, Portugal, and Romania.

The minutes of their prior meeting in Lisbon, Portugal (June 9, 1999), showed that in attendance were representatives from Ericsson and the operating companies in Spain, Romania, Portugal, and AirTouch International of California. That meeting was held immediately prior to the formation of Vodafone AirTouch Plc. Their objectives were outlined in "Vendor-Operator Relationship—Framework for Success":

▶ Streamlined processes for commodity products
▶ Partnership approach for customized solutions for new business development

▶ Trust
▶ Risk sharing
▶ Profit sharing ("carrot and the stick")
▶ Common understanding of operations' long-term network development
▶ Joint advertising campaign and sponsorship
▶ Recognition and acting on common objectives and processes

Interestingly, the objective of this forum was much the same as the initiative that Vodafone and Ericsson had jointly undertaken: to leverage multiproperty (or global) scale, at least in the interest of Vodafone, while simultaneously recognizing changes of practice that facilitate the ability of Ericsson to respond to the commercial requirements. Although certain of the points made were relevant to that process, the key act of globalization appeared to be off the agenda (or was avoided), given that a topic of discussion was "Issues for Local Negotiations," under which is listed "Customs Issues, Inventory Issues, Invoicing Issues, Prices, and Legal Issues."

This introduction served as an interesting contrast to what was presented by me to the meeting, given that issues classified as local were considered the key to leveraging global scale. They actually should have been considered outside the local-country context, as should all items (products and/or services) being sourced in common. Nevertheless, they seemed to take a managed bottoms-up approach, one perhaps lacking in leadership, vision, and strategy as a catalyst and purpose for mutual engagement of the parties, a very operational approach. This very structured approach and inner thinking were entirely contrary to the ethos and ensuing culture that we had established, as would be evident from my presentation.

The first day of the meeting involved only AirTouch companies. A joint meeting was held on the second day with AirTouch and their local Ericsson companies. The meeting host was a member of the AirTouch organization who had been attempting to coerce these companies to work together. However, they were not progressing toward the global paradigm that Vodafone was seeking to motivate them to join, which had more radical ambitions. The general reaction to my presentation was favorable toward their ongoing engagement in the extant Vodafone-Ericsson program.

The two senior attendees from Germany (John Thompson and Dr. Johann Waltar) expressed their pleasure that the existing Vodafone forum included an operating company (in the UK) similar in size to theirs and that they saw this as a reason for their future engagement in such synergy activities. It was agreed that following their return to Germany, they would consider inviting me to Düsseldorf for further dialogue about how we could work together.

My observation of the joint session with Ericsson was that this forum was somewhat less advanced in its vision (this was not in evidence or discussed) and progress toward the realization of aggregation cost synergies compared to that we had established and were continuing to develop between Vodafone and Ericsson. A clear value and benefit, therefore, would result if these teams were so persuaded and motivated to engage, which did eventually happen.

Nynashamn, Sweden

On September 2–3, 1999, the meeting was hosted by Ericsson at Nynashamn near Stockholm, Sweden. Dinner on the first night was followed by much networking. Again the social grouping was not national, Vodafone-Ericsson, or rank based, which suggests that levels of confidence, trust, and friendship were prevailing, much the same as happened in Greece at the previous meeting—all of which enhance the level of accrued social capital. At the last meeting a comment was made about the perspective of now being truly global; this global community preceded all other global activities in Vodafone or Ericsson, and there was now a clear pioneering spirit and camaraderie among the team in evidence. This meeting included the introduction of colleagues from three new companies in which Vodafone now had an equity interest arising from the AirTouch merger, together with the Ericsson corresponding local subsidiary counterparts. Following are the companies and Vodafone's (then) equity interest:

▶ Telecel Comunicaçöes Pessoais S.A. of Portugal, 51% equity interest
▶ Misrfone Telecommunications Company S.A.E. of Egypt, 60% equity interest
▶ Mobifon S.A. of Romania, 10% equity interest

In the Vodafone premeeting I raised the question of how the (virtual) organization of this global forum should be structured, given the increasing number of companies in which Vodafone had an equity interest that were electing to participate in the globalization initiative. This was of particular concern since the program involved only one supply partner (Ericsson) at that time. After the Vodafone-AirTouch merger, consideration of Nokia and Siemens as candidate global suppliers emerged. All attendees were asked to provide feedback, and this subject would be discussed at the next global forum premeeting. Also discussed were meeting reports and a request that when people attended other meetings covering subjects within this global forum, reports were generated and distributed within the "Club," or "Club 7," as it had now been named in recognition of the seven countries that participated. This was an interesting approach from within to give the community a collective identity.

It also was becoming evident that a divide was developing between those individuals who actively participated and progressed actions between these global forum meetings and those who were less engaged in the meetings and/or were not really making adequate progress between meetings. Allowances for the new entrants, of course, should be considered, but the issue applied to certain of the original members. For some, the lack of fluent English may have been a barrier to both meeting participation and clarification of the understanding of the actions and the associated commitments. Further, the seniority, and therefore the authority, of certain Vodafone representatives in their companies may have limited their ability to commit resources to global initiatives notwithstanding the potential financial synergy benefits. Alternatively, the issue may have been that there was a need to engage other departments, although there may have been an element of the local priorities prevailing.

The meetings had become large (thirty-seven attendees at this meeting); however, a consistent observation by participants since the Maastricht meeting was that regardless of the number of attendees, these global meetings were very orderly and without any breakdown or chaos. This observation perhaps gives testimony to the intensity of interest by all concerned in a mutually successful realization locally of the aggregation cost synergy opportunities.

My personal objective was to impart knowledge and experience to the global community and not to create an irrevocable dependency. To that end I began to progressively move my seating location toward the rear of the room, deferring the process and leadership of the meetings to others in the forum. I worked on other tasks, such as sending e-mail, while keeping an ear open to the exchanges in the proceedings. Should for some reason I sense a discussion drifting away from the agreed strategy and/or not moving to a satisfactory resolution, then I would intercede. The impact of this move over time was to transfer the operational and leadership attributes of the forum to others closer to or impacted by the ensuing discussions and decisions, leaving me to focus on the vision and strategy and to assure positive progress. Again, the "others" to whom the implied responsibilities were in effect transferred, save the few who were in my direct team, were the in-country forum members from Vodafone and Ericsson who had no direct or indirect reporting line to me and my team. From my perspective this was evidence of a transfer of initiative ownership and commitment to the local in-country organization, which ultimately would be the source of substantive aggregation synergy benefits arising from alignment in all dimensions of practice, which benefits were not derived from the central teams.

At dinner, in my speech of thanks to the hosts, I pointed out to the team that they represented the most advanced group engaged in the globalization of both interorganizational and intercompany relationships, and that they should be complimented on their positive and continuous drive in this regard. Following the off-site dinner we returned to the conference venue, and again a large contingent of the assembled team stay up to the early hours playing snooker.

Subsequently I received a letter from Per-Arne Sandström, executive vice president of Ericsson, commenting on my after-dinner speech: "Your speech to us in the evening was so to the point with regard to how our [business] relationship has developed over the last two years and the enormous potential that lies ahead of us. What we are doing now is true pioneering in industrial relationships in our business." This was a positive reflection perhaps of the transformation in which we were engaged by someone who had occasional involvement and who was nevertheless a serious and continuing supporter of the globalization endeavor.

Copenhagen, Denmark

A new global supplier prospect, Nokia, with whom Vodafone now had the second-highest global expenditure because of the increased number of equity interests, invited me to make a presentation to their regional management team, which included representatives from locations where they traded with Vodafone. This meeting, held in Copenhagen, Denmark, on October 21, 1999, represented the initiation of the next phase of this journey toward globalization.

I was requested to provide an up-to-date background of the recently enlarged (through the merger with AirTouch) Vodafone organization, as well as background and understanding of the established global cost synergies program with Ericsson. The host wanted all the attendees to receive the same message simultaneously by a Vodafone representative. The attendees received a clear message regarding the vision of the globalization program and the principles through which these ambitions would be achieved.

The discussion that followed was lively; however, the participants did not focus on the overall transformation context but narrowly on the commercial principles and their consequences in regard to their extant business relationships. Without doubt the greatest impact in the short term would be the endeavor to move ahead on a globalization project with Nokia. I had previously met with Sari Baldauf, then president of Nokia Telecommunications and a member of the Nokia Group executive board (responsible for the network infrastructure business) in Finland, and she was resolute regarding the intention of Nokia to become a global supplier to Vodafone. Sari understood, however, that the globalization process was not under way at the time of this Copenhagen meeting.

Cairo, Egypt

The process moved on to a meeting in Cairo, Egypt, on January 11–12, 2000. This meeting included a new company in which the Vodafone had an equity interest, together with the local Ericsson representatives. The new company was Airtel Móvil, S.A. of Spain, in which Vodafone then had a 21.7% equity interest.

At that time the Australian representative for Vodafone was the commercial director rather than the CTO. Changes in representation from either organization in the virtual community were quite normal and did not disturb the flow or momentum of proceedings. For example, the global team working on the "road map" in the virtual workstream process reported progress; however, the action was then reassigned to the Portuguese team, who were to publish the road map inclusive of network infrastructure and terminals on eRelationship. This virtual workstream was then subsequently assigned as an Ericsson central responsibility. Therefore, it was quite normal and acceptable for "baton passing" within the community of virtual workstream assignments for any number of reasons, including resources, specialist skills, and perhaps time availability. Such actions were an accepted dynamic in the pursuit of timely progress.

A general observation of the meeting was that feedback, commentary, and contribution were not at all uniform. Vodafone representatives from Egypt, Portugal, Romania, and Holland took a fairly passive role, and the Ericsson team generally remained passive save when they were making presentations. The level of engagement in later meetings became more vigorous by all concerned, the delay perhaps relating to a lack of initial confidence and the need to develop trust. This meeting, as with all such prior global forums, surprised me with the order and ability to conclude the agenda, include effective presentations, and assign actions. The meetings did not become disorderly even though the introduced changes and transformed practices would have a great impact. A UK participant commented that perhaps this raises the question of individual depth of understanding.

Sydney, Australia

The meeting scheduled for March 21–22, 2000, in Sydney, Australia, was to have a different focus. This was an inaugural forum to review other potential global suppliers besides Ericsson and in categories beyond mobile network infrastructure. Seeking new supplier relationships while continuing with the operating interests engaging in this cost synergy aggregation initiative served to enhance the scope and depth of the emergent global virtual community operating horizontally in-country, notwithstanding the fact that the people visible in the global forums or otherwise engaged in the operating companies substantially "contributed" or were self-motivated from within those companies, at least on the Vodafone side. This meeting included the participation of four new companies in which Vodafone had an equity interest:

▶ Vodafone of New Zealand, 100% equity interest
▶ Mannesmann Mobilfunk (D2) of Germany, 99.2% equity interest
▶ AirTouch Cellular of the United States, 100% equity interest
▶ Vodafone Fiji Limited, 49% equity interest

The stay in Australia was to be eventful and enduring from a social perspective, but also relevant in building on the core relationships that had been developed earlier in the Ericsson global forums and virtual workstreams. The hosts organized some recreational events purposely to bring the team together outside the formal meetings, which included for the daredevil element a tour climbing the Sidney Harbour Bridge, stated by those who participated to be an exhilarating experience. One of the dinners was hosted by the Vodafone managing director in Australia, and another, even though this was not an Ericsson global forum, by the managing director (Karl-Henrik Sundström) of the Ericsson Australia operation; a few other people from the local organizations were also in attendance.

The Vodafone regional CEO, Brian Clark, made an opening presentation in which he offered his continued support for the global cost synergy work and cited the benefits that had already been realized through the established Vodafone-Ericsson global relationship. An executive in my UK team (Tim Williams) led a series of workshops, the first of which was entitled "Definition of Global Supply Chain Management (GSCM) Activities and Roles." The purpose of the second workshop, "Supplier Prioritization and Introduction Process," was to define a list of supplier categories. This would be a first step in broadening the pursuit of aggregation cost synergies for Vodafone.

In the third workshop, "Creation of Supplier Relationship Strategy (Virtual) Teams," supplier categories were defined. Each category had assigned (virtual) team leadership, as did the suppliers that were to be targeted within each category. The leadership team involved a participant and the person's operating company. On a virtual team basis, the assigned leader would engage all other people (operating companies) who had an interest (or the potential thereof) in the products and/or services offered by the assigned supplier.

The next workshop was entitled "Supplier Relationship Strategy." The teams, formed by supplier categories, were requested to outline, based on the activities of the day so far, and with input from those with experience of the customer-supplier relationship, the initial relationship strategies that they were considering. The penultimate workshop session looped back to the subject of the first workshop and sought to allocate the roles and responsibilities that had been previously determined. My own assigned roles and responsibilities were, the "driving force/ownership" for the core supplier category, eRelationship, (global) commercial governance, and internal sponsorship (for the promotion of the globalization activities).

The final workshop was a discussion of the organizational principles applicable to this new GSCM initiative, that is, the structure of a steering group, which was agreed to be an ongoing, evolving activity. It was recognized that this meeting did not represent the entire interests of the Vodafone organization (representatives from eleven Vodafone equity interests attended); therefore, leadership of the various virtual workstreams might change.

My assignment was to engage the CEOs of each of the Vodafone operating companies to introduce and/or reinforce the GSCM program. The primary objective was to set the pace and accelerate momentum toward the achievement of the Vodafone global cost synergy targets, which would require several years to accomplish.[5] I had already embarked on this dimension by creating a social network that was to embrace several key stakeholders with strong operational positions; given that the center did not transact with the suppliers, this was a strategic, influential strand of my activities. This was undertaken to increase business and, in some cases, extended to friendship, asymmetric relationships if judged by hierarchical ranking. I was a director with a group role, but this social network dimension included CEOs, CTOs, CFOs, and other executive management in the Vodafone operating companies and equivalent positions in the supplier organizations. The acceptance of this business relationship by all concerned became another nonhierarchical and influential virtual structure for successful implementation of the global initiatives.

This new type of meeting followed the structure of the original (Ericsson) global forums. As chairperson, I was able to guide and/or influence the outcome and pace of continuing organizational changes and/or transformation. The progress achieved in this forum derived from the experiential knowledge developed in the Ericsson global forum, aimed at broadening the scope of activity and to dispersion of the lead responsibilities of globalization representatives of various Vodafone operating company equity interests. This meeting was the first attempt to begin to formalize a view of roles and responsibilities of the global virtual community, even though not all interests of Vodafone were represented, and leadership might change following the broader community consultation.

The leader of the workshop sessions expressed the belief that this was a watershed meeting. It had become evident that the work with Ericsson, the creation of eRelationship, and the distilled knowledge and benefits from the "Club" approach was easily applicable to other global supplier relationships. The global principles were not challenged in this meeting nor the organizational implications assumed by the assembled group. For the first time the "language" of "global" (even with new members participating) was used without effort, and the concepts used without translation or explanation. The meeting represented real progress with the global opportunities, thereby evidencing a good understanding of the implications of paradigm shift to globalization. It was agreed to continue these exchanges in the premeeting in Lisbon.

Lisbon, Portugal

The meeting in Lisbon, Portugal, was held on May 10–12, 2000. The first part of the (Ericsson) premeeting of May 11 was the introduction and update of the previous meeting in Australia. Thereafter the premeeting was uneventful, save discussing the coordination of activities in respect to the Vodafone Group activities for the acquisition of the next-generation technology mobile network infrastructure, Universal Mobile Telecommunications System (UMTS), for which Vodafone in the UK had recently paid £5.9 billion for a license to operate.

The joint Vodafone-Ericsson global forum was scheduled to run for a day and a half. This meeting marked the point when all the virtual workstreams had achieved progress beyond the concepts and/or ideas stage, and the program therefore advanced firmly into execution (or operationalization) stage at the strategic interorganizational level or beyond.[6] The initial transition phase in the transformation of the interorganizational and intercompany relationships and the shift into the new globalization business paradigm were all now well mobilized. The internal financial evidence demonstrated substantial cost synergy benefit to the Vodafone companies. Vodafone and Ericsson through their operating companies were now engaged in a diversity of global virtual activities and workstreams.

As expected, there were still leaders and followers in the global forum. Of necessity this situation must and did change in the evolution of the next phase of organizational development. The goal for the future virtual workstreams would be for them to more significantly impact in-country processes, practices, and organizations. I concluded that the globalization activity had now reached the stage where a director (or CEO) in each of the Vodafone local operating companies (as a minimum) was required to be engaged in the process. This was to assure that the operating companies both executed and contributed to the initiatives in the global forum, which had become the backbone of this process.

At the meeting in Australia, I had commented that there was now an unacceptable dependence for the success of this program on the goodwill of all involved, the issue being the conflict between this (relatively invisible activity) and the representatives' day jobs. This was also the case for me, as my executive role in the Vodafone UK operating company was director, IT and project management, which included supply chain management and procurement and which involved a combined organization of some seven hundred to eight hundred people. In July 2000 I moved to the Vodafone European organization, which later progressed to a global function, as described elsewhere in this book. Sustained progress needed to be embedded into each of the country organizations and the other supporting organizations like Vodafone Europe Limited and the Ericsson corporate offices. This was to be part of the message that I later presented to the Vodafone (Global) Financial Directors' Conference on June 15, 2000. Dialogue in my key stakeholder social network was also of assistance in advancing such supportive considerations.

Bucharest, Romania

The next Ericsson global forum was hosted in Bucharest, Romania, on October 2–5, 2000. The transition of the transformation of processes and relationships was quite evident at this meeting. About sixty people from the Vodafone and Ericsson organizations attended. The intersession exchanges were intense and entirely nonpartisan; that is, the observed grouping did not relate to country of origin, global virtual team assigned to workstreams, nationality, or whether Vodafone or Ericsson participants; the groupings appeared to be a true mix and varied entirely at each break. On the social side, neither did the groupings in the evenings appear to follow any particular pattern other than one of consistency, namely, being a part of a unique global virtual community that had been formed and developed between the Vodafone and Ericsson organizations. It had clearly developed its own inner momentum and pride of identity consistent with a shared culture. There was no such other comparable innovative grouping in either organization, nor is there today, at least in the Vodafone organization, as later changes eliminated this social network and the accrued social capital. These interactions demonstrated the cumulative progression of global social relationships that became very clublike.

This was the last recorded meeting in the series after almost eighteen months (February 1999 to October 2000); however, the momentum and Vodafone operator support for this aggregation endeavor was unequivocal at this stage. The cessation of the meeting venue rotation was an outcome of the Vodafone executive management direction that all such future meetings, after the AirTouch merger and the Mannesmann acquisition, were to be held in the UK, Düsseldorf, or Milan. This decision was made without prior consultation or consideration of this particular globalization initiative, nor was it taken into account that it had reached an advanced stage of development and was more than satisfying the collective financial objectives set. After all, these objectives could be realized only in and through the operating companies that had been the motivated hosts of these global meetings.

I seek only to record the organizational and management facts without further comment purely for learning purposes. A mitigating factor perhaps is that the entire experiential approach to the transition was counterintuitive and its operations not widely published; therefore, the significance of what had been developed was a well-kept secret, save the collective synergy contributions. This knowledge gained, nevertheless, led to a new, self-adapting organizational stereotype in globalization and the transition thereto (as discussed later in this book), from which future managers may learn.

eRelationship

We identified the need for an inter- and intraorganizational information system (IS) capability given the initial geographic dispersion of those engaged in the globalization endeavor. This topic was introduced at the inaugural Ericsson global forum in February 1999, and a virtual workstream was established under the joint leadership of the Vodafone and Ericsson in-country teams in Holland and supported by the central functions of both organizations.

Progress was to be reported at each of the global forums. At the Maastricht forum held in April 1999, the Dutch in-country team made a presentation on their virtual workstream, "infosharing or Groupware," which proposed the creation of an "e-Infospace" (at this stage of the evolution), with the objective to also facilitate the opportunity to simplify the interorganizational processes. In their proposal, the Ericsson in-country team would maintain an active involvement in the process, which was the antithesis of the intent to improve efficiency. My approach in mediating this situation was to propose to move the dialogue to a higher plane, suggesting that perhaps we should first focus on the strategic intent. The team could then come back with implementation and proposals in support of that strategy.

The proposition was accepted, and Ericsson's Dutch representative was assigned to set up a new breakout (virtual team) meeting. The objective was to maintain the Dutch team in the lead role but to also include selected Ericsson experts and me in this team. My position was that this e-Enablement was critical for the knowledge sharing and operationalization in the overall globalization. It was important therefore to move from a technological and locally inclusive mind-set to something that had a global and strategic, sustainable relevance. By involving other experts and me as complements to the assigned virtual team workstream, we could possibly apply influence to steer the strategy in a positive way within the relevant forum. This approach maintained the integrity of the Dutch virtual workstream leadership in the global forum, while avoiding challenging potential public debates; instead, the reconciliation of views would be kept in this closed forum.

There was no intention of spending weeks and months in developing a statement of requirements and carrying though to planning and budget approvals. The discussion centered around establishing a set of Web-based tools through which the users could "shape" the information (or knowledge) according to the interests of the virtual team clusters and the global virtual community; generally, the latter point extending to both Vodafone and Ericsson. Again, this was counterintuitive and not something ordinarily considered or accepted in company practice. However, this community was known to exist, without any real details of how it was organized or what its objectives were known to any but those actually in or working within.

The next progress statement was in the global forum held at Nynashamn, Sweden, on September 2–3, 1999. Anderson Consulting was invited to make a presentation about eBusiness, intended to be in the context of the potential requirements of the "Club." I had met some days earlier with Anderson Consulting in the UK (this meeting included the UK representative, who was also at the Stockholm meeting). The objective of the premeeting was to review the presentation material. Anderson had also met with the Dutch team in advance of this presentation. An Ericsson director had advised me that Anderson had in the past presented similar material to their headquarters (HQ) organization with limited success.

In my premeeting with Anderson I reemphasized my own vision for the globalization e-Enablement by amending the title of one of their slides from "The Vision for the Supply Chain Operating Model to Build New Capabilities Enabled by eCommerce Market Space" to "The Vision for the *eRelationship* Operating Model …", and the functional example they showed from "eCommerce Market Space" to "eCommerce Space." This was an important distinction in what was being sought in the Vodafone-Ericsson global interorganizational and intercompany relationship transformation. The proposition being described by Anderson Consulting was essentially limited to a supply chain transactional relationship and was not the embodiment of the full strategic scope of what was required in the globalization paradigm. It became evident that Anderson was trying to develop an eBusiness model for "public exchanges," whereas this project required a bi-directional eRelationship portal.

The presentation was considered entirely unimpressive by all. Anderson failed to accommodate the guidance offered by me or the Dutch in-country joint team prior to the meeting. To make matters worse, certain of the content of my prebriefing to them in the UK was presented as "Anderson Consulting Proprietary," a matter to which I took extreme exception, as it was an abuse of confidence in claiming proprietary rights to intellectual input of others. The global forum declined to accept the approach offered by Anderson Consulting, which was in effect a "canned pitch" without any attempt to understand the objectives, perhaps validating this as a new concept.

In a later meeting Kurt Sillén in the Ericsson corporate organization revealed an alternative approach of immense interest. It was surprising that this (relevant) Ericsson project had hitherto not been presented to and/or available to the Dutch in-country team. The initial conclusion was that Ericsson had a project under way that might offer a solution to the requirements of what was now the eRelationship concept as I had introduced it. An additional key factor in the momentum toward operationalization of eRelationship was that Ericsson's corporate organization already had the required infrastructure and resources to develop and deliver the technical platform and would provide them at their cost.

In later communication exchanges it was agreed to focus first on the strategy of the eRelationship concept. This decision created a virtual workstream to replace the original Dutch action, for which a series of meetings followed. This decision became the introduction to what became known as the E-Space Working Group, whose progress was reported at subsequent global forum meetings. This marked the effective commencement of the long-awaited IS-Enablement or interorganizational system (IOS) required in support of this globalization program, which went all the way to the creation of a promotional video by Ericsson to publicize eRelationship within its organization.

IS-Enablement was now firmly on the agenda. Although not critical for the longitudinal transition period, it was considered relevant for the longer-term operationalization of the strategic interorganizational and intercompany relationships. Even though the Vodafone operating companies had already acceded to a virtual center for functions and/or business responsibilities that had previously been local, my concept was that it was necessary to also create a global base of knowledge available to all even if they were not a direct part of the process. This virtual engagement through access to knowledge had the potential to enhance confidence and trust, extending the prospect of reinforcing support for the transformation to take place.[7]

The first of the new virtual workstreams organized by the Dutch team, initially including UK representatives and myself, was held at Schiphol Airport, Amsterdam, on September 10, 1999 (see Figure 3.2b). This was an inaugural (virtual) team meeting of a steering group that was to focus on the Virtual Space strategy, the attempt being to coerce the Dutch team away from the focus on technology and more toward what was required to facilitate the operationalization of the interorganizational relationship, which is concerned with the strategic cooperation between all the partners of the virtual relationship.[8] This was the guidance or intervention I introduced following the lack of appropriate progress exhibited at the global forum held in Stockholm the

	Formative eRelationship working group meetings					
Positions of participants	Schipol 10 Sept. 1999	Schipol 11 Oct. 1999	London 3 Nov. 1999	London 21 Dec. 1999	London 14 Mar. 2000	London 5 May 2000
Vodafone Org.:						
Managing director	0	0	0	0	0	0
Director	1	1	1	2	1	1
Executive	1	1	1	1	2	1
Senior manager	0	0	0	1	1	0
Other actors	1	1	0	1	1	2
Total in attendance:	3	3	2	5	5	4
Ericsson Org.:						
Managing director	1	1	1	1	2	1
Director	0	1	0	2	2	1
Executive	1	1	1	2	1	1
Senior manager	2	2	3	5	9	2
Other actors	0	0	1	0	0	2
Total in attendance:	4	5	6	10	14	7

Figure 3.2b **Composition of participants in and locations of eRelationship working group meetings**

Note: The E-Space working group meetings were a subordinated virtual workstream

Source: Ibbott, C. J. (2001). An IS-Enabled Model for the Transformation and Globalisaiton of Interorganisational and Intercompany Relationships. Doctor of Business Administration (DBA). Brunel University, U.K., p. 319

previous week. I attended all other such meetings. This steering group had been formed because of the technocentric approach being taken by the Dutch team and the absence of strategic vision. A senior Ericsson representative (Kaj Snellman) and I shared this conclusion following discussions. The Ericsson team was expanded to include the participation of additional representatives from Stockholm competent in the topic. I also included a representative from the UK company, as to some extent this was a development of the positive experiences by both parties in the prior two years in the UK.

The thinking had been reset regarding the Virtual Space, and the discussion moved on to the eRelationship paradigm—the vision appeared to have been accepted, notwithstanding the need to consider the contractual aspects of transactions conducted in this environment. One of Ericsson's representatives confirmed that our eRelationship objectives could be realized within the environment that had been discussed in the recent Stockholm global forum. The goal of the representatives was to seek to move the concepts forward to reality at an enhanced pace, given the acceptance of the requirement to support team members in different locations and time zones. The meeting moved on to implementation issues like security and implementation planning and did not spend further time discussing the technology.

The next meeting was again at Schiphol Airport, Amsterdam, on October 11, 1999, which continued the foundation of the previous meeting. A document entitled "The E-Space" (Preliminary Version 1 dated October 11, 1999) was circulated for comment and feedback. One of its chapters, "The E-Space Relationship," was not populated in this version. A prototype of the early stages of the implementation of the eRelationship concept was demonstrated on a server at Ericsson in Stockholm. The summary comment on the Extranet portal presented was that it did not address the eRelationship vision agreed between the parties (in prior meetings), but instead looked very much like a standard Ericsson Web page with the Vodafone logo added.

That said, much positive work by the team had gone into developing the architecture or information structure aimed at meeting the intended requirements, and it was clarified that the required changes were not a major issue. The execution of the vision was perhaps constrained somewhat by the technical management of the process and the Dutch teams who were affected personally by the outcome of this project. The senior Ericsson representative from the global team felt that not enough progress was being made regarding the objectives, especially in visualizing how the global agreement should be integrated and the tools connected for ordering, tracking, and invoicing, all of this being the transaction element of the eRelationship.

There were further meetings held in the Ericsson offices in London on November 3 and December 21, 1999. By the next meeting at this venue on March 14, 2000, the meeting focused on driving the momentum of implementation. In the discussions, participants decided that to promote the usage of the portal (eRelationship) and to get feedback from (potential) users, it was necessary to arrange a number of workshops in both the Vodafone and Ericsson operating companies. The use of the portal needed to be socialized through this approach. Parallel to this, interviews with a selected number of key (to this implementation) players within the different operating companies would be held.

This was an important step toward creating a reality of the vision and putting in place a foundation for the operationalization of this support of the strategic interface between the two organizations. Otherwise, the eventual transformation of organizational practices and approaches, as well as further operationalization opportunities within the companies would be restricted.[9] Three countries were selected for a pilot test—Australia, the UK, and Holland—with a fourth to be nominated. Each market was to be requested to appoint local "owners" for the action, and plans were required to be developed for presentation back to this meeting. It appeared that at this meeting, the drive to implementation planning and renewed pace was a direct benefit of the appointment by Ericsson of Tomas Ageskog as their new eRelationship project manager, who was to join forces and engage with Gary Allen of Vodafone.

By the time of the meeting in London on May 5, 2000, there was approval for the eRelationship vision (release of May 5, 2000). The important point here is that Tomas Ageskog of Ericsson (on behalf of himself and Gary Allen of Vodafone) made a very persuasive presentation taken from their understanding (which was excellent) of the intentions behind the eRelationship vision. I was now convinced that the proposition had traction, having witnessed this presentation by someone who had not been coached by me. As declared by another meeting attendee, this provided the evidence that the team were (now) clearly engaged in the vision, although it had taken the appointment of dedicated resources with the time to position the initiative and to work through the detailed steps. The reinforcement of the strategic intent or vision in this presentation was very clear:

▶ The Vodafone-Ericsson global portal must reflect the entire global relationship, in all its aspects, between Vodafone and Ericsson.
▶ Further, it is the aim that this eRelationship virtual environment become the natural and primary source of information and communications between the organizations, and as such is not constrained by time and/or location.
▶ It is anticipated that arising from this new paradigm will be the mutual requirement for changes in process, practices, and organizations.
▶ In particular, this capability is crucial to the sustainable support of all the global virtual workstreams and initiatives being pursued under the guidance of the Ericsson global forum virtual leadership.

The following relevant statements were also included in this presentation to balance to motivation for the endeavor in the context of "benefits":

The development of the eRelationship is a necessity to reach the following benefits for both Vodafone and Ericsson:

1. To reduce costs in all processes
2. To reduce lead times in all processes or eliminate process
3. To improve quality and eliminate duplication errors
4. To improve the relationship between Vodafone and Ericsson by facilitating an open and trusting environment
5. To support the transformation from a local to global business
6. Both Vodafone and Ericsson have the goal to remain leaders in the use of eRelationship.

Having independently extracted this information from the available knowledge base, the project managers delivered this message with vigor and commitment, which for me was a major milestone in the transfer of the concept into action. The difference resulted from the appointment of the right people, who have passion for the endeavor, are committed, are engaged and willing to immerse themselves in the support activities, are accepted in the role by the wider community, and have the subject matter competence.

There was absolute clarity with the overall eRelationship strategy and a statement that the focus should now be on the roles and needs of the users in the Vodafone and Ericsson organizations; that there should be local involvement in the determination of the specific requirements within the e-environment; and that there should be local and global content on the entry portal. An activity plan was proposed for the remainder of the year 2000 together with clear milestone requirements for the recognition of achievement of the milestones.

The Ericsson project manager made an organizational proposal to set up a joint global eRelationship steering group that would meet quarterly to decide upon global vision and strategy, global program, global objectives, security, and global content. The proposed structure (which includes the topic of local representation) was also included, and I was proposed to be appointed the chairman. In support of this group, it was proposed that each participating local Vodafone and Ericsson operating company also set up a joint steering group that would meet quarterly to be responsible locally for strategy, planning, resources, priorities, and local content. The project manager would prepare and circulate (by e-mail) monthly statements of progress summarizing critical issues and proposed actions, as well as their status. The meeting supported the proposal unanimously.

The proposal was now to move to determination of the requirements and their consolidation to a role-based approach. This meant seeking to populate the eRelationship capability on the basis of functional segmentation, e.g., marketing, planning, procurement, etc. The effect of this approach was to move from the conceptual generic/global approach to the operational specific requirements.

The overall assessment of this meeting was that it had given purpose and impetus to the eRelationship concept, and perhaps more important, the operationalization of the endeavor was now on a firm footing within and between the Vodafone and Ericsson organizations. Although these meetings continued beyond this point, it was judged that the eRelationship conceptualization had been achieved, along with its supporting rationale regarding the interorganizational and intercompany relationship transformation together with the transition to engagement and commitment. The immediate period thereafter was one of implementation for which the commitment in this virtual workstream and engagement of both organizations are now in evidence.

By way of reinforcement that the longitudinal period of transition had concluded and that the implementation phase was under way on this eRelationship virtual workstream, I was invited to make the introductory remarks at a joint Vodafone-Ericsson global eRelationship meeting and workshop in London on October 26, 2000. This meeting was organized jointly by Vodafone and Ericsson project managers and included participants of both organizations from eight of the ten Vodafone operating companies then in the Ericsson "Club." Representatives from Australia and Fiji, for whom there were logistics difficulties, did not attend.

During 2001 the combined number of registered users of both Vodafone and Ericsson had exceeded three thousand.[10] A screenshot of a later version of the eRelationship home page is shown in Figure 3.3.

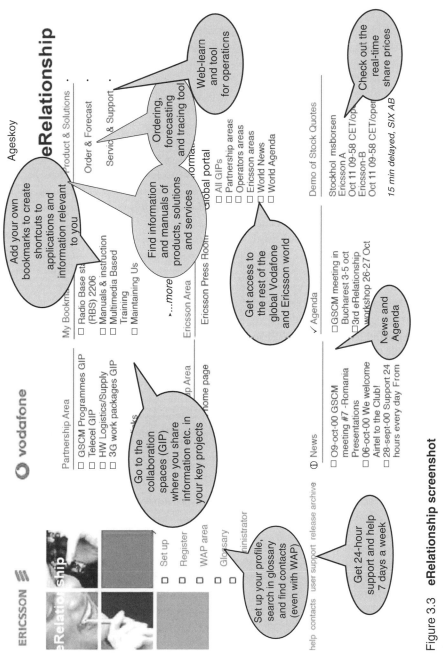

Figure 3.3 **eRelationship screenshot**

Source: Ibbott, C. J. (2001). An IS-Enabled Model for the Transformation and Globalisaiton of Interorganisational and Intercompany Relationships. Doctor of Business Administration (DBA). Brunel University, U.K., p. 323

The Invisible Organization

Orlikowski describes what she refers to as situated change, an organizational transformation situation wherein it is "seen to be an ongoing improvisation enacted by organisational actors [people] trying to make sense of and act coherently in the world."[11] This perspective avoids the strong assumptions that have characterized prior change perspectives because it focuses on the situated microlevel changes that people (or team members) enact as they make sense of the world. The Ericsson global forum formed the formal, in one sense, yet informal in another, backbone of the interorganizational and intracompany transformation and was the ongoing context in which the people made "sense of and act[ed] coherently in the [virtual] world." The focus on the "situated microlevel changes" were derived from the global forum and were acted out or experienced by individuals through their participation in the virtual teams in the various virtual workstreams (which provided the strength) in which they sought to make sense of the globalized world and the new and transformed relationships.

To change an organization's culture, you must first change people's behavior; and although charismatic leadership may grab headlines, steady, consistent leadership results in changes to the bottom line.[12] There was a need to transform the culture in the various companies within the Vodafone and Ericsson organizations in the recognition of the greater group interests. There was also a requirement to simultaneously create a horizontally organized global community with a requisite culture that sought to balance the interest of the global objective with the requirement to assure the engagement of the in-country operating interests for support and sustainable implementation. The leadership was crucial to the momentum and execution of this globalization initiative.

A Vodafone Greece participant (Kostas Megas), who took part in the inaugural global forum through to the Cairo meeting, comments:[13]

> Yes, the Global activity has been a success since the commonly agreed targets (monetary, relationships) were achieved. The success is based on the following:
>
> 1. The reduction in the initial "Club" members to [the initial] four [in-country operations] accelerated the decision making process.
> 2. Definition of Ericsson as a key supplier due to business criticality, volume of business, deployment of future technologies.
> 3. Authority and leadership on the Vodafone side.
> 4. Definition of Single Points of (interorganisational) Contact [I and Nils Grimsmo] between the two organisations, with the relevant responsibility and authority to take decisions and move the whole team forward.
> 5. The quick establishment of measurement mechanism for the synergy benefits and definition of yearly targets.
> 6. Empowerment of the [Vodafone] team members.

Megas went on to state in his note to me that "I believe that the whole [globalization] process succeeded due to your personality, and this is not a compliment. You created a vision strong enough for all the others to understand and not to fear. I was convinced from the very beginning that all movements or decisions were taken in order to fulfil a target. Concluding this story, my own internal majority voted for you. For that reason we trusted you to negotiate a deal for my [Greek] organisation and me. The global forum brought people together from all parts of the world, made them forget their own business back home, and to concentrate on global thinking. The intercompany relationships changed since you created a virtual global team [not yet dedicated, as in full time] to this activity. I think that now is the right time to present an organisation plan for the whole team including responsibility, country, product as we discussed in Newbury in October last year [1999]." And he concludes, "I believe that people like you and your team transformed the part of the Vodafone organisation which deals with supply to a global company, and I'm sure that this model will be used as a reference to globalise other processes of the [Vodafone] Group. I believe that I changed my view for business and relationships. I thank you personally for sharing your experience and vision with me and for your trust to assign me responsibilities within the process."

Since then and commenting recently (2006) on how issues were resolved in the virtual community, Kostas Megas of Vodafone and Dimitris Manolopoulos of Ericsson, both in Greece, said when it appeared that irreconcilable issues were existent that "you (the author) and Nils Grimsmo always found solutions in private dialogue"—a sense of confidence and/or trust perhaps.

Evolutionary change embodies the sociotechnical change approach, and piloting the new processes before IT is used to cement those processes.[14] Participants in the inaugural global forum identified and agreed that a form of Groupware (which later become eRelationship) was required to support (or cement) the overall transformation program. The development and co-evolution of the eRelationship strategy and implementation took place in a virtual workstream that would affect the intercompany and interorganizational relationships required for achieving the globalization objective. On May 5, 2000, in London the eRelationship meeting agreed that there was absolute clarity with the overall eRelationship strategy. Being co-evolutionary and not being driven by a preordained statement of requirement, the development of eRelationship supported rather than dictated global activities or processes; this approach was the antithesis of the norm for such projects or investments.

A philosophy of the transformation process is that the business transformation should precede organizational changes, the principle being an initial focus on business processes and infrastructures and then on organizational structures and systems. The aim is to redesign business activities and structures for performance gains, and to then drive organizational change to align with the new business model.[15] Clearly, this situation was an informal global community not recognized in any formal organizational chart or budget, yet it had aspired to the financial ambitions of the business nevertheless. The eventual formal change documented in Chapter 5 demonstrates that the business in its formalization endeavors (April 2005) did not in fact create such structure grounded in or built on this innovative phase of the journey nor that which followed, as discussed in Chapter 4.

The global forum set a framework around which a number of virtual workstreams were established to redesign the business activities and structures. The successful pursuit of the aggregation cost synergy benefits yielded from this globalization of the supply chain management and the relationships around it were never in doubt. The systems aspect at the strategic interorganizational level is the realization of the eRelationship capability, which itself was developed prior to engaging its capability within the processes.[16]

The Ericsson global forum formed the anchor or catalyst of the Vodafone-Ericsson business relationship globally, notwithstanding the informality of the combined organization. It was the seat of the mutual cultural development and transformational journey toward a new paradigm jointly established in the unqualified or constrained vision of "globalization." It was a learning experience that was to continue for some years. Through their engagement, the Vodafone in-country operations formally had acceded their local decision "power" to this new global forum for all matters designated by the forum as global. In so doing, trust and integrity must have been in evidence within and between all participants, leading to the development of social capital, discussed later.

Persuasion and Leadership

Each organization must appoint a global leader to jointly lead the interorganizational initiative, in this case I for Vodafone and Nils Grimsmo for Ericsson.[17] This leadership is within the global forum, which may be variously an individual or multi-level (hierarchical) group of individuals who join with the global virtual teams from either or both organizations to achieve the aggregation cost synergy objectives; they are all boundary-crossing individuals. Those people, through their informal, nonhierarchical, and horizontal relationships within and between the Vodafone and/or Ericsson organization, are forms of meta-management.[18] This type of management is not set up in the formal hierarchy of a recognized (budgeted) organization but consists of those individuals who are motivated to work together in this global virtual community by a shared vision and common culture. The group positively imposes its will in the organizations from whence each came to leverage benefits in common, which would not otherwise be achievable alone.

Mowshowitz, in outlining a theory of virtual organizations, expresses a set of principles for meta-managing goal-oriented activity based on a categorical split between task requirements and their satisfiers.[19] The essence of the virtual organization is the systematic ability to switch satisfiers in a decision environment of bounded rationality. The (meta) management of such switching is carried out by the Ericsson global forum. The strongest and closest collaborations are in value-chain partnerships, such as supplier-customer relationships, wherein the relationship creates substantial change within each partner's organization.[20] Only relationships with full commitment on all sides (both the Vodafone and Ericsson organizations and their respective companies and equity interests) endure long enough to create value for the partners. In a joint supply chain endeavor the leadership role seeks to develop improvement and/or benefit between the organizations on process, practice, price, and global interorganizational structures and relationships reinforced and supported by the eRelationship (IS-Enablement).[21]

The global forum, the virtual teams, and the spin-off supporting multicountry Vodafone-Ericsson workshops were and are forms and levels of meta-management. They were composed of individuals who subsequently recruited colleagues from within their companies who had the necessary skill and/or authority. The common strand throughout was that the Ericsson global forum did not (and does not) have any executive authority within the hierarchical in-country companies over which it exercised its (or our) influence. The links were horizontal, the hierarchical levels of the individuals engaged were multiple, and initiatives were diverse, all of which had a dynamic and varying degree of influence on the transformation process, which in some cases was quite profound, and all of which were achieved without direct executive authority in the operating companies.

Another meta-management example was the creation and subsequent development of the eRelationship portal, all of which was steered through the E-Space Working Group (in some respects it has parallels with the creation of Linux). The management of the virtual workstream, interorganizational, and company relationships was each a form of meta-management. The role was to influence and motivate the participants and the Vodafone companies they represented to engage in the global propositions (and their co-requisite requirements), while not being in a position to dictate their choices of action. On the Ericsson side the challenge was similar: compliance without adverse consequence in their performance toward Vodafone with the necessity to manage the individual personal incentive expectations.

These approaches involve leading through a virtual center or catalyst, as opposed to a central head office. Such a counterintuitive approach is one in which the vision, strategy, and governance (through the Ericsson global forum) are the lead functions, whereas the envisioning and execution of sustainable operational outcomes are led in-country where the cost synergies are actually realized. This was key to motivating the engagement of the in-country operations in the achievement of the global transformation, notwithstanding that it obliged them to accede local power in preference to building global strength.

This created a situation that was neither central nor federal but a hybrid federal, perhaps. In reality it became a federal bureaucracy, meaning that it was acceptable for the virtual teams to find their own level unless that required some assistance or direction, which I provided. It is clear from the beginning that Vodafone and Ericsson agreed mutually on a common strategy of globalization with due recognition of the asymmetry and timing yields that would result, the basis of the mutual mandate for the individual and community leadership on behalf of the respective organizations; this was therefore a nonnegotiable point although it was never brought into question. Through this engagement people either directly or indirectly by association became part of or formed formative social networks, the collaborative result of which was to develop significant social capital.

TeamNets (virtual teams) will improve horizontal organizational relationships while complementing or co-existing with the traditional prescriptions of vertical hierarchy; they cross boundaries and have fewer bosses and more leaders.[22] Brown quotes Mohrman and Porter, stating that managers need to be both effective vertical (organizational) strategists and horizontal (organizational) strategists.[23] TeamNets combine two organizational ideas: teams (where small groups of people work with focus, motivation, and skill to achieve shared goals) and networks (where disparate groups of people and groups "link" to work together on a common purpose). I am of the opinion that the individuals did not sense that they were in a horizontal organization or that they were required to consciously consider that and their respective roles in their hierarchical organizations. To the contrary, they determined that they were united in a common cause, at least on the Vodafone side; as expressed in the Australian meeting in March 2000, the enthusiasm and motivation of the meeting participants to deliver a cost synergy result generated its substantial strength through goodwill.

Vodafone and Ericsson's organizations did separately contribute resources from within their respective companies and group or corporate functions to participate in multilevel global virtual teams, thus having horizontal relationships with each other. A strong example is the vertical or hierarchical mix of individuals from each of the Vodafone and Ericsson organizations who participated in the global forum meetings and the virtual workstreams. The horizontal virtual organizational structure linked the vertical hierarchies of the various operating companies at a number of levels, given the multiple levels in the virtual teams, even though the horizontal teams themselves did not operate according to hierarchical principles.

Through the global virtual teams and their leadership or virtual organizing of the global forum or virtual catalyst,[24] knowledge was shared and mutual trust developed.[25] Such sharing and trust are said to be crucial in virtual collaboration and are to be developed at multilevels and horizontally within and between all parties engaged on the global virtual stage.[26] There is frequent reference in the literature suggesting that *virtual* and *transient* or *temporary* are synonymous, a point that I would contest in the light of this experience. In such situations individual, company, and organizational boundaries become blurred.[27] Here there were no constraints placed on the degree to which the virtual networking complexity may develop, a point perhaps in evidence at the global forum meetings. It was accepted in the virtual workstream assignments that it was possible to reassign or vary the construct; for example, the reassignment of switching (MSC/BSC) configurations from Greece to Germany; and the variation and development in the structure of Groupware eventually moving to eRelationship, which commenced with Holland and extended to include the UK and Germany.

Although demonstrating transience or perhaps flexibility in the virtual workstream assignments, it does not necessarily follow that this is a transient organization, only that it is flexible and certainly consistent with the views of Mowshowitz. Another view of the boundary-crossing horizontal structure as demonstrated through the global forum and virtual workstreams might be one of multilevel (rank or position of the individuals in the vertical hierarchy of the companies in which they ordinarily work), multirole (the virtual teams), and multinodal (countries); the sum of these elements is a global virtual network or a boundaryless virtual (horizontal) organization, linking the vertical (or country) hierarchy, which is a source of its power.[28]

My leadership focus was on imparting knowledge, which in later years has the potential, when combined with intuition or counterintuition, to perhaps become wisdom. It is said that underutilized knowledge is the largest hidden cost in organizations, but it may be that some people are in some way inhibited by the hierarchical limitations and/or practice of the organization in which they operate to espouse such knowledge. It is also said that careful design and IT do not help if the willingness to share with each other is not there,[29] although a further inhibitor is the centralized authority and structure applied to such knowledge management. Avoiding centralized structure in the co-evolution of eRelationship may have fostered a climate of trust in the global virtual community.

Although trust, identity, and efficacy may be core elements for team collaboration,[30] so too as demonstrated on the evidence in this book is a strategy in common with a mutuality of motivation for the outcome of the joint endeavors. The level of trust in the organization is the most important factor affecting the willingness to share knowledge.[31] An empirical study by Tschannen-Moran,[32] being one of the few studies on the topic, found evidence that the level of collaboration in schools was related to the level of trust: namely, a significant link between collaboration with the principal and trust in the principal, collaboration with colleagues and trust in colleagues, and collaboration with parents and trust in parents.[33] A conceptual parallel here is my role being akin to that of the principal, his direct and virtual management team, and his social network that included many key stakeholders and influencers thereof (equivalent in the hypothesis to colleagues), and the greater virtual community engaged in the collaborative cost synergies endeavors (equating to parents). Although collaboration and trust can be seen as elements of an organization's culture, Sveby and Simons focused on one specific aspect of culture: the values, beliefs, and assumptions that influence the willingness to share knowledge.

The findings of Sveiby and Simons are interesting in this discussion. Older people regard a collaborative climate more favorably than younger people, thereby confirming that it takes time to build up experience and the social networks for effective sharing and that there is a "gap" in terms of effectiveness. They found evidence that new employees, if they do not leave in the first five years, take much longer to become truly effective than has generally been understood; an added dimension may be that this equates also to the development of accrued social capital. A further finding was that the greater the years of experience in an environment, the more likely people are to report a more favorable collaborative climate. Interestingly, Sveby and Simons found that distance was bad for collaboration, a point that runs counter to the experience here, perhaps due to the inclusive and counter-intuitive approach taken in how the global virtual community actually operated—a topic for further research by others.

Based upon an empirical study of a large organization in the 1990s, Cule and Robey propose a process theory of organizational transition that incorporates two generative mechanisms, or "motors."[34] At the individual level they employ a teleological motor, which captures the managerial actions under-taken to promote transformation; at the organizational level they employ a dialectic motor, which captures the forces both promoting and opposing change. The outcome is a model consisting of three phases of transition: cre-ation, destruction, and unification. They also comment that as the new mil-lennium begins, the topic of organizational transformation occupies an increasingly prominent position in both academic and professional discussions and is central to the theme and focus in this book. In this account we are discussing a transformation that emerged on entry to this new millennium.

They continue by noting that writers may have offered a variety of opinions on how "the new organizational paradigm" should be designed, but it perhaps should not be forgotten that it is the contextual placement of the affected people and their mind-set in that domain that are more crucial to success, points most often omitted in organizational design considerations. Arguments therefore about appropriate paradigms for organizations in the future cannot be empirically evaluated until the future has actually arrived, a point of concurrence with the Vodafone-Ericsson and later experiences, which was a progressive and experiential journey paradigm that itself was a seat of learning.

Although theories of transition may explain the processes through which destinations are reached or not reached, destinations are no longer static, thereby making the notion of transition a continuum. A contrary view of transformational organizational transition may be that it is a continuum of iterations, not all of which represent forward progressions, with its success being periodically assessed and determined in the eye of the beholder. Whereas Van de Ven and Poole may discuss generative mechanisms that drive change, I would nevertheless debate whether change is driven or led by an individual, group, or community.[35] Experience in this Vodafone-Ericsson study promotes a belief that transformational change may be effectively accomplished through an immersed leadership, subject to that leadership being capable of embracing the challenge beyond whatever has been modeled on paper and/or expressed as the objectives. There is in the literature a presumption of a preordained or determined organizational state to be reached. I would contest the prior knowledge of a settled outcome if absent of such demonstrable prior experience, which was the situation here.

Cule and Robey state that because the dialectic represents teleological forces in opposition, the two "motors" are coexistent and interdependent. This may indeed be so; however, my experience suggests that through the execution of a journey paradigm there was a mutuality of co-evolution such as to maintain an equilibrium with a positive direction toward the transformational achievements. These achievements were accomplished from within the global virtual community, a nonhierarchical, essentially invisible entity. Cule and Robey's research proceeded without specifying the expected outcome of the organizational transition in advance, which is entirely consistent with this chapter.[36]

Leading Change

Kotter's book *Leading Change* offers his views on reasons why firms fail in transforming organizations.[37] His outline of common errors in such changes resonates with me, but this example perhaps complements or extends his views beyond the boundaries he anticipated. We sought to achieve transformational intracompany changes within both organizations simultaneously, transforming multiple in-country relationships to homogenized global interorganizational relationships—all under the common mobilizing force of globalization to realize aggregation cost synergies. Following are brief comments on each of the eight points for failure advanced by Kotter with a contrast offered between our combined experiences.[38]

Error #1: Allowing Too Much Complacency: The language of "force big change" or "drive people out of their comfort zone" is alien language in the context of transformational and sustainable change. There is the notion of preemption by the organization's management in the actual change and what it takes to transition. The contextual experience in this case would suggest that although hierarchical position is interesting in the context of compensation, it has less relevance in what it takes to transition and achieve transformational change. The emergent horizontal and nonhierarchical organization was collectively the catalyst of leadership to a sustainable transformation change in the globalization context. The vision and strategy were established, which motivated and committed the team both to the ensuing social networks that developed and the financial yield from the aggregation cost synergies. There was no evidence of a forcing factor, and individuals appeared to acquire a new and different comfort zone; the moral of the story is that style may also have relevance—delegation in execution versus a center-driven approach. There is absolute concurrence on the point that an organization's strength potentially is the point of greatest weakness because of complacency.

Error #2: Failing to Create a Sufficiently Guiding Coalition: Here the formative group had a leadership (I and my Ericsson counterpart) who, at least in my case, did not have any direct line of authority over the operations to be affected by the transformational changes. The organization of the leading team and the extended social network were essentially organizationally invisible. This team, in progressively developing and forming its own culture, had sufficiently persuasive motivation to realize its ambitions so that meta-influences prevailed. The collective was "punching white space" in that no precedent had been set, which was believed to be relevant to achieve the corporate ambitions of the Vodafone and Ericsson organization. Part of the approach included self- and collective mentoring as part of the organizational learning through the experiential development.

Error #3: Underestimating the Power of Vision: The nature of the "public discussion" was to be open and visible in the global forum meetings and the virtual workstreams for the purposes of developing a shared vision. It was particularly relevant, however, in this combined customer-supplier forum to take an allocentric, not egocentric, situational view. We had embarked on a journey paradigm, a part of which was to accommodate and make sense of situated change. Again, absent of a vision, strategy and a core relevant quorum motivated through inner belief are co-requisite for a successful outcome.

Error #4: Undercommunicating the Vision by a Factor of 10 (or 100 or even 1,000): The context of "employee" was perhaps superseded in practice with "contributor" in this case—an important attitudinal difference. The engagement was through "subscribing" to the shared vision and voluntarily engaging—mostly on the basis of goodwill, as all participants had day jobs—and becoming the formative or catalyst group taking the Vodafone and Ericsson organizations to a new industry level. The attraction to engage achieved a pull approach (versus push), leading to the realization of an early transformational momentum.

Error #5: Permitting Obstacles to Block the New Vision: The global virtual community were self-motivated and self-empowered, meaning people did not sit around seeking permission to act; one may describe them as enlightened. There was no formal organizational structure of this community. Its informality was perhaps its strength, because had it sought to engage permission for every step of the way, we would still be in dialogue and void of action and therefore results. This informal approach, yet with key stakeholder support for me and the global virtual community I had the privilege to lead and represent, was perhaps another of its strengths and avoided the complex HR issues. The legitimacy of the existence of the Vodafone segment of the global community was in the realized aggregation cost synergies reported, without an in-depth executive understanding of just how all this operated.

Error #6: Failing to Create Short-Term Wins: The early wins from the commencement of the harmonization of the Vodafone-Ericsson business relationship, itself a transformation achievement, stimulated the motivation for further progress, even though changes in practice were required in the in-country operations. Generally, given the election to follow a journey paradigm, there was no plan and therefore no set dates by which certain events were required to be realized, save the economic synergy result. This made the experience somewhat counterintuitive to the normal practice of requiring formal declarations and plans; the urgency was set by the motivation for the realization of outcome.

Error #7: Declaring Victory Too Soon: Here there was no victory to declare; being a journey paradigm and recognizing that the transition was a continuum in that for years to come aggregation synergies derived from commercial terms and changes of organization and practice, the issue was more one of recognition of stepped achievement. The business checkpoint was based on annual achievement rather than targets or expectations of cost synergy contribution realized in the in-country operations arising from this endeavor. Sustainability was defined as embracing the virtual group or community culture, the transfer of practice and the ethos of the few to the global community at large. The virtual community was the catalyst for the reported transformation. That is, the individual became part of a group or nonhierarchical horizontal organization that was the catalyst for transformational change that embedded such changes as necessary into practice.

Error #8: Neglecting to Anchor Changes Firmly in the Corporate Culture: Such changes in behavior have to be something the engaged individuals want and are motivated to do. The skill is in the structuring of the change catalyst and not just engaging those available or in place. Rank or position is no assurance of the skill or leadership sense for a successful transformational endeavor. Assignments were made on the basis of a group's perceived capacity and motivation to perform regardless of country location.

To summarize, the chosen or experientially developed journey documented herein would, although contextually perhaps not anticipated by Kotter, appear to have avoided the pitfalls to which he refers.

Finally, I was of advancing years in this period of responsibility, as were my Ericsson counterpart (Nils Grimsmo) and his operational leader (Kaj Snellman). It was this formative learning experience that became the basis upon which the other three major mobile network infrastructure suppliers (Nokia, Nortel, and Siemens—see Chapter 4) were invited to engage and continue the development of the globalization process. Although I posit that experience, intuition, and the ability to discern the finer situational differences blended with the increasing knowledge that perhaps transcends three distinct conceptual phases commences with discovery in the younger or formative years; leading to déjà vous or "I think I have been here before" or "Was it a dream?"; to the final phase called wisdom, which in the broader frame concludes with "I know I have been here before."

The Emergent Global Network Culture and Requisite Organization

One of the Ericsson challenges was to move from a paradigm of the 1990s that established the current basis of their (global) organizational structure and mode of operation, namely, that the "market is global and the business is local." This paradigm was attributed to the former president, Dr. Lars Ramqvist; I was made aware of that paradigm in an Ericsson meeting in Stockholm on June 29, 2000. I would propose that a contrasting paradigm now being sought through this program is antithetical to the paradigm of the 1990s, namely, that "business is global and markets are local." Therein lay the potential for resistance and potential lack of motivation to make certain changes regarding the approach by Ericsson in managing their opportunities with global customers.

Although there is an assumption of mutuality in motivation and objectives arising from a common strategy, that may not have been the case. The two organizations having agreed to a common globalization strategy were both asymmetric in organizational structure, and impact as a consequence, and with an imbalance in the financial yields and the timing thereof. The position was clear; in the immediate instance, Vodafone was motivated by a financial gain, and the inverse likely the case for Ericsson. This gave rise to a motivational attitude for the Vodafone representatives locally and feeling of resistance on the Ericsson side, although in both situations the decision to pursue this course of action was taken outside the in-country organization.

TeamNets combine the organizational ideas of teams and networks, but they also dynamically balance the decentralizing forces of independence and the integrating forces of cooperative interdependence; however, relationships are essential to binding the team together.[39] The foundation of the Ericsson global forum was the link between two global trading partners seeking to fulfill the common strategy of globalization, albeit for different reasons, the foundation of which was an embedded relationship ethos borne in the social network. The cooperative interdependence consisted of those matters that were actually globalized, and the decentralized forces of independence were the residual local Vodafone-Ericsson relationships focused on fulfillment, quality of service, and services.

In (social) networks, leaders appear at the nexus of purpose and commitment, where responsibility is taken and shared work gets done.[40] Generally, when customers and suppliers separately contribute resources (individuals) from their respective organizations, the individuals will be chosen because of their direct country interest and/or level of expertise within the team of global participants; all such individuals are considered to be boundary crossing.[41] Here, commencing with the inaugural meeting in February 1999 such an approach was demonstrated, with the assignment jointly of resources of the Vodafone and Ericsson organizations (mostly in-country) to global virtual workstreams. The allocation of the opportunities was variously determined by the level of motivation, perceived competence, and experiential knowledge or learning to date. The resulting global virtual teams were resourced from both organizations and composed of boundary-crossing individuals.

These acts commenced the shaping of the experiential culture of this emergent global social network, wherein culture is defined as the result of a complex group learning process that is only partially influenced by leader behavior. Schein restates this in his formal definition of culture: "A pattern of shared basic assumptions that was learned by a group as it solved its problems of external adaptation and internal integration that has worked well enough to be considered valid and, therefore, to be taught to new members as the correct way to perceive, think, and feel in relation to those problems."[42] Schein differentiates between leadership and management, stating that leadership creates and changes cultures, while management and administration act within a culture. Although I may be attributed with the vision, and together with my Ericsson counterpart we may nominally be referred to as leaders, the virtual team was in fact a leadership group forging a new global culture within and between both organizations that had not been experienced before by them or the telecom industry.

The literature, however, does not explore how the individual-level knowledge affects the formation and management of an interorganizational relationship even though they play an important role in the process.[43] The underlying global social relationship was one in which each person was seen as a node connected to a number of other nodes, and superimposed on this social network were a number of powerful arrangements whereby organizations or the individuals in them cooperated across organizational boundaries. Although interorganizational networks (IONs) have the potential to transform the organization of production, it appears that the collaboration being introduced tended to occur within a framework that took the existing primacy as its starting point and was oriented toward buttressing that concept rather than questioning its continued appropriateness.[44] As shown here, the globalization paradigm and the required transformed relationships and practices were determined and progressed solely through the global forum meetings. Countries that elected to enter the collaborative global space were not obliged in the first instance to radically amend existing practices; they were instead accepted into the arrangement, following which virtual workstreams sought to improve alignment to the objectives.

In the virtual workstreams the concept (and reality) was to move to a multileader situation.[45] The only requirement was that the assigned virtual leadership represented the critical mass of the global interest with respect to the supplier in consideration (in this case, Ericsson). This needed to be balanced with the location of the corporate headquarters of Ericsson and the location of their chosen global negotiator or representative. If the two were in different locations and if there was a virtual team member in that location, then they should take a supportive local role to the virtual team leader. There was an objective for both Vodafone and Ericsson to become simultaneously both glocal companies (or organizations) and transnational organizations in order to achieve the mutual strategy of globalizing the interorganizational relationship. These virtual (or horizontal) relationships facilitated both an organizational power and flexibility in the interests of mutual success.[46]

Face-to-face meetings of the virtual working groups (or teams) will complement electronic (e-mail) and other means of communications (eRelationship) to enhance the richness of communications, which in turn enhances the organizational identification,[47] as tacit knowledge cannot be transferred by electronic means[48], although eRelationship was conceived and ordered to overcome or alleviate this difficulty. Evidence supports that rotating the venue of the global forum meetings and such other virtual workstream meetings enhanced the identification of the social networks in which all individuals were engaged. Virtual teams work (horizontally) across space, time, and organizational boundaries within which positive relationships and high trust are important, but nevertheless still require the face-to-face meetings to solidify these teams—by these means management decisions are decentralized.[49]

A real team is a small number of people with complementary skills who are committed to a common purpose, performance goals, and an approach for which they hold themselves mutually accountable.[50] When this criterion cannot be met, then they will rely on individual leadership skills that they have developed over the years, and to challenge one another's thinking is acceptable provided that constructive conflict does not degenerate into interpersonal conflict.[51]

In a comparative discussion regarding the concept of centers of excellence and the experience of this account, centers of excellence imply a fixed location within a group or company that is assigned the responsibility for excellence in a given discipline or capability. However, here the subject grouping was virtual team, both within either the Vodafone or Ericsson organization or a combined team. The leadership role was assigned, but the "excellence" in capability was dispersed among the virtual grouping's total resources, which operated collectively. Temporal leadership was leadership assigned to a given location or company in the group at any instance in time, thereby giving rise to the notion of a "virtual grouping of excellence" in contrast to a center of excellence. Examples of temporal situations include the assignment on optimizing the (MSC/BSC) switching configurations from Greece to Germany, the software convergence project wherein the assignment remained with Australia but later was supplemented or "hosted" within Europe (UK for Vodafone and Spain for Ericsson), and harmonized fault reporting reassigned from Romania to the software project.

There was an initial period of social acclimation reported that emerged in the Ericsson global forum meetings, commencing with the first meeting in February 1999 with thirteen participants, through the meeting in October 2000 with fifty participants from the combined organizations, by which time a global social community had evidently been established through these visible nodes to an extended community beyond them the depth and identity of which was dynamic and unknown. These meetings were structured, well ordered, and successful despite the number of people in attendance. Yet the intensity of the social exchanges between meetings and at the end of the business day was astounding; that is, the individuals' business position, nationality, speciality, and country or organization represented were not considered in forming social relationships. As the transformation achieved by this virtual community increased, there seemed to be a strong sense of participative pride, and the meetings became like a gathering of long-lost friends from around the world. Through this strength, which is difficult to measure, lay the fiber, tenacity, and source of achievement of the total transformation program, thereby suggesting that the balance of the richness of the various media was appropriate to the challenges of the organizational transformations being sought.[52]

Bevan reports that Carr and Johansson conceptualize "culture" as a collection of overt and covert rules, values, and principles that are enduring and guide organizational behavior.[53] Furthermore, "culture pushback" means that people resist radical change, which is the "greatest organisational risk" to the reengineering effort; they warn that only leaders can drive culture change. Bevan further references Hammer and Stanton, who explain that values engender "typical behaviours" that are translated into "cultural norms," from which the challenge is a shift from the traditional (prior) values to transformed (future globalization) values:[54] "Only deep-seated belief in the right values can generate the passion and commitment that a re-engineering process requires."[55]

Here the virtual community was operating in a horizontal interorganizational and intercompany environment for which there was no typical behavior, as the relationships now formed had not existed earlier. Therefore, it was the intent to effect through these horizontal transformational activities changes to the internal culture of the hierarchical organizations from whence the participants came. Through the created cultural strength generated in this new paradigm, it may be concluded that so far, at least in transition, this has been successful, as the hierarchical organizations have acceded to the global propositions.

On July 1, 2000, I transferred out of Vodafone Limited and took the responsibility to create a virtual center function in what was later to become a group (or global) function. I elected to recruit a number of secondees on rotation from the Vodafone operating companies, each for a period of eighteen to twenty-four months. The notion was that candidates would qualify at least on the basis of their in-country management identifying them as highflyers and supporting the secondment as part of their personal development. This represented the commencement of the development of a strong interweaving of the center-led function with the global virtual community being served. This approach achieved an enhanced engagement of the Vodafone operating companies, which together contributed to forming the "glue" and "power" of the collaborative endeavor notwithstanding the continuation of the informal links between the center function, the operating companies, and the Ericsson organization. In this approach the center, while physically in one place, takes on the multiroles of coordinating, motivating, supporting, and meta-managing the global leadership wherever it has been assigned and whatever virtual workstreams arise from such initiatives.

Again, the actual aggregation cost synergies arising from this global collaborative, interorganizational, and intracompany endeavor were only realizable in the Vodafone (and Ericsson) operating companies. The meta-management therefore was through strong motivational-led influence, as no direct line of authority existed between the center-led function and the operating companies, at least on the Vodafone side; the influence was not derived from the "power" of the traditional hierarchy despite my relative hierarchical position. The motivation may have been personal, links through or via key stakeholders in the various social networks, or indeed, purely by the financial benefits for each of the operating companies or the people therein.

Bevan makes references to material on culture, which in the context of change Oblensky debates whether organizations should attempt "changing the culture first" prior to re-engineering or to re-engineer the process first and then "run a culture change programme," as though culture is a discrete variable to be isolated and manipulated.[56] In this description the organizational and intracompany relationship transformations were informally pursued concurrent with the creation of the global virtual community within which rich social networks were embedded. This outcome, while not contradicting Oblensky, does argue that the approach to change may be inclusive, meaning that it addresses the issues of culture and change concurrently in the virtual environment. The general approach taken to set virtual workstream assignments dissipates the proposition that everything is head office–centric, and espouses the proposition of a collective and inclusive ownership to the changes and transformations required for globalization, subject only to reasoned business logic. It is argued that the reason for change has to be closely linked to the business strategy, and it can be and should be accompanied by a strong "people" orientation.[57]

Having established the way of working, and hence the social model in operation, we then had the challenge of transferring this experiential learning of all engaged individuals on to others to lead in the establishment of new and different supplier relationships. This next phase of the globalization program and the endeavor to apply this model in new global relationships is the subject of Chapter 4. The collective virtual team environment (as consolidated through the global forum meetings) may be viewed as an instance of social organization.[58]

This was essentially an informal virtual organization operating within and between Vodafone and Ericsson, perhaps in the language of Jaques, although perhaps not envisaged in this form, a "requisite organization."[59] Jaques defines such an organization as "the pattern of connections which ought to exist between roles if the system is both to work efficiently and to operate as required by the nature of human nature and the enhancement of mutual trust." In discussing the achievement of an effective organization for sustained success, Jaques posits that the way to managerial leadership is through the development of the organization itself; however, what is missing is an adequate organizational framework within which to work and cooperate with each other. These thoughts lead to doing business that releases human imagination, trust, and satisfaction in work. He concludes that our potential unfolds throughout life and that "the art of the good society and of the good [requisite] organisation is to ensure opportunity for the use of their full potential by all of its people."

Although there is a notion of formality and preordained structure in the words of Jaques, it would be reasonable to conclude that exactly such conditions prevailed or were available for those who sought to take advantage of what was a "greenfield" opportunity. There were no constraints to innovative thoughts and actions save their applicability or judged suitability for the matters at hand in pursuit of the strategy to globalize an interorganizational relationship and produce aggregation cost synergies; this was later to change, as will be discussed in Chapter 5. Another variance to Jaques may be that the potential he envisaged in such a requisite organization was within a single company or organization formation, whereas here the horizontal virtual (informal and performing) community existed within and between two global organizations, Vodafone and Ericsson. It would be a reasonable to assume that this depth of knowledge was not in the minds of the executive management of Vodafone as they and their advisers (consultants) planned the later phases of the transition continuum of this experiential journey.

The Ensuing Emergent Requisite Organizational Model

Of contextual relevance to the discussion of this new requisite organizational model is that it relates to a journey paradigm and its transitional continuum toward the globalization of a single interorganizational business relationship of the companies in the Vodafone and Ericsson global organizations. As discussed here and in Chapter 4, it is offered as a counterintuitive stereotype for the consideration by others seeking to lead a transformation transition to achieve the integration of a multilocation collaboration endeavor through the execution of a common strategy, be those locations companies within a single organization or between organizations.

The attributes of this account have been demonstrated to link the variant extant literature although not combined and presented in the form evidenced here. The Ericsson global forum meeting and its leadership form the combined transformational backbone or catalyst. The boundary-crossing individuals are all those who attended the global forum, its leadership, and the Vodafone-Ericsson teams, all of which are included in the organizational model. The meta-management is achieved through the vertical (country) organizations linked through the horizontal relationships, i.e., all the virtual workstreams. The global and local balance of responsibilities is managed through the global forum and mediated by the leadership. The virtual teams (or workstreams) that operate within and between the organizations are the Vodafone and Ericsson global virtual teams. The emerging global social structure is seated in the global forum, although it also includes all those in-country resources of both organizations activated in a meta-way by the participants of the global forum.

The scope of this outcome is set at the strategic interorganizational and intercompany relationship level.[60] In this new organizational model illustrated in Figure 3.4, the local in-country relationships between the Ericsson (S1–Sn) and Vodafone (C1–Cn) companies are retained; however, their role is now changed in contrast to that represented in Figure 3.1. These vertical hierarchies deal in-country with only those matters that are nonglobal and

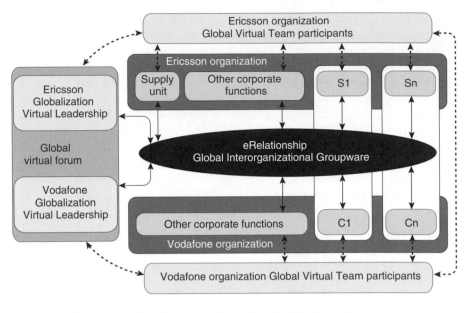

Direct nonmediated interorganizational and/or intercompany
global communication

Company/functional links to multilevel interorganizational and/or
intercompany virtual team initiatives

Ericsson and/or Vodafone multilevel global intercompany and
interorganizational virtual team participants

Multilevel global virtual forum for the interorganizational virtual team initiatives

eRelationship—global interorganizational groupware

Local in-country interorganizational relationship

Companies and/or functions within an organization

Ericsson or Vodafone globally dispersed virtual organizations

(S1-C1) ... (Sn-Cn) represent supplier and customer
globally dispersed in-country resident companies in 1 to n countries

Figure 3.4 **The intra- and interorganizational relationship model: the invisible
and/or requisite organization**

Source: Ibbott, C. J. (2001). An IS-Enabled Model for the Transformation and Globalisaiton of
Interorganisational and Intercompany Relationships. Doctor of Business Administration (DBA).
Brunel University, U.K., p. 222

primarily focus on implementation, quality of service, services, and the local
interorganizational relationship.

A new attribute is added by those in the global virtual teams from both
organizations (*shown at top and bottom of figure*) combining in the global
forum (*shown at left*), which is part of a broader global and virtual community
or invisible organization. This horizontal and nonhierarchical interconnection

within and between the two globally dispersed organizations eliminates the notion of the preexisting mediated communication. So, too, does the introduction of the IOS or eRelationship (*center of figure*) that includes information and knowledge at the behest and under the control of the users or clusters with common interests and global nonmediated access.

The validity of this organizational representation was tested in the original underlying research.[61] The beneficial and ad hoc link between the virtual participants of both organizations independent of the global forum should also be noted; for example, for the pursuit of "low-hanging (economic) fruit" through shared practices. The realization of the aggregation cost synergies was more relevant than who introduced the initiative.

Summary

Going global is a transformational journey. The experiential journey paradigm has demonstrably worked, wherein fix preemptive plans were absent; however, strong leadership and collective motivation to mutual acceptance of a common strategy were primary. The flexible nature of the ensuing virtual and informal organization fostered the requisite circumstances to transition and achieve an effective transformation continuum toward the desired new global state for both previously international organizations with a dispersed global footprint. The emergent situational circumstances encouraged the trust and integrity that were in evidence within and between the two international organizations that were jointly seeking to go global.

Having initially exposed, discussed, and mutually accepted the asymmetry of benefits between the two organizations arising from the agreed strategy, the scene was set for a transparent and end-to-end approach to the derivation of cost synergies for mutual fulfillment. The aggregation cost synergies being pursued, at least by Vodafone having publicly declared such to the financial markets, were nevertheless still to be realized through a now single, polarized collective interorganizational negotiation or business game. This interorganizational global business game nevertheless, was to lead to significant and sustained economic benefits for both organizations notwithstanding the asymmetry of benefits in timing or amount; the longer view of the business relationship was to prevail in the mutual interest of the common strategy to globalize.

Going global means going beyond international. The emergent requisite interorganizational and global organization transcended the complexity of equity ownerships, which on the Vodafone side varied and on the Ericsson side consisted of fully owned subsidiaries. As a result, within Vodafone this gave rise to a requisite and, for the most part, informal, self-governing, virtual intraorganizational outcome save one formally constituted body—informal meaning not recognized or identified in a homogeneous organizational chart and not constituted as part of a visible budget, yet its existence was recognized through the internally reported aggregation cost synergies, the objectives for which were assumed by the author and his minimal direct team.

Recognition within Vodafone team leadership that the cost synergy realization was ultimately the point of the interorganizational business transaction gave relevance to and the motivation for the in-country companies' engagement. Similarly, the joint interorganizational engagement assured that the Ericsson in-country teams also took an end-to-end view, even though for both organizations the business game was managed at the global level for those mutually agreed matters or categories. The impact was that a requisite informal and yet governing nonhierarchical, cross-country, cross-cultures (individual, business, country), and horizontal organization emerged that linked the vertical hierarchies of the in-country companies to operate effectively in pursuit of a common agenda; this was certainly a functional and positive transformational step for Vodafone.

The outcome was the establishment of a new business-performing and global industry-leading team identity both within and between each of the organizations, albeit informal, within which emerged its own culture that contributed to the establishment and development of social capital. The engaged Vodafone in-country companies voluntarily, yet formally acceded hitherto local interorganizational negotiation control in favor of group leverage through this informal structure. Finally, what has been demonstrated is that direct control over all engaged resources is not always necessary to achieve an effective and sustainable outcome; in appropriate circumstances with the requisite leadership and organization, the power of meta-influence may positively prevail.

Going global means working together. Essential for such a collaborative endeavor, which was seeking to simultaneously transform both the intraorganizational relationships and pursue a strategy of the globalization of the interorganizational relationships, is the visibility and access to consistent information and knowledge void of constraints arising from global position. It was demonstrated that the co-evolutionary operationalization of an interorganizational information or knowledge system concept, known as eRelationship, became embedded in the global community of both organizations. The situational application of the eRelationship was guided by the users and conformed to the users' eRelationship strategy. Importantly, a set of tools was established that sought to fulfill the interorganizational (or strategic interface) while leaving open the adoption for in-country interorganizational application (as indeed some did). Such an approach contrasted with the normal IS/IT projects that are preceded with specifications, committees, budgets, etc.

Again, the leadership of this initiative was relevant in engaging the teams to assure that the required functionality and performance ensued. The users established their virtual communities within this knowledge domain, subject only to "rules" of structure. The content was created and maintained solely in the interest of the given virtual team, while generally remaining accessible to all Intranet registered users in either organization, whether or not part of the globalization initiative. This approach, being void of the normal formalities and constraints that encourage people to circumnavigate the system in their own self-interest, is believed to have encouraged the disclosure of tacit knowledge. This openness was more likely to occur in the emergent social network, especially as the social capital developed within said network; this also included selected information that may otherwise have been considered confidential to any of the parties.

Going global involves getting people going. For a successful transition continuum in the transformation taking place within and between two international organizations with a global footprint, success is dependent on those involved and their behavior. The early identification, engagement, and motivation of the key stakeholders and their team members are essential, although the sequence may vary. The stakeholder interest is defined as what affects or influences the outcome of the objective, or as executive management representing the point of realization—generally but not exclusively the in-country operation. Failure of the assigned leader to recognize that motivating key stakeholders is critical. It is through such an approach that a social network develops, leading to the accrual of key social capital brought about through friendships, both within and between organizations.

For the leader such social capital also becomes a reciprocal forum of meta-influence to mutual benefit and thus avoids confrontational circumstances, which may polarize the teams as they follow the leadership example. Such flexible engagement, void of predetermination of who needs to be involved, has been shown to lead to organizational experimentation through experiential learning, all to positive effect. Such cohesion and motivated engagement work together to dispel dissension and help move the process forward in a positive way.

In summary, a community of boundary-crossing individuals was created that together resolved, often in counterintuitive and innovative ways, the merging of practice of those ordinarily and functionally boundary compliant and those who recognized the need to move the game beyond such artificial constraints. In short, a requisite organizational model emerged that served the interests of both organizations seeking to globalize. The sense of collegiate spirit and excitement of engaging in an industry-leading endeavor, in and between both organizations, breached the stereotypical boundaries of management, formality, and control and positively bounded all dimensions of what is known as culture.

4 Adapting the Requisite Organizational Model

Moving the Requisite Global Organization On

At the end of the last chapter, a requisite organizational model for Vodafone's global business relationship with Ericsson was in place.[1] Following the merger with AirTouch, and then the successful hostile acquisition of Mannesmann, cost synergies targets leveraging the newfound global scale were publicly declared.[2] Thomas Geitner was appointed as executive director on May 15, 2000, to "be responsible for the development and introduction of pan European products and services and the achievement of revenue and cost synergies between the operating companies (or "OpCos" as they were known) within the European Region of Vodafone AirTouch"[3]; they (the companies) being Vodafone equity interests ranging from wholly owned, through majority owned, to a minority or affiliate position. I was appointed as director, global supply chain management on Thomas's team effective July 1, 2000, to "strengthen our ability to put synergies in place across the Vodafone Group." Vodafone was to later announce that the "Mannesmann synergies, calculated on a proportionate after tax cash flow basis, exceeded the target of £600 million set for the year ended 31 March 2004."[4] The globalized aggregation cost synergy contribution for mobile network infrastructure discussed in this book was included in that result, contributing both global capital expenditure savings and local (operating) cost savings arising because of the global scale.

Also, according to the same business review, "Group Technology & Business Integration leads in the selection, development and implementation of global technology solutions to support the terminals, service platforms, *network* and IT requirements of the Group. It drives the benefits of scale and scope to deliver enhanced customer experience, increased speed to market and an improved strategic cost position by applying the principle of 'design once, deploy many times' and by working closely with suppliers"; "The Group continues to build its capability to manage suppliers on a global basis and has delivered synergies through negotiating global contracts, particularly in the areas of terminals, network infrastructure and IT"; "there has been continued progress in eCommerce activities, with the Group taking an industry leading position in the effective use of e-auctions." The activities referenced in these comments were initiated and led across the group by Ling Chang from within my team, and I was the executive sponsor for the "Buy-side" eCommerce at that time; the benefit specifically in the mobile network infrastructure business segment was to generate serious global leverage hitherto not considered for such complex systems, hence its being "industry leading."

Although having an economic aggregation cost synergy target within Vodafone, the mobile network infrastructure endeavor (essentially capital expenditure focused at that time) was in all other dimensions counterintuitive: *not having* a formal plan, a budget inclusive of all actually engaged or contributing resources, a visible organizational organogram, a definitive set of roles and responsibilities covering the leadership and all engaged parties, a formal IS specification with statement of requirements for the interorganizational information or knowledge system, etc. Yet it achieved or exceeded its goals!

From the experiential evolution leading to the requisite (yet invisible and virtual) organization in the Vodafone-Ericsson globalization initiative, I formed the view that even though the center had been responsible for vision, strategy, and (informal) governance, it was an inescapable fact that the group's actual cost synergy could be realized only by the in-country operating companies, who, after all, run the networks, acquire customers, and build market share.

The de facto decision we took was to reuse the Vodafone-Ericsson transformational approach and the requisite organizational model—however, with a difference. Given my deep-seated belief, particularly in a services-based business (as a mobile telecommunications operator), that operational responsibilities must be at the point closest to service delivery to the end-customer— the user of the mobile phone, or Terminal, as the industry refers to it—namely, the OpCo. Such proximity to the end-customer also ordinarily coexists as the point of deepest in-country operational knowledge; therefore, seeking to control the acquisition and deployment of mobile network infrastructure and related services from the center was a nonstarter in this emerging new global supplier paradigm, seated in the accrued Vodafone-Ericsson experience.

This chapter presents the advancement by Vodafone to other such relevant globalization endeavors for mobile network infrastructure–related activities. This was to introduce an experiential adaptation of the requisite organizational model established in the Vodafone-Ericsson globalization initiative that affected the intra- and interorganizational globalized relationship, a model that also provided for the motivated transition leadership that resulted in changes in relationships and practice within and between the globally dispersed organizations. Specifically, this chapter deals with the expanded Vodafone globalization relationships beyond that under way with Ericsson, that is, those with Nokia, Nortel, and Siemens.

With the operational lead delegated to the most knowledgeable OpCos came the new term, "Lead Operating Companies," or "Lead OpCos," which will be discussed in more detail. It was through such a move that a generalized model of the initial adaptive Vodafone-Ericsson model was developed to enable a globalized interaction with multiple suppliers in the interest of the various OpCo clusters. What was therefore created was a transformation dynamic simultaneously in operation within and between several international organizations, each with a global footprint, parts of which Vodafone, as the aggregation stimulus and nexus, interacted. The Vodafone OpCos generally participated in more than one of the supplier-based global clusters, each with a common interest. It was through this amalgam that a leading move in telecom industry practice emerged, not to mention a unique cross-organizational case example from which others could learn.

The discussion concludes with the introduction of reverse electronic auctions (eAuctions) as an efficient and effective way of determining supplier competitiveness for the acquisition of mobile network infrastructure and the optimum global market price and cost; the acceleration to the competitive market floor was nothing short of astounding. As part of the eCommerce "Buy-side" initiative, such techniques were also effectively utilized across categories, through which the momentum of an emergent, new global practice was established.

OpCos and Lead OpCos

The Vodafone pioneering team at the inaugural Vodafone-Ericsson global forum in February 1999 was essentially centered on Vodafone Limited in the UK, it having had the longer relationship with Ericsson and greater level of business at the time; the UK therefore took the lead. Essentially, the UK was the Lead (mobile) Operator among the initial and, later, expanding network of OpCos in the Ericsson business-related common interest cluster from around the world and formed the axis of rotation, or nexus, for the Ericsson "Club." Within the "Club" formation through the assignment of virtual workstreams in the community interests, it had been established that transference of the baton of responsibility was quite a normal, acceptable thing to do.

There was a somewhat natural grouping available wherein there were both critical mass and motivation to devolve from the center team the operational and day-to-day dimension of the management of the key supplier relationships. This gave birth to the Vodafone "Lead OpCo" (Lead Operating Company) multisupplier cluster organizational model that would be the nexus and form the axis of rotation, one for each of the key supplier-based clusters. This creation and execution essentially spread the "center" to the customer (mobile phone user) front line. Those to whom the Lead OpCo role was "offered" had the longest relevant in-depth operational and commercial experience with their assigned responsibility, namely, the UK for Ericsson, Italy for Nokia, Spain for Nortel, and Germany for Siemens.

The dimension being introduced here is that the collective economic cost synergies for which the center organization shall be accountable is vested in an organizational form over which it has no direct line control. This is perhaps a test of true leadership and the potential power of a social network, a thriving global virtual community, and the collective power of meta-management. This dispersal of leadership engaged the top management of each of the Lead OpCos in a positive way, of course in their own interest but also in the interest of the virtual community they represented both toward their vendor and the group strategic interest. It would be inaccurate to say that the relationship between the center and the Lead OpCos was never challenged or vexed, because it was; however, given the strategy in common and collective interests, we always found the right way forward.

Essentially, what had been created here were an effective glocal (global-local) leadership, business (and personal) relationship, and decision-making structure. This model may be characterized as the management single global vendor and cross-category or lines of business; that is, the management of all segments of the global vendor relationships with the operators in the Vodafone Group. Given the nonhierarchical nature of the global and virtual communities, there were myriad social networks in play, all acting (hopefully) in the common interest. The only available measure of success was the economic results, they being the contribution to the Mannesmann synergies developed through the virtual workstream endeavors concluded in accordance with the will of the OpCo clusters. This style of management and organizational model perhaps attests to the requirement of the leadership to engage, understand where the boundaries should be set, and delegate, operating thereafter in a meta-influencing role; unquestionably the outcome here demonstrated that direct line of control is not a prerequisite for success.

Figure 4.1 is an illustration of the structure of the Lead OpCo model social networks and the diversity of their formal and informal relationships. The supplier global organization includes their 100% equity–owned, in-country operations trading with Vodafone and the global team, inclusive of such headquarter resources and contributions as they required (*shown at top of figure*). The Vodafone supplier-based cluster comprising the in-country OpCos, with a given global supplier interest in common, is a subordinate segment of the overall Vodafone global organization (*shown at bottom of figure*). This Vodafone cluster is led and represented by the Lead OpCo on behalf of and supported by the OpCo cluster and the Vodafone global team in their transactions with the supplier in global matters. The aim is not to inhibit or constrain intra- or interorganizational dialogue, but the contrary; however, on matters affecting multiple OpCos or global matters, it was important to have a clear point of consolidation.

The joint virtual workstreams comprise in-country resources from both the supplier and Vodafone and such other resources required from either organization. Thereafter the n-way informal social networks develop within and between both organizations with uninhibited communication and association, save the formality between the supplier global team and the Lead OpCo, supported by the Vodafone global team, for matters binding the supplier and the Vodafone OpCo cluster. Both the Lead OpCo and the OpCos in the cluster have social network connections into other supplier-based clusters in which they have a direct or indirect interest. The participating Vodafone OpCos were

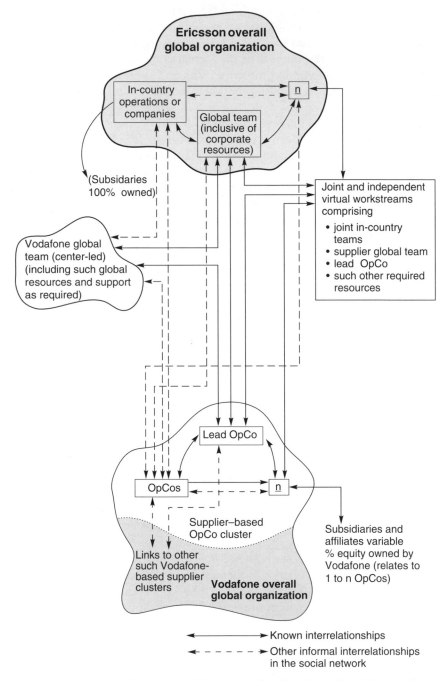

Figure 4.1   **Lead OpCo intra- and interorganizational relationships model**

Notes: The dotted lines: Example of (the) scope of (the) potential social network and (other) lines of communication
The solid lines: Formal channel of interorganizational communication and relationships

of variable and changing equity interests. The interorganizational information system, for example, eRelationship (discussed elsewhere), has been omitted for the purposes of this organizational model illustration.

Sander and Lowney's conclusions of their conceptual discussion in the context of communities may be relevant to Figure 4.1.[5] They discuss bounded communities of common interest wherein one knows the same individuals through multiple strands, for example, within the same organization, although such communities have few links, if any, with other communities, which not so in this case. Sander and Lowney anticipate, however, other communities more akin to this case, wherein numerous people have social ties with multiple other communities—what they describe as interlocking networks. They suggest in the latter scenario that it is more important to look at the level of interconnections between the communities than to look only at the level of social capital within any one of them. Such communities in Figure 4.1 might be the supplier global organization, the Vodafone global organization, the supplier-based OpCo cluster, an OpCo, the Vodafone global team, the supplier global team, and the Lead OpCo.

In a globalization endeavor, although the social capital compounds "strength" at all levels of grouping, not necessarily linearly, it is posited that the level of social capital in the various interconnections builds the capacity for meta-influence or management absent a formal organizational structure to bind the communities. In fact, the benefit here is that the absence of a formal structure provides the flexibility to dynamically adapt to changing circumstances or to respond to situated change, as considered by Orlikowski.[6] Recall the definition of social capital: "the social networks and the norms of trustworthiness and reciprocity that arise from them."[7] The communities, the social capital, and ensuing collective culture that enabled an effective meta-influence leading to the beneficial economic outcome were an outcome, not a planned result; thereby the social capital became stronger as it emerged from the diversity of engaged communities in such a way that motivated and stabilized the informal, or in its greatest scale, invisible collective.

Interestingly, although this organizational model functioned to good effect, there were two aborted attempts, with the assistance of external consultants, to formalize both the structure and the nature of the relative roles and responsibilities between the center and the Lead OpCo. I opted not to pursue the matter further and to continue to capitalize on the developed social and intellectual capital. As indicated in Chapter 3, there was a rich tapestry of cultural mix both in the Lead OpCo leadership (UK, Italy, Spain, and Germany) and the larger global virtual community, from which challenges emerged. Taken in the wrong context, they would have been damaging; but acceptance of differentials in the national and cultural ways combined to give rise to a rich and beneficial outcome, for which experience I remain grateful to the patience and contributions of all my colleagues. Although occasional jousting occurred, the participants always rallied around the ultimate combined objectives for success through our collaboration and elevated their game accordingly.

The characterization of the leadership and composition of the virtual and global collaborative, informal, yet truly requisite, emergent organization has been discussed. Of note, however, is that this combined Vodafone-Ericsson virtual network in operation was an experiential, iterative, self-adapting, self-organizing network absent of the normal or expected command structure. The evidence suggests that this horizontal and nonhierarchical virtual network linking the vertical hierarchies of the in-country OpCos was self-driven in the pursuit of fulfillment derived from a common motivator: the aggregation cost synergies.

Further, the implication for those in this horizontal social network was that there was a mutual integrity and trust in both the leadership and each other, which in turn developed substantive social capital. Evidence for this is that most in this social network at this time voluntarily participated and contributed to the endeavor on the basis of (and on occasions extreme) goodwill, as the responsibilities of many were their daily roles in their OpCos, at least on the Vodafone side. The visibility and potentially the interest of executive management in the social network was not high, save the economic results achieved through the (Vodafone) OpCos; therefore, they essentially had no depth of understanding and appreciation of the "power" and functioning. The virtual global network created, evolved, and established its own culture absent of any preemptive formal act to do so; it just happened.

This was for Vodafone the ultimate requisite organization within which innovation and experimentation prevailed to positive effect—an invisible organization (nonhierarchical, collaborative, virtual social network) within a visible and structured organization in which everyone had a role. The social network or invisible organization, in effect being a third (organizational) force initially within and between an otherwise visible two-organization (Vodafone-Ericsson) relationship, was inclusive and transparent across the community in operation, and later in addition meshed Vodafone with Nokia, Nortel, and Siemens through the Lead OpCo arrangement (in contrast to structure).

A key factor in the ability for the agreed globalization strategy to be effective was that at least on those interorganizational matters in common to two or more networks, the virtual community in general and the accepted leadership (Nils Grimsmo and myself) in particular actually represented their respective organizations. Given the variable equity interest of Vodafone in its participating OpCos and as a matter of good management practice, it was important that those represented formally declare their support toward and acceptance of the outcomes from the global virtual team; in other words, the OpCos had to positively opt in. The opt-in process was the voluntary basis upon which to engage so the aggregation cost synergy benefits would accrue to the participating OpCos. The Vodafone OpCos did formally opt in, normally with a resolution by the board of directors, and in so doing acceded "power" to the center function through the acknowledgment that matters deemed global were no longer considered at the in-country level between the Vodafone and Ericsson organizations.

Through the OpCo engagement this principle was accepted, as the interorganizational leverage had also moved to the group level. Although the interorganizational relationship had been redefined and would continue to be so as more matters were deemed global, it nevertheless did not change the in-country organizational structure or governance Therefore, it was key that to sustain good operation of the emerging new paradigm, there needed to be an effective key stakeholder social network and the social network in general must sustain effective performance so as not to diminish the motivation or incentive. Communication and relationship with the key (meaning with the strongest influence on the outcome) stakeholders were critical in avoiding miscommunication and/or misunderstanding of the attributes and intents of the approach being proposed at any time. I did establish and develop an extremely effective and influential key stakeholder and general social network.

Organizational Transformation

A common mistake in organizational transformation is to presume that activity is synonymous with the pace of progress of the endeavor; it may provide such a perception and is therefore tempting. However, experience would suggest that this is not necessarily true. There is a delicate balance, which is somewhat intuitive. Some years ago when I was in the United States, a colleague suggested that the difference at that time between Japan and the Western cultures was that the Japanese spent 80% of the time contemplating the action (thought) and organizational consultation followed by 20% in effective implementation (action); whereas the Western cultures spent 80% of the time bringing remedy to the consequences of the lack of earlier forethought.

This anecdotal view makes the point perhaps of "less haste, more speed," but there is, nevertheless, a delicate balance between thought or preparation and action: the utilization of the process journey versus the destination journey paradigms. That is, one at least has to have the ability to resolve the preparatory point beyond which the laws of diminishing returns kick in; perhaps therefore, commencing the journey is the best course of action, although there may be consequences to overcome arising from culture, be it national or organizational. Transforming an organization is not an endeavor on which the fainthearted should embark; there must be objective leadership with delegated executive support to see the task through absent of unnecessary bureaucratic or limiting constraint.

There may be counterinfluences to change, namely, those that do not like the change or that have a preference for the continuance of the status quo; such nonalignment arises, I would posit, when relevant parties are not sufficiently involved in the process leading to the implementation of the transformational proposition. True professionals must accept that even though they may not benefit personally, they nevertheless should move in the interests of the business as a whole; such individuals should be viewed as an asset to the company. A resolute determination (analogy of a pilot landing a plane in turbulent weather) and a progressive transition are both required in a multicultural and geographically dispersed organization, which ideally motivate participation conducive to attaining the objective of the change.

Engagement should be encouraged from diverse sources (that is, disregarding ethnic culture, organization culture, size of the participating organization, or the level of success encountered in the past) and not limited to those from whom supportive answers are expected, as they all play a role that finally affects the adoption rate of the new modus operandi. This approach serves to create a magnetic catalyst within which once success is evident (as viewed in the eye of the beholder at this stage), then people seek out "membership," as was demonstrated in the activities of the Vodafone-Ericsson foundation discussed in Chapter 3.

Further, it is important to recognize that progressive contribution is not the privilege of rank or position but of those blessed with the talent to espouse relevant ideas that move the chosen game onward, as demonstrated in the nonhierarchical virtual community formed in the Vodafone-Ericsson cluster. Although not envisaged that way at the time, the Vodafone-Ericsson project was to become a "pilot" rather than a "big bang" or "step change." For a sustainable impact, establishing such a catalyst or nucleus for radical and transformational change has in this case shown itself to be the most effective approach, certainly in the advancement to a broader new multisupplier Lead OpCo model, as discussed later in this chapter.

Multiple Global Suppliers and Adapting the Requisite Organizational Model

As the scale of the Vodafone operating interests expanded beyond the original organizations, through the inclusion of new OpCos arising from the AirTouch merger and Mannesmann acquisition, so did the emergence of other relevant cross-OpCo supplier commonalities. In October 1999 I had been invited for a discussion with the Nokia global sales management team in Copenhagen, in which I presented the current stage of evolution of the Vodafone-Ericsson globalization concept and potential opportunities and associated impacts for Nokia should they elect to engage in this endeavor. Sari Baldauf (CEO of Nokia Networks) later confirmed to me in a meeting in Helsinki that Nokia wanted to participate. In March 2000 the key representatives of the Vodafone OpCos in the global virtual community met in Sydney to open discussions on opportunities outside of mobile network infrastructure, notwithstanding its dominance in capital and operating expenditure for the group. In short, the base of opportunity was expanding, and the need to increase the scope of engagement in the interests of enhanced aggregation cost synergies was clear.

The participants in Sydney agreed to introduce an organizational model variance, namely, to delegate on behalf of the center leadership the global operational and commercial leadership on behalf of supplier-based OpCo clusters towards, in the first instance, the principal mobile network infrastructure suppliers to the Vodafone Group interests. With this move a Lead OpCo multisupplier cluster organizational model was formed within which OpCos could engage in one or several clusters according to their business interests and supplier engagements. The true depth of the informal social network arising from this new structure, like the Vodafone-Ericsson cluster, will never be known except as evidenced in the reported aggregation cost synergy yields. The invisible organization continued with an enriched social capital and diversity of associations.

Given the supplier organization, the Vodafone global team, and the Vodafone supplier-based cluster relationships shown in Figure 4.1, the organizational model shown in Figure 4.2 illustrates the multiple global supplier relationships with the Vodafone group equity interests. Each global supplier has the informal social network within and between its organization and Vodafone, as discussed previously, and its direct interworking with the assigned Lead OpCo, on behalf of the Vodafone supplier-based OpCo cluster that it is both integral to and the representative of. The OpCos in the supplier-based (or group interest) clusters generally participated in more than one such cluster. Selected Lead OpCo teams also managed more than one global supplier relationship and therefore represented such cluster formations with the supplier interest in common.

Communities and Social Networks

From a Sander and Lowney perspective, what is developed is a number of inter- and cross-connected communities each with their multiple-level independent, interlinked, and interdependent interests all within an informal horizontal and virtual organizational framework.[8] The framework was informal, because the organization had no documented organizational representation; because there were no recognized specific roles and responsibilities of most of the individuals participating in one or more of the communities; and because the communities had formed of their own volition a collective culture recognized within the aggregate community. It is difficult to map all the communities and the social networks that prevailed, as the informality provided for whatever constructive frameworks individuals and groups of individuals wished to form in the positive interests of the businesses. As noted earlier, there will be the visible and invisible aspects of the composite social networks however absent of all such elements in the social network it would not function; the key point is that it was not planned, nor was the emergent collective culture defined through any typical such consultative processes—it just happened.

Recall that in this Lead OpCo model the formal dimension of this informal network was the governance structure established, to which the interface was clear; the Vodafone global team worked jointly with and was supported by the Lead OpCos as required. The Lead OpCos and personal and key stakeholder commitment and goodwill were invaluable and were crucial to the success of the endeavor, making the social network critical, along with the horizontal network of the greater community within Vodafone.

The visible social networks present within and between Vodafone and a global supplier organization are illustrated in Figure 4.1. In Figure 4.2 there

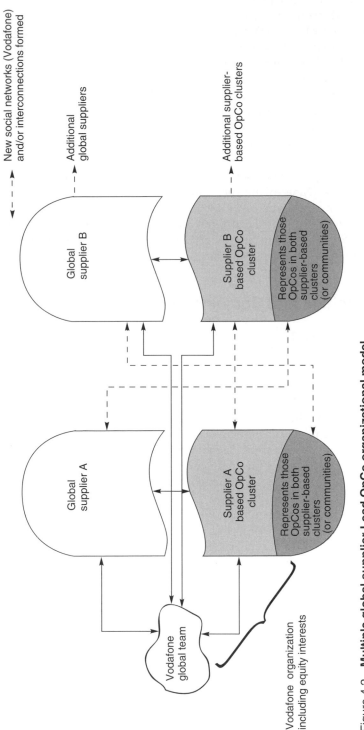

Figure 4.2 **Multiple global supplier Lead OpCo organizational model**

Note: Vodafone global team, the global suppliers and the supplier-based OpCo clusters include relationships, with relationships, and social networks within and between the organizations, as in Figure 4.1 (including virtual workstreams)

are multiple interorganizational global supplier-based communities, as well as multiple diverse, multilevel social network relationships formed by individuals who have various roles and presence in more than one supplier-focused community. As more global supplier-based communities were formed, the time necessary for them to become effective rapidly decreased, given that such communities were formed by an increasing network of able individuals, at least in the Vodafone OpCos. The supplier may have been vexed in trying to adapt the established prerequisite model for such global relationships. A team might be a Lead OpCo in one supplier-based community and yet be an OpCo led by other such Lead OpCos in adjacent communities. To be in a position to document the knowledge gained in forming such a unique and counterintuitive organization, rich in social capital, has been both a privilege and a rich experience.

Any assignment to a Lead OpCo necessarily should be given to the Vodafone OpCo with the greatest design and operational experience of any such given supplier relationship. This criterion serves to make sure that the Lead OpCo is an effective catalyst for the transfer of knowledge within the cluster and becomes the authoritative cluster representative to the given supplier of all operational and commercial matters. Despite the "Lead" dimension of the Lead OpCo, it was nevertheless the obligation to establish and operate an inclusive, engaging approach with the other OpCos in the cluster and the supplier. These motivating and successful practices were learned through experience in the Vodafone-Ericsson transformational journey. Clearly, the momentum improved in subsequent globalization endeavors because some of the participants would have had the early Vodafone-Ericsson experience, increasing the knowledge base. Two attempts were made to formalize the interorganizational relationship, but without success. The informal structure and invisible organization prevailed, visible only in the reported cost synergy savings realized.

The existence of the new social networks in the Vodafone organization between the supplier-based OpCo cluster through engagement of OpCos in more than one such cluster, and the networks between Lead OpCo teams and the global team, served to assure competitive normalization across suppliers and provided visibility for the dynamics to both tactically and strategically engender competition. That is, the hitherto in-country confidentiality between the OpCo and global supplier had now irrevocably moved to the global level within Vodafone, albeit clearly with requirements of confidentiality outside the organization.

According to the above criterion, Ericsson was reassigned to the Vodafone UK OpCo, Nokia was assigned to Italy, Nortel to Spain, and Siemens to Germany. Italy and Germany were the principal axis of knowledge for their respective suppliers; Nortel was a new entrant for 3G or UMTS to Vodafone, and Spain made the most substantive such commitment to them. The virtual leadership retained the corporate and strategic relationship with the suppliers, however, and began to work closely where necessary to facilitate and coordinate within the various new supplier-based OpCo clusters; the Ericsson relationships were ongoing.

For the suppliers, this had an implied impact that also necessitated changes. The impact was somewhat less for Ericsson, as all the actors were already known to them and they had agreed to differentiate between in-country business relationships and global. The Vodafone-Ericsson cluster also had traction and had produced economic, although differential, results to their mutual satisfaction. The potential issue with the new Lead OpCos and associated supplier relationships, from the Vodafone side, was that if the supplier in-country business representative had a dual local and global role, there was the risk of a conflict of interest in responding to the (larger) Lead OpCo customer in preference, bias, or compromise to others in the same supplier cluster. Such an issue would render the OpCo cluster ineffective and serve to de-motivate its members; this could leave open the opportunity for the Lead OpCo to leverage its assigned cluster representation it its own interest and for the supplier to "feed" it with the wrong cultural motivation. It was the role of the center function to monitor such activities for the assurance of balanced representation and yield for the complete supplier-based cluster.

As was experienced in the foregoing globalization process, it was essential for the now tremendously expanded meta-influence of the global virtual community toward the engaged OpCos that a social network emerge within which social capital would develop, a foundation of the community's ability to be effective in transformational endeavors. Given the diversity of the social network, the fact that many actors would participate in two or more supplier-based clusters, thereby enabling comparative judgment (cluster, Lead OpCo, and supplier), was essential to the building of social capital. In the global virtual community there are a number of informal sub- and cross-subcommunities formed, albeit with the collective role to leverage the combined global Vodafone position with the supplier, who, of course, also seeks to leverage the business relationships in its own (asymmetric) interests, ideally in a complementary way. Given the (confidential) cross-supplier transparency to the Vodafone interests, aggregation synergy opportunities arising from "exposed" differences could be more resolutely pursued, often not to the comfort or liking of the suppliers.

Communities and Trust: The Invisible Organization

Sander and Lowney discuss trust in the context of a measure of trustworthiness of (virtual) community members, not gullibility.[9] Some communities exhibit thick trust, wherein trust extends only to known friends and associates; others exhibit thin trust, wherein the trust extends as well to total strangers. Communities with more extensive social networks, such as the Lead OpCo multisupplier cluster organizational model, are more likely to have individuals behaving in a trustworthy manner, since the reputation of untrustworthy members travels fast in well-connected communities. Untrustworthy members pay a communitywide cost for the gains from any such acts on their part. With these norms of trust, people engage in reciprocity, doing for others not with any immediate expectation of repayment. The lessons from the winning strategy are that individuals should initially be open to collaboration and quickly forgiving, but not gullible.

The pathfinders in the Vodafone-Ericsson experience would be presumed, on the anecdotal evidence, to have formed a close bond, analogous to thick trust, but exhibiting thin trust in the acceptance of strangers into the virtual community. Strangers in this case would be those new OpCos joining the original Vodafone-Ericsson cluster, if for no other reason than the extreme pride in being part of the organization and its achievements, albeit the informal status of that social network in either organization. The new OpCo had to perform within the cluster for the aggregation cost synergy realization, which by definition means that the OpCo had to also benefit for the savings to be realized and reported. In the new Lead OpCo multisupplier cluster organizational model, there was mix of the "experienced" Vodafone-Ericsson participants, the newly assigned Lead OpCo leaders and team out to demonstrate their worthiness of position, and all others seeking the benefit already realized in the Vodafone-Ericsson cluster. To that combined end it was not a closed shop, therefore exhibiting thin trust; although the considerations of reciprocity may have lagged somewhat, new relationships were established and developed in the expanded community.

Another observation is that there is segmentation in the social network that can be demonstrated by the following analogies. In years past when studying mechanical engineering, I recall exercises concerning bridge structures. It was intriguing to discover that it was possible to have elements in the structure that were neither in tension or compression, which leads to the obvious question, why are they there? The lecturer suggested the removal of such elements and a recalculation, only to find that the structure was no longer stable; question answered. Much later in postgraduate studies in modern control theory, the nexus of the proposition was to represent systems mathematically; I recall a classic example being a motor-generator set. However, in the mathematics of the complex contour integrals and matrices there were "poles" and "zeros" that required consideration to achieve a stable system. Again, it was discovered that there were elements that could not be directly measured, yet without them the system became unstable. The point is that when applied to social networks, the same logic prevails, none more so than when this social network expanded beyond the formative Vodafone-Ericsson experience to the Lead OpCo multisupplier cluster organizational model.

There may be individuals in one's social network on which there is both a dependency and a trusting and reciprocal relationship. There may also and simultaneously be others in one's social network on whom there is a dependency, yet the trust and reciprocity have yet to develop or indeed have failed or suffered acute setback; like the bridge or the system, however, exclusion is not an option. From my systems engineering perspective and at the conceptual level, human organizations and interpersonal dynamics are just but another form of system entirely consistent with those of an electronic or computing nature. Such challenges are indeed possible in a social network inclusive of social cultural diversity and established corporate cultural diversity, yet not necessarily averse to the globalization strategy or the implementation proposition and consequences of its impact. Certain of my team and others in the supplier-based clusters were certainly circumstantially challenged on more than one occasion for various reasons rooted in the embedded culture of the challenger(s); that is not to suggest that all such challenges were absent of merit.

To complement the move to the Lead OpCo multisupplier cluster organizational model was the requirement to have a center or hub team to fill the social network management or lead role of vision, strategy, and governance. As reported, this team was composed of variously recruited secondees ordinarily for periods up to two years from across the geographic spectrum, including the UK, Germany, Italy, Holland, Portugal, Greece, Spain, and France; a small number of the team members were permanently based in the UK. This approach served well the purpose of interweaving the Lead OpCos and the balance of the greater in-country OpCo community, which now numbered more than twenty across just these four major mobile network infrastructure suppliers (Ericsson, Nokia, Nortel, and Siemens); at that time, included were Vodafone subsidiaries and affiliates (>50% equity holding) and excluded were partner networks (0% equity position, in effect, a franchise).

Previously, a key ingredient to the engagement and "buy-in" of the disparate OpCo community was to rotate the host venue for the global forum meetings. Although this was an approach greatly appreciated by the OpCo cluster and something they engaged in competitively and with pride, the Vodafone policy was changed so that the venues would be the UK, Düsseldorf, Milan, and Madrid. The impact of this change was to require members of all supplier-based OpCo clusters to travel to the location of the relevant Lead OpCo. Perhaps this was a reversal of the customer-centric ethos, in that the OpCos in the supplier-based clusters are in effect the customers being supported or led by the Lead OpCo.

We now return to structure, culture, and specifically the formation of my modest (twelve to fourteen people) center team; coming out of the UK OpCo was a trade of perceived "power" to one of "influence" for success, a major contrast in endeavor. I resolved that to further knit together the leadership of this community in the spirit of the role of the center as described earlier, this function should be small and composed of people with current operator-based experience, some of whom should be on assignment or secondment. Again, this approach was to create strength in the development of the social network and be an important contributor to the growing social capital. The selection criteria included that the assignment to the center was to be considered part of the applicant's personal development plan; there was mutual agreement that the candidates were highflyers; and if they did not have an MBA, the candidates agreed to pursue a course of study without compromise to the assignment. It was not a requirement that such individuals come from the supply chain department in their OpCo, but it was an advantage for some if they did.

This approach was effective and successful in that it was strongly supported by the key stakeholders in the social network, not to mention the

OpCo supply chain global community in general, as evidenced by the results. Perhaps it was a unique construct that carried with it an additional economic burden (the cost of secondment), however, that was insignificant in consideration of the collaborative cost synergy results. Even so, in 2004 the executive management decided to cease the secondment process and instead require the interested candidate to actually transfer and relocate (one way). This decision was, of course, counter to the notion that creating a transient organization attracted people to develop their experience and obliged them to relocate to their originating OpCo, taking with them the acquired global knowledge and experience, or move onward elsewhere in the business, which some opted to do.

The mode of operation of the center team was perhaps unusual too. We were a nonhierarchical team within which position determined compensation; however, it was not considered an assurance of performance. Each person did receive an annual performance appraisal and personal development encouragement. There were no minutes taken at team meetings, the logic being that if team members make commitments to each other, then in the culture of our working it is their mutual obligation to perform; minutes did not enhance that prospect. The assignment of tasks was a matter for the team to agree and propose for confirmation, as was load balancing should a team member become overburdened with tasks. As with the prior stated learning experiences, periodically tasks were reassigned within the team, as was the development of the transfer of tasks or responsibilities to and ways of working with the Lead OpCo teams. The feedback received in the company's annual employee survey was consistently standard setting, leading one to conclude that in that environment the flexible and delegative approach was appreciated.

To summarize, this social network increased as new OpCos engaged in the Vodafone globalization initative and formed to create a unique yet largely invisible network that applied itself to the delivery of the desired aggregation cost synergies. It was and remains a unique experience with demonstrable results that simultaneously combined cross-function, cross-company, and cross-organization, the complete attributes and operation of which were also not visible save the reported cost synergies; how could it be invisible with so many companies and organizations engaged in this social network? Perhaps the very existence of this vast global virtual community is attributable to the combined inclusive leadership that is in alignment with the concept of the requisite organization, within which there is a natural tolerance and resilience to accommodate situated change. In contrast is management that exudes process, control, and a preemptive determination of outcome, which forms the basis of plans and reporting and through which compliance takes precedence over performance, although there are also cultural dimensions here.

Formalization and Governance

What had emerged was a complex yet functioning and performing informal network, save the center team, that was all inclusive in the social network

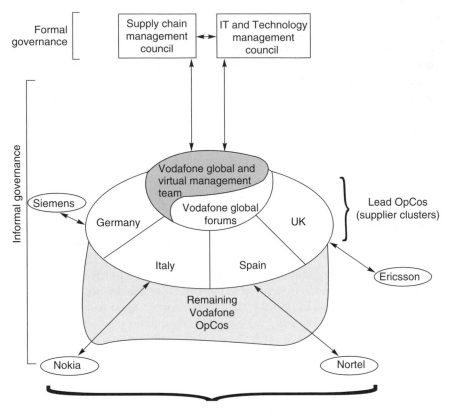

Figure 4.3   **Governance structure**

within the Vodafone organization and between it and its globalizing supply partners. The external-to-Vodafone interface was organized in OpCo clusters of common interest, with most OpCos participating in more than one such cluster. Each cluster had a Lead OpCo representing it that had a delegated operational role with the external partner for and on behalf of those OpCos and my global team. The illustration in Figure 4.3 presents a visual clarification of this organizational structure.

This social network, inclusive of a number of key stakeholders, was essentially self-governing under the auspices of my global role and that of my direct team; although it was informally structured as an inclusive key stakeholder virtual management team to assure relevant input and inclusion in execution. The key stakeholders included were not limited to those in Lead OpCo roles (Germany, Italy, Spain, and the UK); others were invited (as distinct from appointed) who had made or were recognized collectively as having made pivotal contributions to the globalizing endeavor; for example, representation from Japan, Holland, and France was included, none of whom were

Lead OpCos. This emergent informal structure remained nonhierarchical in operation and within the virtual and invisible horizontal organization that included Vodafone in-country operating interests and supplier partners who together formed a globalizing catalyst without which such successful economic performance probably would not have been forthcoming.

It would be wrong to suggest that there were neither moments of challenge nor frustration both within this team and the broader Vodafone OpCo cross-cultural community being served by this endeavor. To the contrary, there were healthy challenges; however, they were in the spirit of retaining the positive legacy of benefits and practices that had been realized in the past and securing them for the future; the depth of resolve and the quality of the outcome were enhanced through the accommodation of these positive "disruptions." Ultimately it was accepted as my role to represent the collective interests elsewhere in Vodafone and indeed at the executive level to the globalizing supplier partners. My position of influence on behalf of the Vodafone organization certainly extended to the buck stopping with me on business matters and the escalation thereof, both within Vodafone and externally. Such "authority," however, was realized through our informal inclusive consultative processes, assuring that all affected operating interests had the opportunity to comment on matters of principle (in effect, global commercial policy), whereas I signed off on all matters relating to commerce. My signature was confirmation of the good work done by the Lead OpCos, my team, and others who made contributions.

In 2001 Vodafone resolved to introduce formal governance in support of the pursuit of the Mannesmann synergy commitment that formalized the relationships between the Vodafone Group functions and its in-country operating companies; this was known as the Momentum Agreement. Under this agreement a number of councils were formed, including functions and representation for and on behalf of the operating companies, the decisions from which were under the agreement binding on the operating companies in the collective synergy interests. Of relevance in this discussion are the Supply Chain Management Council (SCM Council) and the IT and Technology Management Council (ITTM Council); these two governance forums combined to jointly decide on matters of technology—its sourcing and deployment. Important, however, is that although the center functions, such as my own, selectively participated in these forums, the voting members on all propositions for implementation or advancement were the OpCo representatives and the chairperson of the council, the latter individuals having a seat on each other's councils; for mobile network infrastructure matters I regularly attended both councils on behalf of the social network discussed.

The SCM Council was specifically introduced for the formal governance forum. It variously comprised OpCo representatives who were of the position chief financial officer (CFO), chief technology officer (CTO), and director or head of supply chain management. The inaugural SCM Council meeting was held in June 2001 and approximately quarterly thereafter until the final meeting in June 2005, following which it acceded to the Vodafone organizational change discussed in Chapter 5. There were conditions in the structure and operational processes of both the SCM and ITTM Councils on matters of mutual protocol affecting global sourcing and supplier-related matters.

Given that the self-governing globalization activity for mobile network infrastructure had actively been under way since its inaugural meeting in February 2000, the formalization under the Momentum Agreement was welcomed. The SCM Council provided a forum through which matters of governing policy in the interorganizational relationships with the Vodafone global partners could be formally ratified; it was the link point between the formal and the informal or self-governing. Its existence, for us only on matters of global agreements, assured that we had the collective OpCo agreement in advance of taking any such agreement to the SCM Council for formal adoption. Although this occasionally "pressured" both the Lead OpCos and the global functions, it nevertheless combined to good effect in assuring safe passage of each of our propositions. We were effective in communicating our intent in advance of such council meetings within the key stakeholder group (my role), those in their teams assigned to execute relevant diligence for such proposals (Lead OpCos supported by my team), and the OpCo cluster.

The operating impact was to further encourage alignment and polarization in the informal self-governing social network, which in fact continued to operate and function positively through this period to good effect for Vodafone in the pursuit of aggregation cost synergies, given that matters of commerce were not considered to be issues of policy. This positive spirit enhanced the experiential journey and provided the foundation for continued and unequaled success in true globalization, not to mention built substantial social capital throughout this organization.

Engaging the International Suppliers Globally

For the principal suppliers, Ericsson, Nokia, Nortel, and Siemens, the move to the Lead OpCo multisupplier cluster organizational model also meant changes for them. Vodafone and Ericsson together had already embarked on the journey paradigm and now had over two years of collaborative experiential learning toward globalization of the interorganizational relationship. This instance was therefore more of the same toward the transition continuum, as even the Lead OpCo experience was not new for them or the OpCo cluster. For some of the remaining suppliers it was as though the train had left the station and they had to run fast to catch up; however, this would also be the case from a different perspective for the Vodafone Lead OpCo team assignments and their respective OpCo clusters, although individuals with experience of the Ericsson endeavor were placed in these clusters.

As this new organizational model was essentially a multiple footprint of that established in the Ericsson cluster, with a center-led function separated from the OpCos, the opportunity occurred for rapid knowledge transfer within Vodafone and the development of the same model with the new suppliers agreeing to globalize. One had to accept style differences arising from the various in-country company and national cultures embracing this new paradigm for the first time. Again, the aggregation cost synergy results generated by the Lead OpCos and their clusters during the longitudinal period thereafter lend testament to their success and that of the approach taken.

For the new suppliers, on the other hand, although the knowledge transfer opportunity existed, they also had their own corporate culture and ways of working and addressing their markets and opportunities that were not at first aligned to the paradigm being pursued by Vodafone. This difference in position, therefore, required each of them to make structural changes to their organizations to address Vodafone in the manner it now prescribed, from which arose various challenges. A principal difference for them was to now view the Lead OpCo as the largest purchaser of their systems within the Vodafone Group, which now was the global customer. This was difficult as it was no longer acceptable to be deferential to the Lead OpCo in preference to the remainder of the OpCo cluster, a new paradigm.

As outlined earlier, the Lead OpCo was obliged not to take its newfound group negotiating position and leverage its position to its own benefit rather than that of the OpCo cluster that it were leading globally. There were occasional challenges to the logic of the paradigm; however, the global position substantially prevailed and was not undermined by the in-country OpCos. The latter point is often an issue in attempts to globalize, wherein in-country OpCos attempt to demonstrate their prowess in achieving improvements to their position locally. Such detached compromise locally by the supplier in this paradigm took such actions for global benefit; therefore, it was not in their interest to yield locally. The Vodafone social network was very tightly coupled, generally more so than that of the suppliers, leading to no time being wasted in confronting improvement opportunities in the interests of the entire cluster; the group global culture was soon in evidence.

It would not be appropriate to discuss specifics of the other suppliers' adoption and realignment to the formative global model established by Vodafone; however, some observations may be relevant. There is a tendency for organizations with a geographically dispersed multicountry footprint in the same business (conglomerates or enterprises with a dispersed business portfolio are, of course, different) to describe themselves as global, which in the geographic sense may be considered the case. However, in operation and practice the observation is that such are not generally the circumstances. For the Vodafone paradigm, global meant a true cross-country or global transparency with consistent recognition and business treatment for all; the country or in-country operation size was not relevant, but being in the Vodafone Group was. Hence, the Vodafone position was always to leverage in-country requirements on the global stage, meaning to the aggregation cost synergy benefit of all in the relevant supplier cluster; Vodafone was therefore global in this definition.

Initially, and perhaps even now, despite the appearance of adaptation, the suppliers are very head office–centric with varying degrees of decision-making authority delegated to those responsible for the global relationships with Vodafone; in business operation they are therefore international companies, not global. I invested much time with the executive management of these key suppliers and their in-country operations around the world engaging in dialogue concerning the globalization intentions of Vodafone and the meaning of such a paradigm; that is, it was without doubt organizationally transformational for them as well as for the telecom industry. Globalization in this paradigm was not in their culture, be it corporate or national; some may argue the same distinction for Vodafone.

In part such observation may be true; however, its business is a global in-country services business, not product; whatever the determined reality here, this globalization initiative was and is recognized to have been entirely global and, important, not head office–centric, at least in this phase of the evolution (or revolution). On a longitudinal basis the suppliers did nevertheless create an interface toward Vodafone consistent with its requirements despite their inner corporate culture and mode of operation. This positive progress was appreciated, hopefully beneficial for all, and certainly assisted Vodafone in the realization of its aggregation cost synergies in this segment of its business. I developed an excellent personal network within the supplier corporate and global community and developed a number of key stakeholder friendships that still exist.

Certainly, the experience of this further transformational step to the Lead OpCo multisupplier cluster organizational model is the creation of or step to another requisite organization that had become a "force," or invisible organization. This was now an enlarged informal (or invisible) global virtual community in a nonhierarchical multi- and overlapping-stream organization situated within and between the Vodafone global organization and those mobile network infrastructure supplier organizations with whom they worked. It was a requisite organization because given its sustained success, it must de facto have fulfilled the criterion of a "pattern of connections which ought to exist between roles if the system is both to work efficiently and to operate as required by the nature of human nature and the enhancement of mutual trust" as envisaged by Jaques.[10] Social and OpCo cluster networks were somewhat like a self-adapting and innovative amorphous organization, with no formal engagement or disengagement, the impact of which was that these networks expanded or contracted according to interest and/or resource demand by the virtual community or individuals therein for the assurance of success.

Of course, an important criterion would have been the acceptance by those relevant nodes in the existing social network to have established the level of trust with the potential new members. Yet it in its totality the Lead OpCo multisupplier cluster organizational model existed within and between Vodafone and all four initial supplier organizations with which it engaged in this globalization initiative. Although the extant literature generally considers the impact of multiple companies within a homogeneous organization, this model somewhat informally and successfully (from the Vodafone perspective) developed transformational complexities and new social networks within each participating organization (including Vodafone), new interorganizational relationships between Vodafone and each supplier, and such other networks that developed. It would have been difficult to have predicted in advance the outcome, seek to formulate a plan, and drive the organizations to this solution—hence the benefit and value of the experiential journey paradigm, the scope for innovation, and the positive development of social capital therein. This invisible and virtual organization informally existed within and between each and every global organization that became a party to this successful Vodafone-led globalization endeavor that moved the telecom industry itself on to a new paradigm.

An additional forum, a global review meeting (GRM), was introduced, principally arising from the need to aggregate issues and concerns of the operators of the UMTS program rollout. The intention here was to bring the Vodafone operator CTOs (or their assigned representatives) for each supplier-based cluster together in a single meeting with each of the suppliers' teams to assure speaking with one voice. The structure was normally that each side held internal meetings to align understanding and then the operators and suppliers met together, moderated by the Lead OpCo team supported by the center-led function.

Yet another role reversal was my engagement of the principals in the supplier global teams with Vodafone in social events hosted by Vodafone, including horse racing, charity dinners, and Manchester United football events. This created another social network bringing people together as individuals void of their daily business responsibilities, all of whom have Vodafone in common as the catalyst. It was also a way that Vodafone was able to express its thanks for the contribution these key suppliers were making to the successes of Vodafone. Of course, there are always the business rewards (invoices); however there were consistent levels of business and personal goodwill in the actions of these suppliers that would otherwise go unrecognized. I was, in my opinion, pivotal in this social network that collectively conducted multi-billion-euro business annually, who counted many of these individuals as friends outside the business context. Given the composite base of business and personal knowledge accrued in this social network, it clearly attests to the level of trust and integrity that was perceived and actually existed between those individuals and me. I have in effect multiple "Chinese walls" within my own head, across which confidential and personal information does not migrate; pleasingly, a number of these established friendships have survived to the present.

The Complexity of Interests and the Variation Across OpCos

So that the center-led function did not become detached from customer service and for the assurance of OpCo inclusion, in 2003 I extended this management team to informally include the participation of the Vodafone in-country operator supply chain management of at least the Lead OpCos, which linked back to the key stakeholders. The logic is clear: because the aggregation cost synergies are realized by the in-country operating units, taking an inclusive and collaborative global approach assured the contribution, commitment, and consistent execution toward the agreed objectives. The issue that followed was that the cost synergy requirements (therefore the team objectives) to meet the overall business goals were not derived in an analytical way from what was possible, nor did they relate in a definitive way to each of the in-country operations or, more specifically, the supplier-based OpCo clusters. Simply stated, they were top-down stretch numbers that were handed down—not an unusual way of working. Naturally this would cause a degree of angst, as people typically seek to reduce the group objective down to "what does it mean to or for me?"—in this instance the Lead OpCo leaders taking both an in-country and a cluster view.

This virtual and extended global management team, known as the Global Supply Chain Management Advisory Board, gave the Lead OpCos the opportunity for engagement. An unusual dimension to this team under my chairmanship was that the SCM directors of the Lead OpCos (Germany, Italy, Spain, and the UK) were invited to join, together with their team subordinate responsible for the execution of any group decisions agreed for mobile network infrastructure. The other country SCM director members were Japan, Holland (as an original founding member), and France. My direct team were those responsible for the "governance" of the Lead OpCos for each of the major network infrastructure suppliers, the head of eCommerce, the business analyst, and guests from the central technology team. The formation of this team, joined by a strategy in common, was not at all disruptive; in fact, it managed a coherent approach for the realization of group objectives through the actions and contributions of the OpCos together with the center functions. It was a truly collaborative and counter-intuitive endeavor, through and with the engagement of those over whom influence was sought rather than who would be commanded from the center—an inclusive and delegative center-led approach to motivation and inclusion. This team created yet another informal and organizationally horizontal social network of boundary crossers generated by the global synergy economic results being sought by the business.

The complex supplier-based clusters operated in the interests of those engaged in that social network, both the Vodafone interests and those of the suppliers. Seated originally in the Vodafone-Ericsson formative supplier cluster (the "Club") developed to bring about globalization, those original members then migrated into one or more additional clusters according to their business interests. In so doing they were able to evidence their prior knowledge in advancing the new activities of the cluster in which they further engaged. In the longitudinal period, although there were impacts or changes to the Vodafone interests through merger, acquisition, and determined changes in its equity ownership, such changes did not disturb the progress of globalization.

Financial incentives have been known, at least in my experience, to focus the mind and ensuing actions of individuals. The challenge is to align the objectives of individuals to those of the business in the given period and not be stereotypical; however, the objectives should be aligned to a level of granularity such that there is a true sense of positive impact arising from perceived success by the individual. As a benchmark, in all my experience, the financial measurements provided visibility to the collective achievement of those with whom I operated and myself; however, the bridge between those activities and the basis for the annual bonus were somewhat less obvious, as were the incentive structures for those employed and working locally in the network operators; those locally were generally in local program not linked directly to the global endeavors. For all concerned, however, it is suggested that pride in performance of the visible financial collective results was a primary stimulus within which there was a financial benefit for local operations.

Another dimension of incentives is that they may become more instrumental when they form a higher percentage of the individual's target income with the opportunity for overperformance. For example, if the fixed salary is 40% of the desired or target income, then the ensuing performance is vigorous and focused; if 80%, perhaps it may be considered great if the scheme pays out and okay if it does not and may otherwise be considered as payment for attendance that is however potentially void of performance, with no planned extra income by the individual to the domestic finances. It is further suggested that the greater the group associated with a performance bonus scheme, then the greater the dilution of the visibility of individual performance, which somewhat misses the point although facilitates ease of administration. My experience in setting such incentive compensation plans was that the more individual the focus at the operational levels, the better, particularly when the management incentives may in fact conflict and cause tension, which deters the leadership from achieving the optimum results for the business. However structured, incentives should nevertheless assure excellence in operations as perceived and acknowledged by the customer simultaneously with a complementary acknowledgment of the fulfillment of shareholder expectations—a mutual interdependence.

More recently there have been consolidation changes in the telecom industry on the supplier side; the full ramifications and/or benefits to the network operators will only be visible after the integration of the various organizations. On October 25, 2005, Ericsson announced that it was to pay £1.2 billion for the name and most of the assets of Marconi; in the financial year ending March 31, 2005, the businesses acquired by Ericsson had generated total sales of £934 million, and the adjusted operating loss of the business bought over that period was £9 million. Ericsson reported net revenues for calendar year 2005 were SEK 151.821 billion or approximately €16.4 billion.

On April 2, 2006, Alcatel and Lucent Technologies announced that they intended to merge and form what they described as the "World's Leading Communication Solutions Provider"; the combined company, to be headquartered in Paris, would have revenues of approximately €21 billion (US$25 billion) based on calendar year 2005 results. This merger was completed on December 1, 2006 with the corporate headquarters remaining in Paris.

On September 1, 2006, Nortel announced that it has signed a non-binding Memorandum of Understanding for the sale of its UMTS access to Alcatel for US$320 million. On December 4, 2006 Nortel announced "that it has reached a definitive agreement for the sale of certain assets and the transfer of certain liabilities related to the company's UMTS access business to Alcatel-Lucent" and that "The transaction is a US$320 million cash transaction, less significant deductions and transaction related costs". On January 9, 2007 Alcatel Lucent announced the completion of this purchase on December 31, 2006.

On June 19, 2006, Siemens and Nokia reported the merger of their respective network infrastructure divisions to form a 50/50 joint venture, i.e., no money changed hands. The joint venture was registered in the Netherlands, headquartered in Finland, with board control held by Nokia; the new entity was named Nokia Siemens Networks (NSN) and had calendar year 2005 pro forma revenues of €15.8 billion (Nokia €6.6 billion, and Siemens €9.2 billion). Later "Nokia announced today (April, 2 2007) that Nokia Siemens Networks started its operations on April 1 (2007)."

On July 26, 2006, Motorola and Huawei announced a new collaboration to bring an enhanced and extensive portfolio of UMTS and HSPA (high-speed packet access) infrastructure equipment to their customers worldwide. These industry changes will, at least, impact the distribution of market share and therefore potentially the competitive landscape as seen from the operator perspective; there may also be impacts arising from the newly integrated supplier attempts to consolidate and rationalize product lines to achieve cost synergies.

The Creation and Implementation of Network Infrastructure Reverse eAuctions

A further noteworthy activity was the mobile network infrastructure industry's innovative advances made in the eCommerce area beyond the foundation of eRelationship discussed in Chapter 3. In the Vodafone Group eCommerce initiative, I was the "Buy-side" sponsor and had a small team leading this initiative for the broader applications in global supply chain management in general.

In advance of the Olympic Games in Greece in 2004, Vodafone Greece initiated a paper RFI/RFQ process leading to contract award for the initial deployment of a UMTS/3G network. The Technical RFI was issued in November 2001, leading to a cross-vendor normalized network model agreed to by the four key vendors (Ericsson, Nokia, Nortel, and Siemens) as of May 2002. Compliance with the Global Terms & Conditions (GT&Cs) and the Global Price Books (GPBs) was declared as a compliance requirement to join the RFQ. The RFQ was issued to all four vendors in June 2002 and was to become the manual precursor to the eventual reverse electronic auctions (eAuctions).

The vendors were obliged or given the option to respond in five RFQ rounds with feedback being given of their position relative to best bid in each predefined category (product and services), save the final (fifth) submission; clearly, as this process was manual, it extended over a long period of time. The key point is that given the cross-supplier product/services normalization process had been completed and agreed, the only separator to be resolved between the equally qualified and acceptable vendors to the requirements of the operator was cost. A point to note is that not all vendors adjusted and/or bid in all rounds of the RFQ. The shortlist was developed and the final selection decision taken in January 2003, with the Letter of Intent (LOI) issued in February, leading to contract completion by May 2003.

The Core Network was awarded to Ericsson (who also supplied the GSM Network), and the 3G Radio Access Network (UTRAN) was awarded to Siemens. The commercial launch for business trials was scheduled for April 2004 and the network (or system) to be "Olympic ready" by June 2004. A noteworthy point that may appear foresight but was indeed luck is that in advance of the RFQ rounds was a bid protocol, or rule, that any supplier RFQ bid affecting its GPBs was automatically to become the new global price; the logic was that should the supplier consider its GPB competitive, then there would be no requirement for a different bid; therefore, de facto a bid to reduce pricing was tantamount to an acknowledgment of being non-competitive. This thinking stimulated the multiround RFQs; although the suppliers were not terribly grateful for this protocol, they nevertheless agreed to participate in the process. The somewhat penal impact of this approach was that suppliers both competed for the local business while conceding at the global (another operator where they have already business) GPB level, win or lose on the in-country (Greece) business; the benefit for Vodafone was that it yielded amplified benefits.

In the period April 2003 to March 2004 (Vodafone fiscal year) the eCommerce team successfully stimulated sixty-eight eAuction events in the gross amount of €587 million, yielding savings of circa 50 percent globally. There were two industry events in that period related to network infrastructure: the first in October 2003 for the award of business to a second radio (UMTS/3G) vendor in the UK (awarded to Nortel) and the second in March 2004 for the UMTS/3G network vendor(s) award for the combination of Australia and New Zealand (awarded to Nokia). The process followed and the protocol were exactly as for the Greece multiround RFQs, save this time the bidding and feedback processes were automated, using a Web-based capability supplied by Emptoris. The precursors were also Web based, namely, the eRFI and eRFQ, leading to the next eAuction process only having to request variance information from the suppliers particular to their network topology or services requirements. These two network infrastructure eAuctions were a tremendous success that led to savings globally in excess of the available business locally, clearly a game that does not have an extended life. However, the pricing floor is reached rapidly when one has willing players and goes well beyond the bounds of classical negotiation both in amount and time, no matter how great players believe they are at negotiating.

Another key factor, other than we elected to run these events off-site, with no audience nor administrator access to the system for the assurance of no "leakage" inadvertently or otherwise, is that the award decision was presented and consulted upon following verification of the economic outcome (in accordance with the protocol), normally now within two to three hours; the supplier bidding behavior and our controlling of the event were deemed commercially confidential. Clearly, the approach in general to the application of reverse eAuctions is very contextual, complex in opportunities, relevant for the application of game theory, but not a topic on which to embark here.

In the subsequent twelve-month period to March 2005, there were 1,148 eAuction events, exceeding €1.0 billion and combined savings overall totaling in excess of 50 percent.[11] In this fiscal period, in April 2004, another network infrastructure eAuction was run for the award of the UMTS/3G network infrastructure award for Vodafone Hungary (awarded to Siemens). In the period after March 2005 another major business award for Microwave in the UK was conducted by eAuction, the award going to Siemens. There was a subsequent UMTS/3G award for Vodafone in the Czech Republic (after my retirement) that did not go to a reverse eAuction, perhaps signaling the expiry of the value of this approach to the game. Earlier, and without disclosing commercial confidential information, I had observed that perhaps with the lack of substantive new "buy-decisions" combined with the auction protocol, the supplier interest in actively participating in such events with the potential of commercial sacrifice for no gain was less interesting. The converse being that the adverse business impact to the supplier companies in engaging further with Vodafone in the eAuction events and not being successful was too great and, or the supplier risked winner's remorse even with a successful outcome.

The Actual Benefits of Globalization to Vodafone, to the Suppliers, and to the OpCos

One multistream endeavor with which we were successful, although it took many years to develop and establish within the global virtual community, was the establishment of all the Global Agreements (GAs) and Global Price Books (GPBs); some were somewhat dismissive of the diligence required to see this through. There were more than four such mobile network infrastructure global supplier agreements with up to twenty OpCos, many participating in more than one; for simplicity, each OpCo had to create (a pro forma) a Contract of Adherence locally that admitted the global documents to be adopted under local law. These agreements required the collaboration of the local SCM and legal teams, those of the supplier and the same for both at the global level. In summary, this was a substantial amount of work with multiple iterations for the assurance of global and cross-vendor consistency. All were successfully completed, and most important, we had in fact created, with the support and contribution of the OpCos and the suppliers, what was referred to as a "global constitution." All prior agreements with the vendors locally in-country were at this point superseded and replaced by aligned and normalized Global Agreements that created governance at the global level (center/Lead OpCo) variously for 60–80% of the relevant in-country expenditure with the global vendors.

This again shows the power of the relatively new established and counter-intuitive, but with limited generalization, Lead OpCo multisupplier cluster organizational model. Subsequently there were those that elected to try to restructure the Global Agreements and not take account of what had been achieved here, although they were met with resistance by many who had actively collaborated and contributed to this body of work. To say that what had been achieved could not be improved upon would, of course, be incorrect; however, to advance the game, it may have been relevant to consult with those who had achieved these agreements and consider their foundation work before seeking to impose changes as those announced in 2005 (not a point of further discussion here).

Vodafone realized through this endeavor a truly globalized virtual organization in action that delivered collectively and realized through its operating interests aggregation cost synergies above its expectations. The issue perhaps is that this organization was not visible or publicized except its beneficial economic outcome, yet all the OpCos were engaged, albeit some more so than others. This nonhierarchical horizontal organization was dynamically bounded by a boundary-crossing virtual organization of individuals that formed their own social network within which substantive social capital was developed. These links also crossed multiple supplier-based OpCo clusters, wherein OpCos were generally engaged in more than one such cluster. This type of engagement assured the transfer of knowledge and an accelerated inclusion of new suppliers after the initial activities of the Vodafone-Ericsson strategy of globalization.

Delegating a Lead OpCo role to frontline in-country OpCos assured the availability and commitment of talent both close to the end-customer and with expert knowledge of their assigned supplier to work in the interests of the collective and share knowledge. The combination of the Lead OpCos with those represented in their respective clusters and the center-led function created a power and effective asset for the business in negotiating and managing the business toward the global suppliers. Without doubt these facets combined to the interests and benefit of Vodafone in general and all participating OpCos in particular in the realization through globalization of the aggregation cost synergies. It was in its own way a global network that formed a collective requisite organization with interlinking organizational supplier-based clusters that also represented requisite organizations, albeit none of them recognized in their totality on paper. The group culture that emerged was results driven and self-motivating, substantially supported from the OpCo perspective by and through the goodwill of the individuals and the key stakeholders involved. This goodwill was relevant in the engagement of new suppliers to the global activities of Vodafone beyond the initial and beneficial encounter with Ericsson that was to set the endeavor in motion.

The industry-leading interorganizational information system, eRelationship, provided the nexus of a substantially open and transparent information system to the entire organization for sharing knowledge and practice, not being limited only to those closest to the globalization or localization of certain activities. This E-Enablement later moved on to the introduction of reverse eAuctions for the sourcing side of the business in general and the industry-leading pursuit with respect to mobile network infrastructure in particular. The experience of these activities—eRFI through eRFQ leading to a reverse eAuction—was the challenge of creating a cross-vendor optimized network model to facilitate the application of an eAuction; the effective realization of this was the industry-leading step. The benefit that flowed from reverse eAuctions in general is discussed in the literature; however, the specific benefit for the acquisition mobile network infrastructure was that it provided for the acceleration of financial cost synergy yields locally and globally and the timing thereof that could not otherwise have been realized through the traditional negotiation methods. Having the eRFI and eRFQ online availability meant too that subsequent network infrastructure eAuctions focused only on differences and changes and not the complete process, thereby improving efficiency.

As for the supplier cost synergy benefits and therefore intensity of motivation, I can only speculate. However, they too moved their organizations to a differential global team accountable for the total business with Vodafone, supported by the in-country teams around the world. On the basis that each stayed in the game for the duration of my presence in the globalization endeavor, it is therefore assumed that a synergy benefit was being realized and that they had a consistent interface globally into Vodafone. They were nevertheless on occasions challenged locally in ways diametrically opposed to the global paradigm, which the Vodafone social network was always quick to pick up on and attempt to leverage. The administration of the contractual relationship was simplified and consistent with the onset of the Global Terms and Conditions and Price Books and the implementation of the global constitution, replacing the varied history with a consistent future cross-Vodafone.

5 Resetting the Social Capital

The Accumulated Social Capital

After 1998, when the journey documented here commenced, Vodafone merged with AirTouch and later acquired Mannesmann of Germany, as well as enhancing its equity interests in certain properties and disposed of others. The impact of those activities on the globalization endeavor was to vary the number of Vodafone in-country properties (OpCos) engaged (at one stage, as many as twenty-three) and to enhance the scope of the international supplier interorganizational relationships available to be globalized. The journey hitherto and the ensuing intra- and interorganizational model commenced with Ericsson (Chapter 3) and subsequently engaged Nokia, Nortel, and Siemens (Chapter 4) with Vodafone at the center.

Organizations are often referred to as being global when in fact they operate as international organizations with a global footprint. Intra- and interorganizational transformational change and the transition between states may be embarked upon as a journey, absent of the formality of definitive plans and budget, yet guided by a common vision and strategy among all the voluntarily engaged parties. Various intra- and interorganizational forums may be established in an informal way by those affected by and motivated for the realization of the strategy, in this case the achievement (at least by Vodafone) of aggregation cost synergies that may not otherwise have been achieved by the parties individually. The idea of this strategy is that the executive of the in-country operations will voluntarily accede otherwise local commercial business decisions to a global collective and their local resources will be so motivated as to extend goodwill beyond the call of their local duties to bring collective success.

We did not break any "rules" in the informal social network that we de facto made or set through collaborative practice; it was a self-governing network focusing, through collaboration, on the beneficial economic output for all parties involved: Vodafone and its globalizing mobile network infrastructure supplier partners. Time was spent working on the identified tasks toward the globalization of the intra- and interorganizational relationships, the alternative being to face inward and engage in protracted dialogue aimed at a documented protocol prior to action. Schein says that "consensus on the core mission does not automatically guarantee that members of the group will have common goals";[1] however, it would seem on the evidence thus far that in a positive social network, unusually in this case forming an invisible organization, as suggested by Jaques the common attributes of individual and group goals can lead to success in a requisite organization.[2]

On the supplier side there was also an acceptance of asymmetry in the synergy benefits arising from globalizing the interorganizational relationships and without the requirement to share data mutually regarding such yields. The richness of the emergent, culturally complex, yet informal social networks led to high levels of social and, perhaps, intellectual capital arising from the mutuality of trust and integrity of the leadership, which may have had to be experienced to be believed. This nonhierarchical horizontal social network linked the vertical hierarchies of companies and served as a powerful meta-influence in pursuit of the global aggregation cost synergies.

It was important to recognize that engaged leadership is that accepted in the eye of the beholders in transformational change situations and, as such, is more relevant than being exercised by the "power" of rank or position in a hierarchy. The former, as in this case, objectively creates a sense of community purpose with collective motivation arising through the engagement, whereas the latter may tend to leadership by command, or perhaps management. Ultimately, these attributes created a global, virtual, and largely invisible intra- and interorganizational system that aspired in its various stages to perform as a requisite organization. It also variously established a culture and sense of community values created by the leadership that co-evolved and strengthened throughout the longitudinal period, as distinct from being solely a matter for the leader.

The concept of interorganizational IS, initially known as eRelationship, was created to bridge the impact of time and geography and provide a presence regardless of location, the functionality and application of which co-evolved (with no formal specification or budgetary process) over the longitudinal period.

The acceptance of a structure wherein the vision, strategy, and governance were led by (not controlled by) the center and all the operational dimensions were assigned in-country was the approach; the center team was the only part of the (social) network that existed on an organizational chart that had a budget and was the catalyst for all aggregation synergy targets and the reporting thereof. The modest (ten to fourteen people) Vodafone center team was also substantially staffed by contributors on secondment from an in-country operation for periods of around two years as part of their personal development and for the bonding and assured empathy by the center to those over whom it sought to influence through the collective network. Focus on the personal development of individuals through academic pursuits, principally the MBA for the center-based team whether on secondment or not, and the development in-country through delegated responsibilities at the global level created a strong interweaving in the social network that led to the emergence of enhanced social capital and access to a meta-influence through the informal social network across the vertical in-country operations.

The center devolved interorganizational responsibilities to Lead OpCos (Vodafone lead in-country operating companies) as a means of accession to a second global organizational model to facilitate Vodafone's engaging in several such interorganizational globalization endeavors; whilst this created enhanced social system complexities with now multiple intra- and interorganizational informal relationships, it was nevertheless functional and objectively successful in operation. Attempts to formalize the nature of these various relationships, particularly that of Lead OpCo, failed; yet the informality of the loosely coupled federation exceeded the financial expectations. The Lead OpCos represented clusters of in-country operations with a common global supplier interest, whereas the Lead OpCo representatives, along with other key operators, informally joined the Vodafone center team (led by the author) to assure a collective and executable leadership across all in-country operations.

The limited formal governance in this social network was in the form of a forum (SCM Council) within which the Vodafone in-country operations were cemented. We have seen that the form of individual and collective leadership throughout the transition continuum was absent of a stereotypical prescriptive assignment and predetermined view for the parties engaged; it was an innovative initiative focused on the fulfillment of a globalization strategy in common. In short, this was a unique and innovative ground-breaking experience that transformed many of the telecom industry paradigms, set new norms, and created organizational transformational models and the transition thereto from which others could learn. The expectations of Vodafone were more than satisfied through the aforesaid organizational approaches.

Transformational Change

It is perhaps important to recognize that the agent or intermediary for the transformational change and the management of the transitional continuum thereof was a nonconfrontational stimulus to otherwise far-reaching changes. That stimulus was the collective pursuit of the agreed-upon vision and strategy for globalization, which was focused around the realization (at least for Vodafone) of the aggregation cost synergies. The economic performance of all in-country parties would benefit from the synergies, the motivation for the goodwill of their engagement perhaps supported additionally by the key stakeholders and, later, Lead OpCos, leading to the collective results being sought. The focus, therefore, was not on the performance of the countries but on the community's realization of its aggregation objectives; in so doing they were motivated to deal transparently with situated change to positive effect.

This transformational transition continuum included a multilevel (in the hierarchical sense) engagement from within and between the Vodafone and supplier organizations and their operations affected by the mutual pursuit of a global paradigm. The global leadership accountable for the realization of a successful economic synergy outcome had strong a meta-influence to achieve success, quite independently of an organizational chart or ordinarily declared responsibilities. The roles of the people involved in the social network were potentially at variance to the individual or departmental roles that would be created in the future.

The scope of what was intended in the new definition of the organizational role of each team perhaps went beyond the current boundaries into unfamiliar territory. Management in the local in-country companies affected by change or transformation activities must be seen to exude commitment in spirit and action; otherwise, there would be seeds of doubt (or hesitation) and the initiative would risk compromise, leading to a reduction in pace of execution of the initiative. The advantage in this case was that the period of transition had been redefined and had a foundation upon which to continue to build. There was a balance of judgment to be made between using energy and, more critically, time in mitigating the affected management requesting them to step aside in the interests of the progress of the business as a whole.

In any change or transformational endeavor it is important to recognize the views from the vantage point of any affected parties, consistent with an allocentric perspective in game theory. The likelihood is that if such views do not make sense, create unworkable discontinuities, or appear unworkable, therein lies the answer to the merit of the proposition and its potential for success, notwithstanding how it may look on paper. In consideration of the design of the transformed organizational structure, it is essential to clarify the relative roles and responsibilities for the successful realization of the paradigm shift and to seek feedback from selected individuals who are in roles that will be affected in some way by the proposition. In the ideal case such individuals would be those with whom a relationship has been developed over time, within which there is trust and friendship and the integrity of the individual is respected and supported. It is posited that in such a transformation the legacy (past practices) should support the future or the future should not be constrained by or have obligations to the legacy; the game, after all, is to look and move forward in the image of the vision for the future. Often a continuing challenge is that many people's vision is constrained by the boundaries of the construct of their own stereotyped thinking, seated in their own experiences; however, the engaged and collective approach taken here largely overcame such issues in a positive way.

As with most successes, luck and timing, no doubt, had their roles to play; however, you make your own luck in the relentless pursuit of opportunities. I am sure that even though we attempted to apply "science" in this endeavor, luck played its part here too.

One Vodafone

The original catalyst for the derivation of aggregation cost synergies for Vodafone arose from the declared Mannesmann synergy objectives. The multifaceted portfolio of responsibilities through which Thomas Geitner as chief executive, global products and services was to pursue said synergies included global product management, brand management, IT and technology management, supply chain management (SCM), account management, and Web enabling.[3] My mobile network infrastructure role and the discussion in this book were included in the SCM function, whereas the eCommerce "Buy-side" sponsorship was a contribution included in the Web-enabling function. The realization of aggregation cost synergies for mobile network infrastructure by Vodafone was derived from intraorganizational operational and process conformance, interorganizational alignment, and the reduction of diversity of the network element requirements; that is, essentially operating within and between the organizations while not imposing conformance of process and practice in the Vodafone operating entities. How OpCos organized within to achieve the collective global agreements was essentially a matter for them, meaning that as there was no direct reporting role, the metainfluence and motivation within the globalization initiative nevertheless prevailed in a beneficial way.

In a press release dated June 23, 2003,[4] Vodafone announced that "Thomas Geitner, currently CEO Global Products and Services and a director of the Company, will be head of Group Technology & Business Integration, as Chief Technology Officer. The purpose of Group Technology will be to lead the implementation of a standardised architecture for business processes, information technology and network systems. This will support the next generation of products and services and the critical role of introducing and operating 3G capacity," reporting to Julian Horn-Smith, group chief operating officer. Forbes.com reported that Thomas "was appointed to the Board in May 2000 during which time he established and managed *Global Products and Services*.[5] He *was responsible for* (the achievements of) the single Vodafone brand, Vodafone live! and Vodafone Wireless Office and the partner networks franchise. Effective July 2003, he was appointed Chief Technology Officer (to be) responsible for the rollout of 3G, the consolidation of data centers and service platform operations and the *establishment of the Global Supply Chain organization*.

The subsequent globalizing initiative called One Vodafone, focusing on the period after the realization of the published Mannesman acquisition strategies, was a major business integration project initiated in October 2003 and intended to lead the group through a business transformation process spanning up to five years.[6] The service delivery platform, which in part delivers Vodafone live!, is one early example of the group's "develop once, deploy many times" concept. This approach permits the architecture, design, and development of core-enabling technologies to be undertaken only once and rolled out to many countries, saving on costs of design and development in each country. On September 27, 2004,[7] as part of its analyst and investor day, Vodafone said that it "will also disclose its expectations of the *financial benefits of its One Vodafone programme* to deliver the benefits of scale and scope. The One Vodafone initiatives are expected to achieve GBP 2.5 billion of annual pre-tax operating free cash flow improvements by the year ending 31 March 2008. Cost initiatives are anticipated to generate improvements of GBP 1.4 billion, with a further GBP 1.1 billion from revenue initiatives. Further details of the anticipated benefits of the One Vodafone programme will be given in the full presentation and related materials (Ken Hydon, Finance Director)."[8]

At the Vodafone group analyst and investor day held September 19, 2005, Andy Halford (CFO) spoke again on the topic of One Vodafone, in which he illustrated an overview analysis of cash flow improvements.[9] He espoused that "network will drive cost savings," making a 26% contribution to the incremental cash flow improvements and that "Terminals [mobile devices] [will drive] revenue based improvements" for a 38% contribution. He then noted that "Network" is 48% of the "Combined mobile Opex and Capex," of which 60% is Capex and 40% is Opex; operating expenses are those costs with direct impact to the P&L whilst capital investments are subject to depreciation and amortisation and therefore have a lesser immediate impact to the P&L but have a direct impact to cash flow.

Under the One Vodafone program, there were later created the departments, or divisions, of Global Network Technology (G-NW) and Global Network Supply Chain Management (G-NW-SCM). I was responsible for the latter. However, the principal discussion here concerns the continuity of the journey toward the newly named G-NW-SCM department. What was to become the centralized form of these two newly defined (center-controlled) departments was implemented effective April 1, 2005, with a progressive organizational rollout or resource transfer thereafter.

My recollection is that for G-NW-SCM, the first internal discussions of One Vodafone and its ambitions in which we were engaged was at a global meeting around June 2003 in London attended by SCM representatives from at least sixteen of the network operating companies from around the world. I had invited Arun Sarin (CEO of Vodafone Group Plc) to make the keynote speech in which he would disclose One Vodafone. Network-related activities would commence shortly thereafter, leading to options for departmental organization with recommendations for the consideration by the executive management team. The development of the chosen organizational option would evolve in the ensuing period.

It is perhaps appropriate to reemphasize, concerning the preexisting, albeit invisible, organization, that my (our) metainfluence was directed to coercing the OpCos to accept changing process and/or practice so that collective aggregation synergies would be realized; however, they had both flexibility and choice. It is important where preexisting businesses converge by using agreed-upon strategies that common actions and alignment should first be accepted by all. The paramount point is that thereafter, what is newly introduced is not compromised to accommodate the legacy; to the contrary, the legacy should be varied to preserve the sanctity of the stated objective. In the network supply chain management actions and the company vision, progressive moves toward an eventually aligned outcome will be realized, thereafter facilitating true cross-boundary consolidation; this point is relevant for the One Vodafone ambitions, as the structure created formed or developed into a federation of companies within the organization, leading to the ultimate synergies of having a homogeneous and consolidated back office (invisible to the customers), while accepting that the front office, or customer face, may require local variations.

The conceptual performance objectives of One Vodafone from the network supply chain perspective were to progressively achieve convergence of process and practice, initially cross-OpCo within a given vendor cluster and then cross-vendor clusters, to the extent the physical architecture permitted, for the purpose both of operating efficiency and the realization of group-level cost synergies. The existing activities, it could be argued, were principally delivering cost synergies derived from a collaborative sourcing strategy and had yet to move toward affecting end-to-end process and practice alignment cross and within the OpCos; the opportunity for such in the future now existed under One Vodafone. Even though *supply chain* were words used on many occasions, executive management and others thought and acted as if sourcing were being discussed; the theory was that this thinking would now change. This would lead to the development of process and practice in the supply chain once and the deployment thereof many times, not new, for example, to the automobile or any other production-based industry.

In my logic, the deployment of the mobile network infrastructure was conceptually a virtual manufacturing proposition, the output of which was for a service in common to the end-customer; therefore, variations between country and vendor should be limited. In practice, selective tolerance would be required given that level at which interchangeability between vendors was possible (the granularity thereof) and the legacy of the already existing network; after all, we were dealing with a proposition going forward, not one trying to reverse out of the established network, which served no economic or service purpose—the network had, in fact, been operating and delivering service to customers for many years. In the period before April 1, 2005, there were initially sixteen OpCos engaged in One Vodafone with the addition of SFR, France (a Vodafone affiliate, meaning less than 50% equity position), although they were not obliged to go along with the organizational changes; thereafter Romania and the Czech Republic joined the quorum following Vodafone's purchase of the majority equity stake in those businesses.

A perhaps cynical view for some is that we embarked on the One Vodafone journey, as is so often the case, with an appointed external management consultancy. Such an appointment is typically occasioned to be an agency with whom the, or an, executive has had a prior business relationship—perhaps a comfort factor. In this case (network infrastructure supply chain management and network technology) the location of the leadership for both Vodafone and the chosen consultancy was to be Düsseldorf, Germany. The early One Vodafone organizational options considered (with specific focus on the network infrastructure SCM) were development of the status quo, a centralized solution, or a hybrid solution midway between the boundary options.

Executive management were preemptively minded, it would seem (the advice of the consultancy is not known to me), to a solution tending toward centralization as evidenced in the ensuing outcome implemented; there was no serious attempt to forward the merits of the status quo, which brings into question more generally management, their sources of advice, their own experience, and the situational circumstances, should one believe that automatically defaulting to a stereotype (possibly culturally, too) may not be appropriate. So a short philosophical diversion, with perhaps a hint of reality, may be of value to discuss the preparedness of management to lead a business through changing and challenging times and the engagement of consultants.

My view on consultants is that they tend toward set-piece scenarios of the day in the practice, often with contextual mismatch that becomes the basis from which management selects and after which the data are collected. Perhaps the word *consultant* is being misused, much the same as *engineer* in prior years; a medical consultant position can be achieved through many years of learning, practice, and experience in a specialty: the consultant diagnoses, prescribes, and remedies through surgery, drugs, or a combination thereof and engages one minimally. So-called consultants in business often do not aspire to such standards of excellence, many never having held an executive line position or having had enough experience to actually have an executable qualified position.

So what does the client pay for or get? Very often the opportunity to hear a reconstruction of knowledge, experience, and remedy preexisting in the business and the opportunity to pay the consultancy for the opportunity to take away the developed knowledge for reuse elsewhere; and, of course, yet again the missed opportunity to have delegated to a selected management team the opportunity to develop its own basis of experiential learning. It may be, as is sometimes the case, that the outcome is aligned with the management's ambitions that were declared up front, the purpose being to use the third party to legitimize their intentions. Yes, cynical though this scenario may be considered to some, it does seem on the evidence available to me that this is how it works, and none more so than for One Vodafone.

When faced with an organizational decision or business challenge, what determinant factors may be in play for the executive management as they choose the way forward? I might suggest a few characteristics gleaned from my own observations, in no particular order of relevance, which will be discussed with illustrations of important points:

► Age
► Experience in role with changing market forces
► Domestic versus international and/or global operational experience
► Telecom industry background
► Natural sources of advice
► Developed for or appointed to the role now occupied
► Team builder, team leader, and/or coach
► Cultural background
► Hierarchy in action
► Control versus delegative style
► Own career aspirations or ambitions
► Degree of postgraduate continuous management training
► Self-confidence and perceived security
► Trusting, innovative, and/or entrepreneurial
► Actual diversity of decision-based experience involving transformational change
► Personally developed relevant global social network.

It is not my intention nor assumed position to critically analyze any of my former superiors or colleagues with whom I had the privilege to work, only to suggest that I observed at least relevant considerations of the aforesaid characteristics variously in play with the different team decisions that formed the basis of the chosen One Vodafone network infrastructure SCM organizational model, the implementation and staffing of which I led. Recall that the corporation had engaged a consultancy based in Düsseldorf (the seat of executive management at the time) throughout the One Vodafone development and planning phase outside the global cross-cultural virtual community in which I was positively engaged at the time.

So perhaps with additional insight it would be a business exercise to rationalize and attempt to develop the elected scenario. In the different review bodies, I essentially represented my direct boss, with his occasional attendance; I also worked closely with the assigned external consultancy in developing the organizational logic for what became the eventual implementation. I engaged the ad hoc advisory board with whom I worked from my social network to both presell and take implementation guidance; it was also a useful source for resolving who should fill the leadership reporting to me and the constitution and sizing of their teams.

This approach on my part was consistent with the prior and successful collaborative methodology, at least with the key stakeholder organizations. In the early stages of the functional design of this next step in globalization, it was resolved to move away from the Lead OpCo model, which essentially meant supplier management cross-category (e.g., access and radio network, core network, etc.), within which their products were utilized, to leadership on a category basis whatever the cross-supplier structure. The Lead OpCo was perceived on occasions to create an internal vendor competition between the lead country representatives, which did not or may not lead to convergence in process and practice, an essential requirement of One Vodafone.

The categories in the first instance for my own department became Access and Radio, Core and Transmission, Physical Supply Chain (taking an end-to-end view for the alignment of process and practice and defining the eBusiness support required), Passive Equipment, Service Enablers and INTP Planning (to complement the activity being led in the Global Network department, adding costing and process requirements), and Advanced Technologies (an SCM role engaging in the evolutionary process at standards formulation to assure a commercial competitive outcome).

This category approach was consistent and, broadly speaking, aligned with the structure of the global network organizational structure. It was decided that the new Network SCM organization would track the same locations chosen by the Global Network Technology department. The head of the G-NW department with whom I directly worked on the organizational development was German and a management peer of my boss; prior to the global role, this individual's formative telecom experience led to being named CTO of Vodafone Germany, the largest of Vodafone's European operators. The cross-operator planning methodology was developed through an aggregation process for the network capital and operating investment and expenditure plans, referred to as the Integrated Network and Technology Plan (INTP), which was a great advance under One Vodafone toward a globally aggregated cross-operator transparent budget and planning process.

The INTP (covering an eighteen-month window in detail and up to three years in outline) served as an outline budget document from which the in-country network operations would develop a detailed budget; this process and documentation were also known to the network infrastructure supplier community.

So, given all of the foregoing descriptions, styles of management, and background information and history, how would you have structured the center organization and its relationship with the sixteen OpCos affected by this new organization? A matter perhaps to be a researched for later analysis by the scholars of the future, then having the benefit of 20/20 hindsight—often a great vantage point; however, in the evolution of Vodafone only time will tell.

As hinted earlier, the determination to create centralized organization was relentless, as was the accompanying stereotype, at least in principle—the notion of command and control (my words). For me in my area, the notion of conformance and operational convergence of both processes and practices was not in debate; what was in debate for certain other key stakeholders was the manner in which that was to be achieved. We had developed, by all measures of performance, a successful global virtual community in the area of network supply chain on the principle of centralized vision, strategy, and governance; in short, that success was neither examined nor seriously considered. It was as though this history did not exist, or to the extent it did, the reset button had been pressed and all erased in the consideration of organizational options. Those in favor of further developing on the foundations and business relationships established over the period since 1999 were, alas, in the minority at decision time. I nevertheless moved vigorously to execute the decision and will of the executive management, the outcome of which I shall now describe in brief and on which I shall offer constructive comment.

Figure 5.1 shows the One Vodafone network relationships, i.e., the INTP relationship to each organization and the relationships between organizations. Figure 5.2 shows the changes in these relationships, as in the following discussion. For the purposes of the organizational development my function was considered parallel with that of the G-NW director, although he was my boss's peer. The categorization of the technical functions formed the basis of alignment for my global supply chain team, as did each of the two principal locations in which these roles and teams were to be based; we further sought to have the functional leaders located together. Unlike the Lead OpCo model that had for some years operated successfully (center led with distributed execution), the decision now was that although the center resources would be drawn from the OpCos and would be in the same place locally, the designated global resources were explicitly no longer a part of the OpCo.

In my organization, both for those who reportedly directly to me and those who would form their teams, the objective was to seek to attract contributors who had worked with us over the years and other supporting resources. The approach, although laudable, had a flaw: the resources (people), should they be interested in joining the global team, had to move to the locations of preference chosen by the network technology team. This clearly

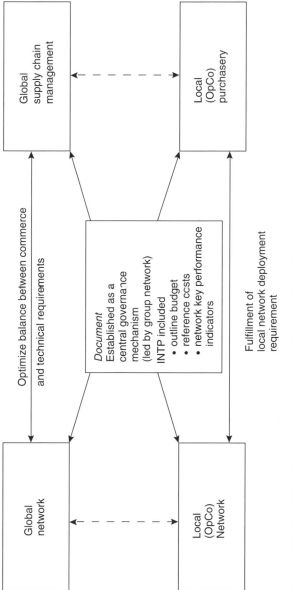

Figure 5.1   **One Vodafone network interfunction relationship**

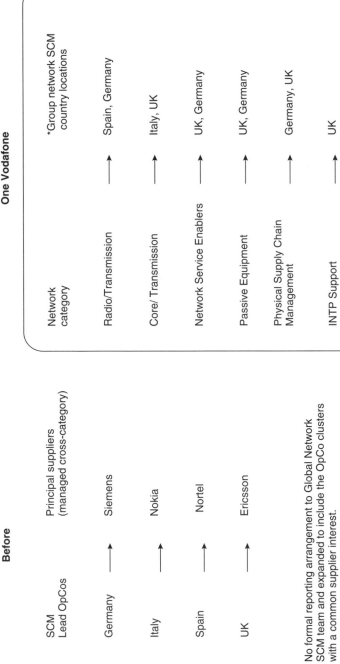

Before

SCM Lead OpCos		Principal suppliers (managed cross-category)
Germany	→	Siemens
Italy	→	Nokia
Spain	→	Nortel
UK	→	Ericsson

No formal reporting arrangement to Global Network SCM team and expanded to include the OpCo clusters with a common supplier interest.

One Vodafone

Network category		*Group network SCM country locations
Radio/Transmission	→	Spain, Germany
Core/ Transmission	→	Italy, UK
Network Service Enablers	→	UK, Germany
Passive Equipment	→	UK, Germany
Physical Supply Chain Management	→	Germany, UK
INTP Support	→	UK

All resources in Central or Group Network SCM

Figure 5.2 **Changes in network interfunction relationships**

* Was subject to variation. However, candidates were required to move to be located in the designated countries

provided an advantage for those so situated and a disadvantage for those who may not have been able to relocate, notwithstanding their interest in being with or continuing with the globalization development.

The global organization did not have direct-line management authority over the OpCos, a break from my perspective that had been created in the social network and capital built up over the years and, of course, the goodwill. My organization was located in Newbury in the UK (location of corporate headquarters), Düsseldorf in Germany, Madrid in Spain, and Milan/Ivrea in Italy. I was assigned to manage the suppliers in the global relationship cross-category and was supported by a small team. All vendor activity in any given category would be the responsibility of the head of that SCM category. I had throughout the period managed the network infrastructure suppliers at the global corporate level, although that role became subject to challenges after the October 2004 Vodafone investor conference, when the responsibilities of my manager were reduced with the assignment of global terminals SCM to group marketing.

The diagrams in Figure 5.3 and Figure 5.4 show how the distribution of the functions and governance changed, as explained in the following discussion. This approach and structure changed the dynamic and nature of the relationship between the center function and the OpCos for my area, with the risk of creating a fat center but not really materially changing the OpCo-based resources (over which the center had no jurisdiction anyway), given they had an operational dynamic and responsive role that could not possibly (nor was it intended to) be managed from the center. In IT terms, there is the notion of a "thin client" and "fat client," with the center being the complement; in this case, in my view was that a "fat center" AND a correspondingly "fat client." In IT terms, at least, this situation does not work, and I think the same applies for global organizations.

The governance model also changed from the former SCM Council (paralleled by the ITTM Council) to an arrangement that more or less by intent had the group CTO as the final arbiter on technology choices and supplier strategy and selection. There were different levels within which the network and network SCM were combined, although with an asymmetric balance of representation and the financial function omitted, somewhat analogous at this point to the inmates running the asylum figuratively speaking, but very reflective of a center-controlled arrangement. There was a single global SCM representative on the network board chaired by the global director of networks (a peer of my boss), who was initially my boss. Later it was decided that I should attend and represent his position, given the network focus.

The balance of that forum included CTOs from the large OpCos and a collective representative for the smaller OpCos and Société Française du Radiotéléphone (SFR)[10]; the bias or balance of power clearly leaned toward the larger OpCo representatives. In the forum at the next level, my boss was the sole representative for the global SCM. The forum was chaired by the group CTO and attended by all the One Vodafone OpCo CTOs. At the next level was an even smaller forum that included the group CTO (and I believe all those who reported directly to him), the major OpCo CTOs. Finally, the

130

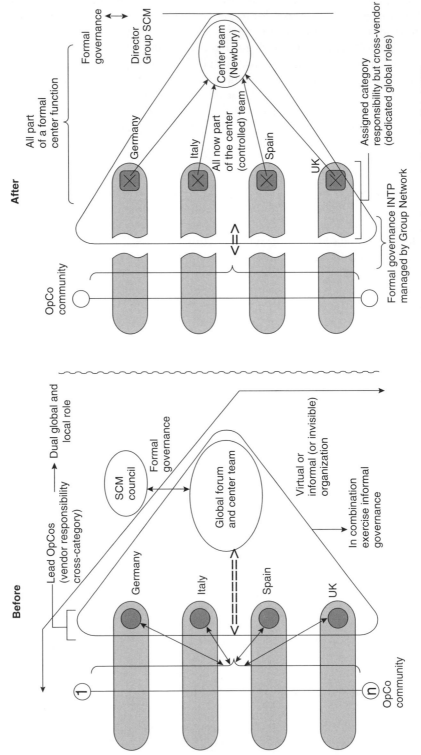

Figure 5.3 **Global SCM relationships changes in distribution of functions and governance before and after April 1, 2005**

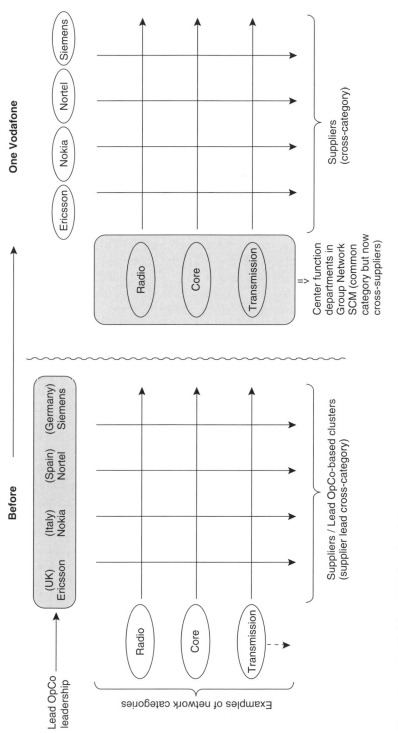

Figure 5.4   One Vodafone SCM functional change

Group CTOs management team met in a forum. Given the positive experience of the SCM Council and the benefit derived from the presence of key CFOs representing the finance community, it remains my opinion that they assured a balancing business view that was now lost, not to mention the complexity of this new governance structure that may be eventually be judged as somewhat self-serving.

The concept of governance is a form of checks and balances, in which the business or financial balance in decision making was less obvious in this structure, save the will of the larger OpCos (France, Germany, Japan, Italy, Germany, and UK). The fact was, for good reason, that it was clear that should proposed global technological alignment work for the larger OpCos, then the motion would carry; otherwise, they of necessity would push ahead in their own best interest. This was always the case, however, with the SCM Council; there was business-balanced participation capable of rationalizing the issues to hand toward an acceptable solution; it was not always perceived in this way by others. The complementary council, ITTM, which was populated primarily by technology people from the center and the OpCos, continually struggled toward consensus and for aligned time frames of implementation. The decision-making challenges of the day were well espoused, and those matters on which the mobile network infrastructure sourcing category required formalization through the SCM Council governance structure enjoyed unabated success.

My new (One Vodafone) organization was established in accordance with the plan and commenced functioning on April 1, 2005, while still recruiting, notwithstanding my views on what I had been charged to do by the executive management. As part of the introduction of this organizational model, we in SCM also ran a global vendor day to explain the changes, outline the impact to them, and offer clarity of the chosen way forward in the vendor relationship.

At this point, the social and perhaps intellectual capital were firmly reset. The notion that somehow and by some means the newly formed organization would function in the same manner as that which it replaced would not represent sound thinking. Also, to have eliminated an organizational structure (the mobile network infrastructure category) that was economically producing in line with the stated objectives of One Vodafone, albeit in an informal or invisible way, and that had already successfully globalized, may indeed be counterintuitive, but not in a progressive way leading to a foundation for the future. That is, the functioning social network may be eradicated at the stroke of a pen, whereas the reversal thereof would take orders of magnitude more time to recover, if indeed that is possible. To discount extant people in the performing social network who do not sit in the selected primary resource hubs of Düsseldorf, Madrid, Milan, and Newbury and are unable or unwilling to relocate is a novel approach. Let time and the scholars of the future be the judge of the wisdom of such recommendations that became decisions.

The entrepreneurial journey of almost ten years in the firm had come to an end, and I determined that I had now effectively designed myself out of the business, leaving the principal onward track to a younger team with whom I had the privilege and joy to work. In the summer of 2005 I was staring at the upper age limit of retirement for a director in Vodafone UK (sixty years). Although I had an offer to extend my employment, by exception, for at least two more years (subject, of course, to performance in the normal way), I announced my intention instead to take retirement and seek my future fortunes elsewhere.

Senior Management May Not Like What It Cannot Formalize

Two respected colleagues and key stakeholders of the mode of engagement of the One Vodafone consultative process, which led toward the management team proposals or recommendations for the successor global organizational model being sought by the executive management, observed that sometimes the incumbent thinking is so entrenched in the status quo of the current operations and organization that the individuals are unable to see or envision beyond those boundaries. In this instance the issue was to see beyond sourcing and to a newly defined supply chain management function, with the exception of the formalization and organizational construct not in variance to the one currently in place.

A key question here concerns where management sees its role in the spectrum from control through facilitation and on to guidance and support and progressing to delegation; that is, the formal versus the informal, in which certain managers move from comfortable in the former to unsure in the latter. From a dimensional perspective, perhaps control is the antithesis of inspirational or motivational leadership that results in innovation or counterintuitive and positive outcomes. Further, are organizational successes due to management or leadership, or do they result in spite of either or both, not to mention luck? Whatever the relevant combination is, without doubt a leader's ability to stimulate and motivate the social network (or not) will impact the outcome somewhat regardless of the organizational chart. In other words, a disconnected manager can only guess as to why things work out when they do, meaning that all too often success occurs in spite of management and not because of it.

Some in management take the view that when things go wrong they need through their chain of command to be able to attribute blame. Unfortunately, a blame culture does nothing to stimulate or motivate people. Such style leads to a conformant command structure in which the management should actually shoulder the blame for what goes wrong as they oblige their people to act like monkeys. A competent leader with positive business logic and rationale will always find good reception in the team, even if there are adverse impacts to them, because they will be engaged and have the opportunity to understand and contribute to the potential outcomes. It is a sign of weak management if the only logic for the pursuit of the endeavor by the team is on the basis of management's command. If managers have grown up in formal, hierarchical, process rigidity and enforced compliance to organizational structure, why indeed would they believe there was any other way to manage?

I have observed that national or company cultures also have their roles to play. Schein states "the unique talent of leaders [note, not commanders] is their ability to understand and work with culture." Schein goes on to say that "to distinguish leadership from management or administration, one can argue that leadership creates and changes cultures, while management and administration act within a culture." He concludes with his definition of the culture of a group: "a pattern of shared basic assumptions that was learned by a group as it solved problems of external adaptation and internal integrations, that has worked well enough to be considered valid and, therefore, to be taught to new members as the correct way to perceive, think and feel in relation to those problems."[11]

The discussion here does not concern command; the discussion instead concerns what "was learned by a group," which does not set or mention a natural boundary of management and other individuals or, indeed direct reports, or the need thereof in pursuit of a cross-functional, cross-boundary, or cross-operational endeavor. I would posit that the statements of Schein are borne out in the narrative of Chapters 3 and 4, in which the links in the performing social networks in consideration of the aggregation cost synergy requirements. Because they occurred in an informal organization, certain management failed to understand and could not or would not accept them, save the economic contribution.

Ineffective or Globally Inexperienced Management May Tend Toward Control

Age, although a taboo topic these days, is nevertheless an important factor or determinant of the measure of experience and applied knowledge potential; the issue or question then arising is its relevance. There may be a de facto assumption that by having attained a certain (hierarchical) level, an individual is competent at that level. One therefore has to be careful to distinguish those who claim credit by association (or indeed the boss or leader that was swept along with the tide, figuratively speaking) from those who in context can demonstrate where they actually made a difference. Context and timing in this global case may be important. For example, prior success bounded by a country and then moving to a global function provides an interesting cultural (in all aspects) challenge. So too does the market timing, as a rising market provides boundless opportunities, for success whereas a maturing market is the opposite.

Jaques provides an important adjunct to age, that is, the exploitation of the full potential of a leader, which he summarizes in four propositions:[12]

Proposition One: *Our potential capability (time horizon) for work we value is likely to mature along an unfolding pathway within a maturation band represented by modes on the time-horizon progression array.*

Proposition Two: *There is a substantial range of differences between individuals, and individuals are quite aware of those differences. It is not true, in short, that everyone has the natural ability to be President.*

Proposition Three: *This maturation process is strong enough to override all but massive catastrophic events that might befall a person. That is to say, everyone's potential capability will mature in the ordinary hurly-burly of dealing with life's problems, despite any lack of educational, socio-economic, or occupational opportunities.*

Proposition Four: *If we can learn to recognise the highest level of complexity of mental processing we are capable of using at a given age, we can locate the mode within which we are most likely to mature naturally in the everyday dealing with life's problems.*

In short, our *potential* unfolds throughout life. The art of the good society and of the good (requisite) organization is to ensure opportunity for all its people to use their full potential, which is the best stimulus to innovation, creativity, and sound morale. Jaques discusses individual maturation bands ranging from mode 1 (shop floor and office) through mode 5 (business unit president) to mode 7 (CEO, COO), embraced in his Stratified Systems Theory. He also distinguishes between the nature of the working capability of a person: *applied capability* is "the level at which a person is actually working now in a role which may or may not call upon a person's exercise of full potential"; *potential capability* is "the very highest level at which a person could work now, in work that was strongly valued and for which the person had had the opportunity to gain the necessary skill knowledge."[13] It is the potential capability that matures in a broadly predictable manner throughout life into old age. The issue or question therefore becomes whether or not the management appointee has reached the maturation level consistent with the hierarchical appointment and demonstrates adequate contextual and boundary-crossing experience. The complementary and critical issue, of course, is whether management has the ability of leadership in general to identify the relevant traits. Ultimately, everyone has a boss who should be held accountable for the performance or the lack thereof of the appointee; the underlying assumption is that they appropriately engage.

Sveiby suggests that the propensity of people to share knowledge and experiences in contrast to retention for one's own personal gain changes with age.[14] The young up-and-coming individual sees information and knowledge as "power," whereas the more mature person is more likely to share these attributes and, where experience is evident, add the dimension of wisdom and share all such knowledge. Logically, such factors affect management style and/or the degree to which the management will engage in the material matters at hand. Such style or approach may vary from delegative to strictly hierarchical—the latter tending to be a defense mechanism, particularly in circumstances in which one is unable to persuade the audience. Ultimately, the individuals, not merely the hierarchy itself, validate (or not) a published organizational hierarchy; coaching, self-confidence (a factor influenced by past successes), nationality, and cultures also contribute to style, some of which may lead to such adverse management styles of too controlling or micromanaging.

For experience in a role with changing market forces, there is a stark difference between reading of the experiences of others (which I would always encourage to broaden the intellectual capacity around the challenges of management), being on or associated with a team that engaged in a diversity of situational challenges and dealt with them to positive effect, and having personally been in the saddle and having had to manage and lead the team or company through the "rough." Having to lead a company through the impact of a recession and/or major downsizing or reforming for other business reasons is a sobering experience and one essentially absent on the operator side of the telecom industry. In contrast, in the 2001–2003 period the mobile network infrastructure supplier side went to hell and back and probably had greater depth and substance from the unfortunate experience.

Personally I have experienced three such states of turmoil in my background. In the telecom operator domain the 1990s was a period of explosive growth, both the rate of growth of the number of mobile operators and the capital investments they were making; I would characterize this as a period driven by mobile voice and text messaging, wherein success was easy and failure was more difficult to achieve. In this decade, with many major markets (certainly European) reaching saturation, average revenue per user (ARPU) not growing so readily, government-induced in-country competition through the issuance of more (3G) spectrum licenses, the financial burden of these licenses, regulatory interest in general to drive down the cost to the consumer, and shareholder pressures to evidence flare while growing the shareholder value (that is, a combination of share price growth, in which a major factor is the excitement for the future, and dividends), we enter a period of reversal. Now it is easier to fail than achieve success, a contrasting experience for those executives of the former period who never had to successfully and demonstrably deal with such challenges.

As a reminder of the substantial risks, at the present time the affordability of the 3G, the nonvoice services propositions, and all the device innovations are being supported from the operator revenues of the prior-generation (GSM) technology; there appears no evidence to suggest an uptake of significance, in accordance with the objectives of the mobile operators to avoid being perceived as a "bit-pipe." In fact, this function will always be present and drive focus on declining costs (and prices); the issue is how to create a services-based overlay (e.g., mobile TV, Web browsing, etc.) that at least arrests the current level of ARPU and ideally creates growth. Perhaps the protective "walled garden" approach is perceived by the end-customers as a "trap" or "tariff black hole." I do not believe that historical evidence supports success with such defensive strategies (at least that did not work in my former times in the IT industry). A market dominance, on the other hand, can avail a controlling strategy to good effect, particularly when the supplier or services choice creates an upfront lockin such that switching costs and/or risks are prohibitive, e.g., application software embedded in one's business or personal use (such as Oracle, SAP, or even Microsoft).

Contextual experiences, whether domestic or national versus international versus global operational, are important experiential differentiators as this business opportunity is very specifically global. In this perspective *international* means in the image of the corporate home country and culture regardless of the offshore location; *global* means consistent with the corporate stated vision and strategy but locally adapted as required for effective delivery to the customer in consideration of the shareholder investment to do so. In this case, given the preexistence of established in-country businesses (OpCos), although the legacy decisions should be respected, they should not unreasonably limit or constrain convergence in the future. I would further posit that the situational context needs to be taken into consideration. For example, manufacturing facilities, regardless of location, perhaps need to be in the image of each other; for a services-based industry (as telecoms) the infrastructure and back-office capabilities invisible to the customer may be highly integrated and geographically independent, save any regulatory requirements. Management in this organizational regard should be stereotypical only in situational circumstances in which it has determined the likeness or consistency of circumstances; otherwise, leadership should defer to innovative alternatives for the purpose of the business endeavor.

It remains an interesting question as to which is more beneficial for leadership or management appointments: relevant direct-industry experience or relevant situational experience. Companies have the tendency to pick from their native industry segment, thereby assuring to some degree the continuity of the legacy rather than the injection of new and perhaps noncompliant, consistent, or even radical thinking. The former tendency is seated in a presumption of safety, which it may well be; however, there is no assurance of the candidate repeating the former success, which is often contextually inconsistent anyway. I always keep in mind the expression that industry familiarity breeds contempt with limited assurance of success. On the basis of my observed experiences and those of others, therefore, I am not convinced of the relevant industry experience in a given business as qualification for a management position. However, what is of relevance is a demonstrable track record wherein candidates can evidence situational circumstances in which they actually were the lead decision maker, not by association or through subordination, but actually in the driving seat.

As a demonstration of the point, although the reader can exercise his or her own judgment, Vodafone appointed the current CEO (Arun Sarin) from within the industry. His former roles and experience were at AirTouch, and he was a Vodafone non-executive director at the time of appointment. Ericsson appointed their current CEO (Carl-Henric Svanberg) from an unrelated industry background. He did not have direct knowledge of the telecom industry; therefore, one would posit that he dealt with business matters rather than focused on technology, i.e., running a company as distinct from a telecom company. Telecom experts, with their natural biases from their own former telecom experiences and opinions, were of course already employed in Ericsson; however, the new CEO would be obliged to his own business judgment based on his former business experience.

Whatever the reader's view is, the same logic and questions apply to all levels of management, perhaps also including the candidate's degree of financial independence, which must be perceived a factor for motivation or commitment. Given the dynamic of business, companies tend to recruit on the issues of the present and the expectations for the future; however, there is a (conceptual) case for the argument that certain roles in companies should be reserved for "portfolio executives" fitted to the purpose for the phase of a given situational circumstance (growth in market, turnaround, reinvigoration, etc.). This is not a new idea but is not yet evident in general practice in businesses. Few globally visible leaders have started businesses and sustained success through multiple phases of the business over the long term; notable and very respected founder-leader examples in the IT industry include Bill Gates (Microsoft), Larry Ellison (Oracle), John Chambers (Cisco), and Steve Jobs (in-out-in Apple).

What evidence does or can the management demonstrate of previously self-initiated and executed leadership changes and/or transformational changes across cultures, countries, and organizations? Being what may be described as "old school," I seek to differentiate between those who were swept along with the tidal flow or associated therewith but are shy on evidence of direct personal impact and those who were the prime movers and boundary pushers—the latter class will be in the minority, whereas the former, particularly coming from a corporate background, will be in abundance. Certainly in my career, recruiting the (apparently) accomplished candidate from larger enterprises to the middle-sized businesses in which I was working at the time mostly resulted in disappointment. The new recruit absent of the equivalent of their former support organisation, may have the tendency to none of the expected accomplishments, a good test of the individual's mettle. The company took the view that such candidates were of greater interest and potential after they had worked in the company for a while, by which time they will have (hopefully) survived the period of adjustment and figured out what it is like to manage or perhaps more importantly lead.

Businesses, especially those going global (and even nonglobal enterprises are impacted by global competition), are faced with a dynamic and challenging landscape within which to create their successes. A "developed" appointment means either one who was "groomed" in the succession process, which may have the risk of continuing the status quo because of lack of relevant and comparable or superior experience in other companies, or a person appointed from the "ranks." The issue in either case may be the experience of the management making the appointment in having previously navigated similar terrain, which forms a boundary condition. The alternative is someone who is "appointed," that is, an appointment external to or from another function within the company. When this is done with relevant consideration of the challenges in the path ahead, it can make a significant difference to the business outcome.

Following are examples of mobile telecom industry CEO appointments for the readers' contemplation and judgment of performance in role: the Vodafone sequence of Sir Gerald Whent (the founding CEO) to that of

Sir Christopher Gent and on to Arun Sarin; the Ericsson sequence of Dr. Lars Ramqvist to Sven-Christer Nilsson, Kurt Hellström, and currently Carl-Henric Svanberg. Jaques concludes that large organizations are inclined to underestimate the numbers of Modes (Individual Maturation Bands) 8 (super corporation CEO), 7 (corporation CEO, COO), and 6 (strategic groups, business unit executive vice presidents, or headquarters business development executive vice presidents) executives they need to have coming up the pipeline if they are to remain vibrant at the top and sustain their competitive edge in the long term.[15] The effective working capacity (maturation level) of the corporate chief is far and away the most important factor determining the growth, contraction, or stability of an organization—contrary to the consensus belief that economic or market conditions produce those effects. Additionally, the problem with CEOs choosing their own successors is the risk that a successor less competent than the CEO will be found. The readers must draw their own conclusions on the merits and consideration of the succession paths and the appointees.

Evidence by a manager/leader of having developed and/or created an original successful and performing team is an important attribute in my opinion. Some accept and develop or replace as appropriate to the future challenges, whereas others have a comfort or preference to repeat history and recruit former colleagues and/or subordinates, possibly in an aligned culture. In my view a true leader is the former. I see the potential of risk with the latter strategy, added to which it brings into question the competency of the leader and is perhaps indicative of operating in the comfort zone and/or a having a sense of insecurity or a competence issue. I am strongly of the belief that whatever you create behind you should stay behind and provide your former "stable" with a sustainable and survivable organization, the mark of a true professional.

A question of management style is whether one is a team leader and/or coach. A team leader knows that to be a star, the leader needs a star team, who should publicly be given credit when relevant. Leaders do not need to be a star in any one of the functions for which they are responsible; however, they should be able to identify, select, and delegate to those who are and motivate them through a clearly espoused vision and strategy. A propensity toward micromanagement or control, on the other hand, is a management characteristic that destroys the concept of an organization and team. My observation was that style has a close correlation to (national) culture; in some the organizational hierarchy is well documented, but in practice all decisions (often major or otherwise) route to the top of the business and through a number of management layers, which is not a recipe for success or the development of tenacity or experiential learning within or for the team. Mobile network operators, independent of their global scope, are nevertheless in-country services businesses, leading to the conclusion perhaps that business decisions that affect customers or shareholders should be made at the point closest to the customers being served, which for an international business attempting to go global is a worthy consideration.

Cultural background is an interesting topic that in my observation and experience was a controlling factor in the evolving game such as to occasionally become a detrimental factor, often impeding the path of positive progress. Culture, of course, has many facets, two examples of which are corporate culture and the national in-country company cultures. For a global business, such characteristics can become either major roadblocks or success points, depending on how one deals with these realities. Derived from this experiential learning, I certainly found it very useful having received mediation accreditation (in the context of dispute resolution), which I combined with my own management style (delegative) and moderated by my own intuition or, indeed, occasioned with counterintuition toward a positive outcome. It provided a basis of tolerance in seeking to achieve the collaborative aggregation objectives, while recognizing any realities of the cultural differences. Most important was that whatever the solutions, as the journey progressed, they had to be seated in the mind-set and commitment of those in the operating companies, not the center organization, thereby building mutual trust that was to be earned not assigned. The reality was always delivered by my colleagues in the operating companies, which was a guiding ethos for all of my actions.

A great idea is interesting; however, if nobody is willing to move to action, what is its value? My observations would indicate that there exists a serious lack in this dimension. The corporate culture clearly has its role, but if people do not see the espoused culture in action through the conduct and practice of their management, then the following becomes limited. A further observation is that managers, particularly those who do not have experience outside their own country, have a tendency, when faced with such a new challenge, to operate in that in-country image. This observation pertains more generally also to international (and sometimes global) organizations, e.g., in Germany, the United States, or Italy. This becomes a boundary limitation; whereas all must be equal in objective and international or global ambition, at the in-country level the absoluteness of conformity must depend on the nature of the business.

For example, in a manufacturing environment of the same product in multiple locations, one would expect conformity as a given. However, for a services-based business, one might anticipate the necessity for a degree of localization while not comprising the collaborative strategy, in this case aggregation synergy benefits. So, too, in country norms of management there has to be a respect such that the global leaders do not impose on the local team save the mutual agreement of the "what" (objectives), leaving the "how" (implementation) to the local management. Another consideration on the enforced national culture or approach on the global stage is the degree to which the company has market dominance; an example of this might be Cisco, who operates internationally in my opinion and experience but not globally, as everything reverts to the acceptability and/or conformation of their U.S. headquarters.

The career aspirations or ambitions of the leader or manager can also be a crucial point for the subordinate team. How often do managers credit the team as a source of contribution to whatever it is they are stating or proclaiming? The person that sees himself or herself as the sole leader will intellectually rape the team in an aggressive way, all in the interests of self-promotion, which leads to the question, what is the substantive contribution of such managers? A true leader, on the other hand, is perhaps one who sees his or her success vested in the performance of the team. For example, for football coaches or managers, although they do not play the football game, their success is nevertheless measured in how many goals their team scored and whether they won.

I have learned from experience that there is a void of developmental training for executive management, which results in their having bounded thinking or perspectives and/or vision borne in the limits of their own experience or those whom they choose as advisers. The argument follows that such considerations also set the framework within which they exercise (or not) intuition. In my view no manager is so good such that further education and continuous training is something to talk about and others to do. It is a sad reality that if business leaders or managers get it wrong, they may suffer personally as a consequence of their lack of foresight, but such consequences are often more devastating to the innocent workforce operating under their leadership. Perhaps in a philosophical way, management has a duty of care conveyed in actions. The captain may be obliged in old chivalry to go down with the sinking ship; however it is not the captain's role to sink the ship and take the passengers with him or her.

Luck does not run in a way such that managers or leaders move from company to company as their career progresses and somehow their former experiences are locked in a time warp, assuring that they will always perform on the day. Life is not that easy, and the situational backdrop changes and, these days toward globalization, at an ever increasing pace. Perhaps in contrast, the rigorous training of soldiers, airline pilots, or doctors, wherein the promotion and progressive appointment process has mandatory rigor absent of circumstantial attributes or reward system, even they have to deal with and manage the unexpected. Perhaps there is also something here for business management to learn.

In the context of egocentricity and perceived security, how many managers will act in the interests of the business and in effect design themselves out of their position? I managed to do this three times in my career, the last being my retirement from Vodafone in October 2005. The question is, in whose interests do managers generally operate: themselves, their team, the customers, or the shareholders? I would posit that the true professional working in a company owned or financed by others (meaning not one's own business) should not be primarily operating in his or her self-interest to the consequence of those other stated attributes. The competent professional operating as suggested, I would posit, has little to fear. I have always held the view, which is consistent with my personal experience and the observations of others, that operating in the greater good actually makes individuals more valuable contributors to a company's health and wealth. Should their opportunities expire in their existing employment, then I am quite sure they will realize their rewards elsewhere with a positive reference from the former employment, or even more luckily, arising from industry recognition for their achievements. My observation is that certain managers operate in a self-centered way, yet they accept the salaries and rewards for contrary actions.

Trust is a topic about which much is written; however, from a management or leader perspective it is fundamental and linked, may I suggest, to management style. There may also be a co-dependency or determinant, meaning one has to earn trust. However, does earning trust mean that a trusted person is one who would do as a manager says, faced with the same set of circumstances, or does it mean that the right thing will be done even though it may not align with the manager's view? Perhaps the answer may be resolved by the objective of the manager: does the manager wish to have a trained monkey or a thinking person? The dilemma comes when the manager wishes to have a thinking person but then obliges the person in practice to operate as a trained monkey—not terribly motivating and can put physical distance between the two, resulting in a mission impossible for the subordinate. This approach then knocks on the door of micromanagement, wherein ultimately there is a reporting or information flow demand that operates on a time scale such as to assure never having any time to complete the actions before progress is being inquired about. Such experiences are not unusual, unfortunately, having experienced such traits.

Being innovative or entrepreneurial is not a job role. Such achievement is probably in the truest sense a once-in-a lifetime achievement for those people who aspire to such recognition, and history shows not too many individuals have such repeated success. There are, of course, notable exceptions other than those mentioned earlier, like Sir Richard Branson. Concerning the business world I offer two observations. First, innovation is likely to be inversely proportional to the size of the organization—the larger organizations are more bound in process compliance than allowing flexibility, whereas smaller organizations are driven more on innovation out of continued pressures for survival, meaning the "need factor" is greater. Second, to follow that point, an innovative environment is diametrically opposed to a strong process-driven organization.

The management style of individuals who are innovative may be formed around the degree of latitude they have had in their former experiences and whether those organizations were receptive to actually think the unthinkable and try out a new idea. Or they may operate within the boundary constraints of set-piece processes, and no matter what their title or seniority, they are actually an operative in a system that is unable to accept an extreme view. I would say that my experience generally has not been bounded by process, thereby offering me free reign, subject always to performance, to do as I and those with whom I worked thought appropriate for success. That door finally closed as we moved to and executed my delegated centralizing task under One Vodafone by taking the former center-led globalized function to center control.

Given that everyone has a boss, this management characteristic shows the kind of top team and those they attract to join them. In the extreme one must be compliant in every dimension rather than have a core compliance that is flexible to take on board great ideas for success. If everything I, together with my colleagues, did was subject to approvals, processes, and budgets, then I would not be writing and attempting to pass on to readers these powerful learning experiences. There may have been a culturally based stereotypical prevailing view that center control is somehow synonymous with a directed positive result, while ignoring the performing informal or loosely coupled and virtual organization or community.

Actual diversity of decision-based experience involving transformational change is perhaps the degree to which the management has set pace versus trailed pace, an important distinction. I have met many people who proclaim success by association and few that actually were the prime mover in the reported success. The former will be those that tend to surround themselves with familiar people and possibly of the same culture; however, this is symptomatic of a weak form of leadership in my view. Another relevant point is that a good practitioner is not necessarily synonymous with a good leader, yet these distinctions often are muddled in management and leadership appointments.

This experience has shown me that having a relevant or perhaps requisite and global social network is a paramount precursor for developing a successful transformational change toward true globalization. I do not refer to being in meetings with many others; I mean direct personal contact outside the business. Such thinking, I am sure, would be very familiar to people in the diplomatic service, for example, where significant preparation takes place in advance of any visible meeting. That is, the objective and the responses thereto are crystallized and agreed in advance of their formal adoption. A public debate (meaning managers in the presence of their subordinates) can lead to win-lose scenarios or visible power games, which are not helpful. My observation is that transformational endeavors cross-companies and cultures, lead to public displays of different opinions, in this case at the highest levels, which were not all helpful.

Cooperation Versus Competition Always Involves Tension

With the decision taken to create under the One Vodafone banner a center-controlled organization, it became relevant to quantify the resources within the preexisting informal and virtual organization or social network. However, it is perhaps not surprising that the responses provided did not reconcile with expectations, given the expectation that such numbers would likely be debited from the local team numbers following the formation of the center function. In transformational transition, when synchronization is lacking throughout the chain of affected parties, there is a risk that "surplus" resources (people) from the former structure that remain in place may serve as "antibodies" and challenge every progressive move.

Regarding Lead OpCos versus the One Vodafone centralized approach, the previous distributed and delegated management approach under the vision and strategic leadership of the center and the governance of the SCM Council served both to engage the affected operating units and to minimize the potential of natural tensions that prevail in a stereotypical central organization seeking an operational influence or control; but this approach was not used in a centrally managed organization. My experience of the implemented center-controlled organization was that it certainly involved a sea change in the attitude of the in-country operator business relationships with the new central (command and control) functions for network infrastructure. However, the preexisting personal relationships in the social networks survived to some degree, certainly the case for me.

I would like to posit, as a practitioner and researcher, the notion of an "embedded manager or leader" as being relevant in cases in which there is an expectation of transformational change such as the one I had the privilege to lead and on which my initial qualitative research was conducted. Critical to the notion is that intuition, interspersed with inspirational flashes of positive counterintuition, is seated in the experiential learning and knowledge derived from within the journey paradigm; this is an inside-out view rather than a detached outside-in view, as is often the case when management is distant from the reality.

I would further posit that there are few who enjoy the background experience and leadership qualities to act in this role, leading to the argument that often managers seeks to bridge their own shortfall with the engagement of others (external consultancies) because of they lack the ability to identify what is actually required to support and/or develop the manager's own businesses. Furthermore, the executive is perhaps already being compensated on the presumption of prior knowledge and experience, not as consultancy coordinator. Perhaps managers see what they want or need to see and are blindsided to the factual realities of the situational circumstances. The engagement of external and unrelated parties in itself contributes to a counterproductive tension when many in the organizations under discussion have more than adequate intellect and experience to bring solution or remedy, given the invitation to do so.

In a situational sense, albeit within one organization (Vodafone), a game was taking place, as in the game theory sense. On the one hand, the resolve to globalize and to optimize or maximize the global cost aggregation synergies across the Vodafone properties created the necessity to *cooperate* to validate such opportunities. On the other hand, there was somewhat of a *competition* between the in-country operations to lead such endeavors (virtual workstreams, as discussed in earlier chapters), particularly as the number of engaged properties expanded. Nalebuff and Brandenburger refer to this tension as *co-opetition*, although in an inverse context to this case, they suggest that "creating value [aggregation cost synergies] is an inherently cooperative process, capturing value [leading the virtual workstream] is inherently competitive" and that "to create value, people [the center function] can't act [or resolve] in isolation."[16] Were there games played? Of course there were. Did tensions arise? Of course they did, although in the collective spirit of the overall endeavor outlined in Chapters 3 and 4, such tensions were naturally dispersed through dialogue, painful though that may have been at times, perhaps because the underlying ethos was one of cooperation in the collective interests. The notion of a large center function seeking to exude or perhaps impose "leadership" may find lesser fortunes. It is difficult for those with past or even no operating experience to presume credentials superior to those actually in the role, which then introduces "antibodies" into the game that are obstacles to cooperation.

It is of interest to consider "centers of excellence" versus "competence centers" and perhaps to add an "orbit or constellation of excellence." A center of excellence was intended as an authoritative and generally central function, whereas a competence center had an advisory or consultative role, the guidance being offered not treated as mandatory. The former has the potential or risk to introduce tensions, perhaps of a counterproductive nature, whereas the latter encourages dialogue and exchange of ideas. A bridge between the two, orbit or constellation of excellence, may characterize the social network discussed in Chapters 3 and 4 in so far as it involved consultation and ultimately yielded executable and sustainable decisions that were followed. Although this approach had its emergent tensions, given the community motivation for collective success, such differences were generally mitigated for the good.

Centralization May Be Driven by Stereotypical Experience and a Conformist Culture

Choosing a center-controlled organizational structure over that discussed previously in this book demonstrates the executive management's lack of in-depth appreciation or understanding of the power of the social networks and the accrued social capital beyond the economic results resulting from the latter type of structure. Such a decision would be a preemptive move, not one arising from any acknowledgment of the approximately seven-year intra- or interorganizational history and achievements of the extant virtual community. Perhaps the extant social network would actually represent a functioning example of the globalization ambitions being sought by the One Vodafone initiative.

Although I fully endorsed the concept of One Vodafone, disagreement arose on the emerging organizational approach that discarded the experiential learning to date. Further, management failed to understand that retaining people in-country yet assigning them from a local role to a global role changed the nature of their local relationships. This was very clearly pointed out to me by an Italian executive; I understood the point both then and now, a sanguine lesson. My conclusion was that the center-controlled organizational model disregarded all that had successfully gone before and terminated a long period of innovation under the former management, which made retiring to private practice an easy decision.

I would posit that the richness of sustainable knowledge and experience is borne in practice and direct (rather than by association) accountable line responsibilities as opposed to the advice offered by others (consultants, for example, whose vision is bounded by the observed experience of others)—IF the leadership paused for reflection, but circumstances generally deny such pause. There are, of course, professional exceptions. One can be confident, for example, that with senior airline pilots, fighter pilots, police, doctors, or military commanders there is a valid presumption of skill, experience, and capability as the structure of their discipline requires. Such rigor is not at all evident in the process to achieve senior positions in business management, especially highly compensated executives who have a dependency on external consultants; the notion here is that development of resilience and experience of management teams is usurped by such practice, often to the disappointment of the up-and-coming future leaders.

The stereotypical approach to change and/or transformation is often grounded by practice in the experience of others. This "formula," however, by no means assures repeat performances of past experiences of the people involved, especially if one is dealing in a global situation in which de facto there is a cultural and ethnic mix of custom and practices. My observation of consultancies supported by the opinion of others is that consultancies tend to follow the "practice" formula, processes, and methodologies without fully considering the actual circumstances. Life and people are just not that simple.

My observation over the years is that systemic cultural roots in cross-cultural organizational and business transformations are all too often ignored. The ensuing organizational options are driven from the knowledge and experience of the management and maybe the set pieces from the library of former endeavors of an external consultancy, all leading potentially to out-of-context choices of stereotypes. In such a case management is less often seated in the vision, strategy, and logic of the extant social and intellectual capital; instead, management opts to hide behind an independent party, which I posit is an abdication of management responsibility; after all, they should be closest to the people impacted or on whom they depend for success. It is often as though people in the business are unaware of the issues and unable to provide alternatives for remedy if or unless they bare their sole to the consultants. In the discussion in this book, the cultural asset was diverse and complex yet rich in the potential of contribution and perhaps had the capacity to obstruct if motivated to do so, just to keep the balance.

What is the role of human resources (HR) in such organizational designs? In this case, the role was more one of conformance to the process and legal labor relations obligations than depth of challenge of the logic of the pursuit. Given the relative newness of the mobile telecommunications industry (which began in the mid-1980s), many of the early risk takers who were in mobile operator start-ups remained in the business, as did their spirit. This was the case for the Vodafone companies, those with whom we merged at AirTouch and later those who joined the family from the Mannesmann acquisition, in all a rich diversity of cultures and perspectives.

The foundation of the structure was the individual country or national culture with its extant local and global hierarchical legacies, the founding and emergent mobile operator culture, later the impact of the group culture

(Vodafone, AirTouch, and Mannesmann), the emergent culture following the business transactions, and finally the culture that we in the mobile network infrastructure SCM category informally and successfully developed leading to the informal social network. The final stage of these organizational transactions had created something that was counterintuitive and nonconformant to the stereotypical experience of managers and their advisers. In the case of the advisers, the advice was normally seated in the richness of their client experience rather than in innovation on their part. No one attempted to understand what was existing and its merits before proposing going-forward scenarios to the executive management; in fact, such suggestions perhaps fell on deaf ears and strong management cultural biases ensued.

In the final analysis and irrespective of the organizational ambitions or power games, the objective was to realize and maximize the aggregation cost synergies in the interests of Vodafone. Given that the roots of the group business were discontinuous and not organic, and that whatever the center function perceived as its capacity to contribute to the scenarios in which to yield aggregation costs synergies, such yields were principally materialized and transacted in and through the in-country operations. Therefore, failing to adapt and selectively engage leadership in the cultural and performance richness of the in-country roots of the group rather than forming a very large center organization may perhaps in hindsight be judged a lost opportunity in both time and economic yield—given the eventual organizational paradigm recommendation and final choice, so much for innovation and extended goodwill of those who contributed to the success of what was about to be replaced.

Yet More Unfinished Vodafone Business Perhaps?

As a postscript for the period since my retirement from Vodafone in October 2005, the old firm continues its process of self-discovery with a number of movements at the executive level, challenges to the authority of Arun Sarin, and issues of clarity of strategic direction and the approach. There have also been asset (equity) disposals and new acquisitions.

On the people side, on January 31, 2006, Vodafone announced that "Sir Julian Horn-Smith will be retiring from the Board at the company's Annual General Meeting in July 2006. Sir Julian, 57, has enjoyed a career spanning more than 22 years at Vodafone and has held a number of senior posts including Chief Operating Officer and currently Deputy Group Chief Executive, which includes responsibility for global business development. He was closely involved in all of Vodafone's major transactions including Mannesmann and most recently the acquisition of businesses in the Czech Republic and Romania, the disposal of Vodafone's Swedish subsidiary and the purchase of a stake in India's Bharti Tele-Ventures."[17]

On March 8, 2006, it was announced that Peter Bamford, the group chief marketing officer, would be leaving effective April 1, 2006.

A news release on April 6, 2006, announced that as part of a "new organisational structure" Bill Morrow was to be appointed to the new position of CEO Europe (which included global technology and global marketing) on his return from Japan, where he was president of Vodafone K. K., effective May 1. 2006. Also included in that announcement was a change to the role of Thomas Geitner, who was to relinquish the role of group CTO to become CEO New Businesses & Innovation. The third plank of that same announcement was that Paul Donovan was appointed CEO Central Europe, Middle East, Asia Pacific, and Affiliates.[18]

On July 24, 2006, Vodafone announced that Bill Morrow had "decided to leave the [Vodafone] business to return to the US for family reasons." It was reported in the media on July 24, 2006, that "the abrupt departure from Vodafone of Bill Morrow, a key executive and a man regarded as a potential heir to Arun Sarin, is yet another blow to the world's biggest mobile group."[19] On August 15, 2006, Pacific Gas and Electric of California announced that it had elected Bill as its president and COO, effective immediately.

Vodafone announced on August 1, 2006, "the appointment of Steve Pusey as Chief Technology Officer with effect from 1 September 2006. Steve Pusey will be responsible for all aspects of Vodafone's networks, IT capability and supply chain management. He will report to the Chief Executive of Europe and will join the Group's Executive Committee." Steve was previously one of the most senior executives at Nortel and is "currently Executive Vice President, and President, Nortel EMEA."[20] He had been with Nortel since 1982.

The company announced on September 5, 2006, that "Vittorio Colao will join the Board on 9th October 2006 as Chief Executive of Vodafone's European region" (the former position of Bill Morrow) and that Vittorio "will also succeed Sir Julian Horn-Smith as Deputy Chief Executive. In this role he will assist the Chief Executive in external representation, in particular with political institutions and regulatory bodies."[21] Previously on June 23, 2004, the company had announced "that Vittorio Colao informed the Company, yesterday evening of his intention to resign from the Board of Vodafone Group Plc with effect from 27 July 2004";[22] at that time Vittorio held the roles of chief executive of Vodafone Italy, regional chief executive, and main board director.

On October 13, 2006, the company further announced that it is "devolving the activities of the New Businesses and Innovation Unit into parts of the organisation closer to the customer. The new structure will simplify the organisation and enable the Group functions to work even more closely with the businesses. In the new stream-lined structure, the Group functions reporting to the European Region together with the operating companies will execute the mobile plus strategy, and a Group Strategy and New Business function will identify new business opportunities and key partnerships. As a result of these changes, Thomas Geitner, CEO New Businesses and Innovation will step down from the Board of Vodafone at the end of December 2006 after the transition to the new structure."[23] The notable contributions of Thomas have been recorded earlier in this chapter.

For the record and notwithstanding the dynamic appearance of the management and leadership of the firm, the fiscal performance should not go unrecognized. For the fiscal year to March 31, 2006, it is true that the company posted a pretax loss of £14.9 billion; it also reported a positive free cash flow of £6.4 billion. The media reports tend to lead on pretax loss, much of which is valuation adjustments of former ("paper") transactions that should not be confused with having lost (or wasted) actual cash expended. The positive free cash flow, generally ignored by the media, tells a (for some confusing or contradictory) story that I suspect may be the envy of the telecom operators for some time to come.

I am delighted to have had the opportunity to record a part of the experiential learning that has played its relevant contribution and role in the successes of the Vodafone quest for aggregation cost synergies, to convey to the management and leadership of the future a base of learning, and to broaden their knowledge in providing this platform from which they may further extend thinking through practice for themselves and their successors. This book captures a longitudinal period in excess of seven years and is supplemented by over thirty years of international strategic and operational business experiences.

6 Building Global Relationships

The previous chapters have presented a journey—a journey in the construction of global networks, both the supply chain for the infrastructure that allowed Vodafone to create networks, and the invisible social network that created the relationships that drove forward the transformation. What now follows is a thoughtful reflection on building these global relationships in such a way as to enhance or indeed even make possible positive outcomes when dealing with performance or transformations that focus on a global context.

This is a personal chapter. As stated at the end of Chapter 5, this book has captured seven years in the transformation of Vodafone's supply chain but also over thirty years at strategic levels in global organizations. Chapter 7 presents some general findings and compares them to some of the literature. Here I allow myself the luxury of reflection, assertion, and speculation.

Managing Distance and Time

The notion of people separated by distance and time conjures up for most the perspective of extended distances and the crossing of one or several time zones. It is important to clarify that the same logic applies if individuals have offices adjacent to each other and for whatever reason their schedules do not allow them to be there at the same time. Therefore, although the narrative in this book encompassed a significant geographic and cultural diversity in the virtual community, certain of the principles learned may well apply even in circumstances when the physical proximity and diversity of people are substantially less.

An anecdotal observation is that the positive impact of management, particularly those perceived as "HQ," traveling to and engaging with distant operational resources and activities has the sense of being a long-lasting benefit in and of itself, especially in the minds of those visited. Size of operation should not dictate the significance or relevance of such management investment of time, and perhaps to the contrary, in that smaller operations are usually under greater pressure to perform and appear to be more innovative than their (necessarily) process- and procedure-driven larger counterparts.

Having worked in leadership roles away from HQ for many years, I should report that the solitude from being out of sight and out of mind is not bad at all, although a tenuous link was maintained to the company president, and the opportunities for corporate "interference" were minimized. Of course, there is a catch: success is what breeds the exclusivity of self-determination within the framework of the business strategy, which fortunately I and my extended team had. In the Vodafone world my proximity to management was local, quite a change for me after so many years of being in a leadership role and being detached from the center function; however, the space for entrepreneurship and innovation prevailed among those with whom I worked up until April 2005. So in a global and virtual organization, geographically dispersed independent traits are nested, particularly in acquired operating companies regardless of their size; the strength of these traits may and frequently do increase with distance from HQ to positive effect. The issue arising therefore is, in such organizations how does one capitalize on vibrant energy in those dispersed operating units, wherein the time shift and geographic spread extends from Stockholm to Fiji, while balancing with the teams that are closer?

In such a globally dispersed and interdependent cross-cultural cluster of companies, the style of management or leadership becomes important. The initial and fundamental decisions that impact style and thus motivation are the differences between task or management delegation and control and being the boss or leader. To examine these points, it is helpful to resolve the locations of actual operational transactions leading directly to economic global aggregation, a clue being that they are unlikely to be at, or solely at, HQ in a globally dispersed in-country services business. Even if the in-country operations are subordinated in the hierarchical dimension to HQ management, as a practical matter in a requisite organization one would be advised to adopt a meta-management influence, meaning delegation and not control. The reversion to control, sometimes reinforced with micromanagement, may be seen as a sign of weakness and/or insecurity and possibly absent of substantive or convincing logic to the proposition or direction being given. Those distant from reality and/or past practice, seated in HQ, lead and coordinate the vision, strategy, and governance with input and support from the affected parties (the globally dispersed business units), whereas the in-country operations lead the operational execution and compliance with the strategy in support of the short-term business goals without compromising the longer term.

Control, Management, and Leadership

This book has demonstrated that control does not have to be synonymous with direct lines on organizational charts; to the contrary, the dominant discussion here has been around an essentially invisible organization through which substantive and dependent economic performance was yielded. This invisible grouping, meaning the extent of which was not at all visible structurally or in a budget, transcended the boundaries of vertical hierarchies within and between companies and organizations. It became a catalyst of voluntary, yet motivated transformational change to true globalization arising from which roles and "authorities" were changed and in some cases transformed. To the extent that "control" was required in this formation, it was through substantially informal governance that was not an alternative route for a questioning micromanagement control regime, to which some cultures are occasioned. So, being a boss is easy, but there is no assurance of leadership or indeed that the inherent potential is present to aspire to and deliver the requirements of the objectives. Leadership, on the other hand, is something that is natural to the individual, a role earned in front of the team either for which one is directly responsible or more broadly the extended virtual team on which one is reliant for the realization of business objectives – an outcome not an appointment.

A manager must be self-confident and competent to delegate such as to exude confidence in those to whom they have delegated; those delegated to must be at the relevant level with the necessary potential over time as prescribed by Jaques.[1] In the informal world of the nonhierarchical and virtual organization that emerged, delegation of tasks was to those accepted by that community as being most qualified or relevant to perform that task and lead it to a successful conclusion. Such assignments were by mutual consent, not arising from an interview and formal appointment process. Delegation on the basis of perceived or expected competence by the virtual community took hierarchical rank out of the equation and introduced capability; the lesson here is that rank is interesting but by no means an assurance of a diversity of skills in all areas and at all levels, nor should it so be. Hierarchical position is a determinant of compensation and should be reflective of leadership capabilities, although that this is often not so. Delegation, of course, leads to motivation; success leads to self-confidence, which then leads to a mutuality of trust that enhances the requisite organization. As a complement, delegating to the operational point closest to the end-customer is conducive to service experience and satisfaction, with the HQ function in the background to assure the aggregation of synergy benefits consistent with the strategy and in the sustainable interests of the shareholders.

Taking this debate full circle then, concerning the impact on teams in various locations but with tasks in common, delegation with confidence is important to those to whom tasks are delegated or objectives assigned because they have participated in the rationale and logic of the debate leading to these assignments; commands do not work in general and certainly not for remote parties in particular. Such style engenders in the individuals a positive and motivated resolve with the necessary goodwill to deal with situated change, all in an optimal way to secure the desired outcome.[2] In such cases it appears that the recognition and opportunity surpass matters of compensation, although incentive compensation is not to be trivialized. This style is demonstrative of true leadership.

A boss, on the other hand, issues commands that may drive egos and instill fear; however, it is definitely not a performance enhancement approach whatever the hierarchical level of those in the team. In a globally dispersed organization requiring management across distance and time with relevant consideration to cultures locally, delegation is essential, which means "hands off" but not "let go." The delegate must own and be responsible for local operations, that is, must give latitude in execution absent of "Please do it my way" or "What I think is." This style leads to management accepting that there is always more than one way to approach an objective or task; the acceptance of the local proposition, although not assuring a successful outcome, does nevertheless induce a motivated and sustainable commitment to the result. Through such an approach that allows for experimentation, the result from time to time is failure, which contributes to a more robust and experienced management team.

Through such delegative approaches a tangible and intangible team identity emerges within which a separate culture evolves that may be at variance to that of the in-country operation.

Organizational and Interorganizational Structure

Effective organizational relationships and cultures within or between organizations cannot be preempted or imposed. Such positive outcomes emerge if the organizational situation is conducive to such. In this case the organization that emerged was not conformant to any preemptive stereotype.

In pursuit of global relationships it is unwise to independently create an organizational structure absent of the consideration of the people and their accrued tacit knowledge; I would posit that many organizations through practice fail to access their extant and rich talent pool often in preference to third parties. To promulgate the practice of management or leadership appointments on the basis of current position, past performances, or tenure is unwise. It is preferable to permit a degree of informality for a period and observe where and who the natural leaders or opinion formers are. Although the idea is not new, companies, particularly large ones, are less inclined to experimentation and learning and more inclined to process, formality, and hierarchy, which is a somewhat self-fulfilling prophecy, perhaps with continuance in the comfort zone.

By outcome rather than by plan, such natural conditions brought about the achievement of the desired economic results and minimal formal governance prevailed. It was also the case that we twice attempted to voluntarily formalize the relative roles and responsibilities at the team level and failed, resulting in the continuity of the functioning and performing status quo. With One Vodafone, the parties then supported what had been previously rejected, in contrast to the emergent strong desire by many for centralization without consideration of the truly global and performing organization developed over a six-year period, despite clear internal visibility of the collective financial contribution. Administratively we had moved to what I earlier referred to as a global constitution, meaning that all former interorganizational local business relationships had been superseded with a homogeneous global arrangement, all developed in collaboration with the operating company clusters; this too was not considered.

The Vodafone mobile network infrastructure SCM organizational structure discussed in the earlier chapters, although including a center function under my leadership together with a direct small team, provided a catalyst and coordination for the collective vision and formative strategy and informal (interorganizational) governance. Such arrangements did not seek to impose operational structure on the operating companies. The center team constituted a number of individuals who as part of their personal development were seconded from their operating companies for a typical period of two years; this facet of the organizational structure was to create a strength and "binding" of the operating companies to the actions required for success. Until terminated by directive, the embracing of the operating companies through the rotation of venue of the global meetings was also a relevant adjunct to the operation of the organizational structure.

The organizational structure in operation was the outcome of co-evolution of the progression of the cost aggregation endeavor and our chosen or experiential approach. It functioned within and between those other international organizations with a global footprint that became part of this industry-leading initiative.

Change and Leadership

Change is not a linear and nonrecursive process; to the contrary, in a globalization endeavor it is thwart with potential complexities, leading one to conclude that it therefore cannot be considered a detached process and delivered by or through third parties aside from management. Such approaches, although considerate of the requirements of the business (often cost focused) and absent of contributions from those affected, miss the tacit knowledge input and the opportunity of a motivational stimulus in support of the endeavor by those on or through whom delivery is dependent. This case was not a transformational change driven through a restructuring or operating cost reduction; the objective for Vodafone was to leverage aggregation cost synergies arising from the emergent global scale, whereas the requisite and, in this case, virtual organizations or communities were an experiential outcome, not the subject of any preordained organizational design. So the objectives were economic, which were substantive and visible to the financial community for a period. In regard to network infrastructure sourcing, it affected and transformed the intracompany relationships within the Vodafone organization as it did the interorganizational relationships with Ericsson, Nokia, Nortel, and Siemens. The organizations, through the co-evolving intra- and interorganizational global relationships, collectively performed in the common interests of Vodafone and its chosen approaches in the commercial game.

However, the issue of the organization is also a game, albeit of a different kind, a key factor being the style of the leadership. Let us now discuss a differentiation between management and leadership conveyed in the experiential learning shared in this book. It may be asserted that management and leadership represent two boundary conditions that may be observed in practice as having two different styles and outcomes. Management may tend to imposition of authority or power, the need for recognition, hierarchy, control (what and how), direction, and possibly micromanagement. In contrast, leadership may be the willingness to share a vision, gain collective agreement of a strategy, delegate execution, provide governance over execution, inspire trust, and accept input and debate from a broad school while mindful of the requirement of the organization to perform.

It is, of course, important not to create an "us" and "them" between the center and those in the operating entities over whom one seeks influence; management might prefer control, whereas leaders are satisfied with positive influence. Seeking to operate as a homogeneous whole with delegated tasks to the in-country operations assures that the ensuing proposals will be executable by the cooperating cluster with the common interest; in the examples cited this also functioned well interorganizationally. Such an approach places the task at the nexus of relevant critical mass that resulted in a motivated momentum toward delivery. A further step that bode well as an example of a performing organization was the establishment of the Lead OpCo. What would otherwise be considered intra- and interorganizational center functions were delegated or assigned in operation to key Vodafone stakeholder in-country operating entities, with the center taking a strategic, advisory, and background governance role.

At this point of the organizational evolution and development of global relationships, there was only one formal governance forum, the Supply Chain Management (SCM) Council, all else being informal, invisible, and a form of self-governance with key stakeholder engagement; again, the economic results known internally to Vodafone attest for themselves as to the value of such effective global relationships. None of these developments were instituted on a "big-bang" basis; they were emergent and developed from the early Vodafone-Ericsson interorganizational and globalizing endeavors. Such an approach facilitated the social network to develop and reach states of equilibrium; the accrual of social capital engendered the notion of the requisite organization throughout the transition.

Management tends to drive or control people (subordinates), whereas leadership creates scope for innovation and contributions for achievement absent of inhibitions introduced in hierarchical schemas as anticipated by Jaques in a requisite organization.[3] Daft, in the context of transformation and boundary-crossing individuals, provides a consolidated view that "Transformation leaders are characterised by the ability to bring about change, innovation, and entrepreneurship. Transformation leaders motivate followers not just to follow them personally but [also] to believe in the vision of corporate transformation, to recognise the need for revitalisation, to sign on for the new vision, and help institutionalise the new organisation process."[4]

Daft also asserts that transformation leaders build a coalition to guide the transformation process and work to develop a sense of teamwork among the participating group. Such a coalition should include people from all levels of the organization who can engage the commitment of others (within their company and/or organization) and successfully guide the transformation process (to the achievement of the realization of the business objectives).[5] The key words are *coalition* and *guide*, leading one to the thought that the manager perhaps seeks conformance whereas the leader seeks to create trusting relationships from which innovation arises and in which interpositional competition is not a factor. To allow confrontation, of course, is healthy to stimulate debate; however, experience has shown that it is important to guide resolution through the logic or strategy of the business endeavor and to avoid directly stating that an individual is right or wrong, as these set up power plays and point-scoring exercises that can be regressive.

Many in management have the notion that the absence of visible activity is somehow synonymous with lack of progress and linked closely with the idea of any form of consensual leadership. However, given the notion that change is a form of organizational game in pursuit of the business objective (in this case) within which one needs to consider the cultural dynamic, the need for sustained outcomes, and the opportunity for the leader to guide the coalition, then a form of federalism is unavoidable. However, the leadership results in this case have adequately demonstrated that the expression "less haste, more speed" has relevance, and time was not lost in delivery. To recall, the collective works in accordance with the common globalization strategy within and between the engaged organizations, and through this approach all participants balanced the mitigation of risk with the requirement for organizational performance. Those engaged from the Vodafone side that were not in my center team remained sufficiently motivated to engage and deliver substantially on a goodwill basis in addition to performing their normal day job.

The Performing Invisible Organization

The posited requisite (invisible and virtual) organization through which global relationships were developed became an environment within which the individual self-interest was manifested in working toward the collective globalization outcome, perhaps stimulated by a motivated engagement and contribution thereto. The horizontal organization that transcended the vertical hierarchies of the companies was nonhierarchical, which led to ideas being considered solely on merit and with no regard to the hierarchical position of the contributor. Good ideas are not solely the prerogative of management, and dare I say many of the best ideas probably may come from the extant team globally, not through the engagement of third parties; the latter, in fact, tend to aggravate global relationships.

The challenge for the leader is to guide the prioritization in consideration of the "pain-gain" logic (the level of difficulty of implementation versus the realizable benefit), knowing that the proposers will, with motivation, make it happen given that they are working their (ideally collective) ideas—a question in such circumstances of harnessing the energy rather than having to stimulate it. A leader allows the views of the quorum to flow and avoids the injection of personal fixed or preemptive views and ideas, focusing instead on the what and simultaneously accepting that there is "more than one way to skin a cat," as the saying goes—a difficult proposition for some in management positions or leadership roles.

The challenge then becomes the selection of the appointed leader and placement with the organizational structure to shape a performing organization pursuant to the company strategy and its required performance. Jaques clearly states, "The effective working-capacity [maturation level] of the corporate chief is far and away the most important factor determining the growth, contraction, or the stability of an organisation—contrary to the consensus belief that economic or market conditions produce those effects."[6] However, the same logic prevails for anyone in a position of management authority or leadership other than a CEO. Another related thought is that "leaders are made, not born, and how they develop is critical for organizational change." Rooke and Torbert discuss the seven transformations of leadership giving rise to the question of currency of level and the capacity of the leader to aspire to the relevant level for the role in this context.[7]

In discussing the paradigm espoused in this book leading to the performing organization with an acquaintance who is a business consultant, the initial response was that a serious limitation to that paradigm is that there are not many who have the skill and capacity to aspire to the demands of the role and thereafter to attract those who can engage and fulfill a given strategy. The response, of course, should be that the path to the future in this ever global world is pitted with situational challenge to which a performing organization must respond without diversion. Failure to recognize that in the appointment of leadership and instead opting to retain the status quo and operate in the comfort zone will assure a ho-hum performance, leading to an eventual downfall that impacts everybody. Such a choice is tantamount to an abdication of responsibility for which, unfortunately, the incumbent is likely to be compensated on exit, unlike those impacted in the organization—a perverse logic. A true leader of high integrity would accept that the peak of performance has passed, deferring instead to imparting wisdom and coaching individuals with more aligned skills but without the experience of the demands of the new paradigm.

Finally, in the emergent performing global and virtual (or invisible) organization, absent of preemption or prequalification, to which I was assigned the task of globalization and aggregation cost synergy benefits, inclusion was the order of the day, both within the Vodafone organization and those others featured in this recount of events. This was informally extended to key stakeholders, all those contributions and commitments that were crucial for success, the engagement by invitation of those in operating companies in my extended virtual management team, and in several organizations dealing at one stage with more than twenty of the Vodafone operating interests. I traveled the world extensively (the old-fashioned banker approach) as did my team and many others in the Vodafone operating companies and the partner organizations, all to assure a continuum of engagement, the acquisition of feedback, ideas for betterment and for the assurance of effective communication, particularly for the most distant entities. Interestingly, the greater the distance of the journey, the greater the impact and welcome, as was the residual benefit.

A relevant point from game theory is that you "cannot yield more from the game than you put in."[8] The period of profound learning recounted and reflected upon from the longitudinal experience in this book lends credence to the establishment of an alternative, new organizational paradigm that, notwithstanding its challenges, offers a solution to the management of the transitional continuum to globalization (or multilocation alignment)—the performing organization. This multiple interorganizational structure that led to Vodafone at the hub developed its own collective culture, despite the various backgrounds of all those engaged, within which there was a uniformity of objective and collective ambition. What followed was the emergence of a profound social network. The cultural alignment combined with the emergent individual and collective trust led to a substantive social capital that fueled the success. This social capital was perhaps unwittingly lost or "reset" through lack of insight by those who preferred a center-controlled organization that ran counter to all the best learning and practice documented herein and led to a lower-performing organization not representative of situational excellence.

In summary, leadership will prevail over control in the development of a performing transformational organization; however, the appointment of a relevant and natural leader is paramount!

Experiential Learning

A key factor in the success of the globalization initiative conveyed in this book is the notion of the journey paradigm. This must to be collectively self-driven in pursuit of the strategy and objectives, in contrast to seeking to specify and plan something for which the approach and outcome are uncertain. Just such an approach led to a number of counterintuitive outcomes that may otherwise have not been recognized or achieved.

Experiential combines the notion of experimentation to seek and define new and extended boundaries of capability and achievement from which organizational or experiential learning is forthcoming. It is through this approach that business and friendship relationships were established globally and in which the majority of people are necessarily boundary compliant; that is, they operate in accordance with set policies, processes, and practices—all reference for change would be seated in the status quo. Another group of people consists of the boundary pushers, that small number of individuals operating on the edge that identify clearly the need for change (transformational or otherwise). They see the importance of getting on with the task and of not being bounded in committees and approvals, all of which introduce delay but not necessarily an improvement in the quality of the outcome. A third group consists of those who are boundary spanning, also relatively few in number, who recognize the need to pursue the intuition or counterintuition of the boundary pushers yet empathize and align somewhat with the compliant mainstream. The boundary spanners, very important contributors, take the role of catalyst or bridge to invoke reality. Such roles and people emerge in practice; their classification is an empirical outcome and not by appointment. These various roles and interrelationships at the leadership level serve to simplify complex ideas for clarity of communication and ease of understanding.

The emergence of the horizontal and nonhierarchical virtual community while achieving a strong meta-influence over the operating entities also became a great setting for the exchange of ideas, wherein the merit of the idea, not the person, may be challenged. This type of exchange provided the stimulus for out-of-the-box or counterintuitive, innovative ideas and actions, all being experiential contributions resolved in the context of the vision and strategy.

An interesting adjunct to experiential learning is espoused by Senge et al., who posit that the "core capacity to access the future is presence," which they define as deep listening, of being open beyond one's preconceptions and historical ways of making sense.[9] They present a relevant metaphor that lends credence to an experiential approach:

> *It's common to say that trees come from seeds. But how could a tiny seed create a large tree? Seeds do not contain the resources to grow a tree. These must come from the medium or environment within which the tree grows. But the seed does provide something that is crucial: a place where the whole of the tree starts to form. As resources such as water and nutrients are drawn, the seed organises the process that generates growth. In a sense, the seed is a gateway through which the future possibility of the living tree emerges.[10]*

This metaphor can be related to the experiences and learning shared in this book: the "seed" may be considered analogous to me and the eventual direct center-led team; the "resources," the emergent social network or global virtual community (the invisible organization); the "living trees," the interorganizational relationships formed and the Lead OpCos grafted to the "seed" that together organize "the process that generates growth"—in this experience "growth" being synonymous with the aggregation cost synergies for Vodafone, perhaps the leaves on the metaphorical tree. The rate of growth is fueled by the "water and nutrients" that may equate to the rate of engagement in and the expansion of the nonhierarchical, cross-company, cross-organizational, horizontal social networks and the social capital; the global relationships; and the mutual experiential learning therein—altogether, a powerful learning experience.

Management and Leadership Development

Trying to determine the relevant management or leadership development attributes necessary for success in groundbreaking endeavors such as that discussed in this book is an interesting conundrum. I posit that, borne in this and prior experiences, change, and transformational change in particular, is something that one leads whereas management is something that is more a steady-state circumstance.

Management may be slowed down by relying on past practices or legacy, whereas leaders are drawn to the opportunities of the future; that is, the future (not seated in the image of the past) sets the going-forward agenda, and the obligation of the legacy is to adapt and move on. The depth of need regarding management is clearly impacted by the point in the market cycle, in this case for operator success in the telecom market in the 1990s, which saw rapid proliferation of operators and strong in-market growth in which success was relatively easy and failure difficult. In the 2000s, on the other hand, with the number of new operators in sharp decline, consolidation, and emerging market saturation all leading to intensity of competition, the converse is true: the prospect of failure in financial performance is elevated, and success is ever more challenging, if for no other reason than paradigms have to change and move. These are conditions in which leadership needs to take precedence over management.

Management in business, unlike other professions (medicine, law, military, aviation, etc.) has no recognized process through which to demonstrate individual management or leadership competence and capacity or potential. Rising up the hierarchical ladder is as much or perhaps more a matter of "being in the right place at the right time" than positive selection for role, a limitation being the eye of the beholder. The evidence would suggest that as one climbs the ladder, there is an increasing propensity to utilize external agencies (consultants) to bring remedy or direction, yet Jaques sees the (appointed) leaders themselves as setting the boundary of organizational performance.[11] It reminds me of my early days when people said that "you could not get fired for buying IBM or Digital" and now when it comes to transformational organizational changes arising for whatever reason, "you cannot get fired for engaging McKinsey," or so it seems. Is this approach demonstrative of management or leadership? Is it not the case that such outcomes are relatively self-fulfilling or stereotypical and perhaps out of context, all guided by the brief? Does this get the best from the extant and in this case global organization? What happened to the intellectual and social capital embedded in the organization?

For management and leadership to build a global social network within and/or between organizations, lead transformational change, and create a successful and sustained outcome, then surely it is a co-requisite to demonstrate one's own capacity for leadership through the development of and influence within one's own social network. Does the engagement of McKinsey actually deliver innovation and have sustainable and motivated outcomes? There is a school of thought that says no. Is such engagement demonstrative of leadership or competence in management? Many within the organization argue definitely not. Ultimately, the business is about people, and leadership is about delegation and empowerment at the point of greatest influence for positive outcomes, a point to which all the aforesaid discussion delivers a short circuit. The accrued intellectual and social capital embedded within an organization is ignored or improperly considered in deference to the pursuit of something totally economic or idealistic, the manifestation of which is a compromised or flawed outcome.

Having an effective social network within which one has strong business or personal relationships is not synonymous with control or micromanagement; to the contrary, through the development of such a network, an embedded common culture emerges from a common strategy; cultures of trust may develop, as this case demonstrated. It is difficult, however, to build global relationships if bounded by a leadership vision that is conformant with or aligned to a national, corporate, or, indeed, an inadequate cross-cultural experience in said leadership; this is particularly so in a globally dispersed services business such as a telecom operator. Where is the motivation for global relationships and the engagement therewith outside the HQ? After all, collaboration is implicit in the practice of meta-management, or the management of management;[12] and given that the operational management is in-country, relationships globally are a prerequisite for a positive meta-influence (and not rejection) toward aggregate success.

In transformational endeavors it is likely that ways forward breach the boundaries of current and past practice, and such counterintuitive rich outcomes are more likely to emerge from or be triggered by the engagement of a social network that transcends the operator boundaries within which positive relationships are maintained. Daft promotes the view that "each part of the [global] organisation can serve as an independent catalyst, bringing together unique elements with synergistic potential, perhaps other firms [for example, suppliers] or subsidiaries [and/or affiliates] from different countries to improve performance."[13]

The interpersonal and social skills of the leader are paramount. The social network and the emergent social capital therein is not a "tick in the box" exercise; rather it relies on integrity, chemistry, influence, and mutual trust, all of which may be developed only over time and not as an outcome of a single visit or the pronouncement, "I am in charge; read my lips." It further relies on embracing the views of key stakeholders and rationalizing individually or collectively as is appropriate to a converged view in the context of the agreed strategy; it is a people game, and you want them to engage and to play your game (the strategy) but not necessarily requiring it be done your way, that is, allowing flexibility in the in-country teams. Leaders allow, invite, and encourage debate, whereas managers may tend toward suppression, defaulting to command or control. Leaders are self-confident even in uncertain times, whereas managers place a greater reliance on the hierarchical position and, when pushed, default to "this is what I have been asked to do (by the boss)."

The merits of the journey paradigm in dealing with transformational change in uncharted waters are exemplified in this book; however, a leader would be comfortable with the proposition, whereas a manager would likely be less so. A leader can deal with and probably thrive in uncertainty in the evolutionary search for the new paradigm and the transition continuum thereto; the manager wants to somehow preplan what has yet to be discovered and create the perception of certainty and control. Yes, a sharp division in roles is asserted here, but this forces the debate on suitability and preparedness of appointees to lead transformational change. To be even more blunt, this is not about appointments made on tenure, he or she is a "good guy," safe pair of hands, worked with them in the past, same nationality, chosen to achieve a demographic balance; all such arguments are interesting but irrelevant. Such thinking is dated and likely will result in a mismatch between the appointee and his or her role; what is relevant is that a requisite appointment be made, which may be bonded by the level (Jaques language) of the CEO. Such global transformational assignments are not for political appointees but for someone who has the smarts and energy to develop and maintain a diverse, broad school of global relationships, or better still, who has in another role already done so.

This book has recorded a transformational journey that was anything but a shift between two states, the before and after. Because it was an experiential journey for which there was no industry precedence, I have characterized it as a transition continuum, comfortable for a leader but challenging for a manager. Nortier (p32) quotes William Bridges, who even in the mid-1980s considered that "like the rest of us, executives have been wise about the mechanics of change and stupid about the dynamics of transition. That stupidity is dooming many of their [transformational] change efforts to failure." Nortier himself says that transition "belongs to the realm of the subjective" and "is a process internal to the individual, slow and progressive, not demarcated in time and directly related to what the individual is living through."[14] The context for these comments appears to be with respect to moving between the present and a second predetermined state, whereas the complexities espoused herein further compound such issues, adding to the dimension of challenges for the leadership. What is clear concerning these views and the experiential learning is that leadership needs to engaged and to be seen doing so with vigor and commitment to build the diversity and depth of the social network and the ensuing relationships. These relationships may range from personal to general awareness through the grapevine, rather than engaging with and seeking to execute transformational endeavors through a third party.

The question remains as to where and how one develops the requisite skills and capabilities to effectively operate in a global domain, leveraging a range of relevant global relationships in the common collective interests. Absent of any quick fix, I can only posit that such skills are developed through maturity and a diversity of operational cross-cultural experience within which the manager or aspiring leader can directly evidence where he or she actually made the difference. In my view, many individuals, even of senior ranking, have been swept along by inertia having done the job and claim success by association, yet have not taken a direct in-line risk themselves that lead to a transformational paradigm outcome in practice. So I leave this debate to be continued yet record the fact that this is unequivocally an issue of relevance in this increasingly transparent and globally diverse world.

The experiences discussed in this book would lead me to believe that being tough and assertive are not the formula for success. Being a leader, visionary, strategic in approach but with a balance for the here and now, consultative, persuasive, cross-cultural by background, and accepted as a natural leader in contrast to being an appointee are all relevant attributes. For the magnitude and diversity of such transformational tasks discussed herein, we are perhaps, in the language used by Jaques, discussing a rising Level 6 as a minimum, and in that of Rooke and Torbert, a Strategist or Alchemist, meaning by their sample individuals in the top 5%.[15]

Let us return to Senge et al. and specifically what I see as their reinforcing views, what I describe as modern leadership:

> As models of leadership shift from organisational hierarchies with leaders at the top to more distributed, shared networks, a lot changes. For those networks to work with real awareness, many people will need to be deeply committed to cultivating their capacity to serve what's seeking to emerge. That's why cultivation, "becoming a real human being," really is the primary leadership issue of our time, but on a scale never required before. It's a very old idea that may actually hold the key to a new age of "global democracy."[16]

A personal reflection on the "good old days," to which they are so often referred; at that time hierarchy was everything and in many cultures, national or corporate, it still is. Today, however, and not just to the thoughtful person, although the hierarchy is interesting, it may not be defining for the ensuing actions or direction. Position alone cannot overcome the extant cultural mind-set in the absence of a reasoned strategy, logic, or the stimulation of collective motivation. Interestingly, a closing view from Senge et al. is that "what distinctive power does exist at the top of hierarchies is usually skewed toward power to destroy rather than to build. In a few weeks a CEO (management) can destroy trust (and therefore social capital) and distributed knowledge that took years to build."[17]

The Benefits of Age and Experience

At this point, as no doubt the reader has already determined, I do not physically fall into the category of "young man." This leads to the notion that I therefore do not need to theorize on the benefits of age and experience but can instead recount from the accrued knowledge and experience that in some instances may transcend to wisdom. However, not to make the mistake of anchoring myself in the past, its value is that it provides an excellent base for the inquiring mind to dig into and experiment for the future, a part of which has been shared in the experiential outtakes recounted in this book. On one aspect I am irrevocably fixed—achieving success; on everything else I remain open and flexible, subject to it being legal. Venturing into the domain of the hitherto considered impossible is, of course, the most exciting opportunity and a chance to gain new knowledge.

I am at the stage of personal development wherein it is more relevant to delegate and mentor than to attempt to "steal" the glory of the achievement of others. I would posit that it is important that in your personal inventory you have the range of experiences that will positively equip you to guide the team to new levels of challenge and success in pursuit of leadership and excellence. My experiences suggest that a mature experienced leader, in contrast to manager, should do the following:

▶ Push the boundaries of organizational experimentation, while being of good standing; accede to failure as required and be receptive to the contributions of others, a positive team play.
▶ Delegate and recruit the heir apparent on whom personal development should be focused to move the individual's motivation and enthusiasm to greater levels of achievement.
▶ Do not create an isolated center organization; instead, intertwine resources from those entities over which you seek to have implied or meta-influence.
▶ Maintain a currency of operational knowledge in the center team through engagement of the principal stakeholders and their relevant team principals.
▶ Engage said key stakeholders in the decision cycle for global strategies; after all they that to implement the strategies for the realization of the economic benefit (at least in this case).
▶ Engage face-to face, regardless of the geographic diversity, and carry the message of the transformation, and accept, not necessarily with the obligation to implement, all input and feedback offered.
▶ Avoid confrontation, as opposed to debate, in open forums; be a diplomat and take such controversial matters offline in advance. Do not be afraid of hierarchal asymmetry in the intra- or interorganizational relationships. Be bold to assure being connected with the seats of influence and control; it can only be to your benefit. Organizational hierarchy is interesting only when it supports what you are tasked to achieve; its lack of relevant functioning cannot be used as an excuse for failure.
▶ Attract and recruit the best and, ideally, those whose grasp of the topic is better than yours, so as to embed sustainable strength to your team. Being recognized, at the group executive level in your own and partner organizations, as a cross-cultural and cross-entity global catalyst for performance will enhance your and the teams' social capital and deliver committed support far in excess of any formally visible deployment.
▶ Seek counterintuitive outcomes, as they are likely to differ from the performance of the organization; in this context intuition is bounded by prior knowledge, experience, or awareness and may therefore miss the competitive advantage. Be aware, to repeat an earlier message, that the social network has to be relevant and requisite in the context of the objective, which means that all key stakeholders must be engaged for success, not just those whom you like and get along with.
▶ Finally, be bold enough to recognize when you have passed your useful "life" in a role, and make way for younger person. Failure is to not recognize where you are in the cycle; wisdom is to take stock and move to other roles and continue to leverage your accrued knowledge, experience, and experientially derived wisdom—of course, to be applied to the future and not anchored in the past. As is said about financial investments,

"Historical performance is no guide to the future performance"; build on the past, but do not try to relive it, as the passing of time will have changed the context anyway. In this way your global social networks and the relationships therein will survive, of course, the assumption being that you were deemed to have integrity and trust.

In conclusion, I recently asked a Jaques devotee to carry out an assessment of me just as a reference or baseline for others who choose to study more closely the experiential leadership approaches and the journey discussed in this book. To quote Mattias Forsbäck, vice president of organization strategy, Ericsson AB:

> The basic principle of having the possibility to succeed in a role is to have the right capability. This is primarily built of knowledge/experience, values or commitments and potential capability. The potential capability matures with each individual and the larger potential capability the more complex roles you have possibility to succeed in. Both the level of capability and complexity of roles and organisations can be measured in absolute levels—Stratum. Smaller companies on stock markets are typically led by CEO's with a capability at Stratum 4 up to the largest organisations like GE and US Armed Forces headed at Stratum 8.

> Professor Christopher Ibbott has in his career history in Vodafone held corporate level positions which equals to head of a business unit in a multi national or global company (Stratum 5). By driving the globalisation of the supply chain, he did not only transform his own role but also how the company and industry operated as such. This goes beyond the complexity of the formal role and could not have been done successfully without excessive potential capability. Such capability is normally shown by COO's or heads of divisions (Stratum 6) in these kinds of companies.

> Having worked close to Professor Ibbott, and during a longer period of time screening his capability, he has been found to have a potential capability at Stratum 6 and is likely to have been so for at least the last 10 years.[18]

Culture and Stereotypes

Culture is a complex topic, especially so in a globalizing endeavor wherein there is an n-way dimensional transformational change in the intra- and interorganizational relationships that emerge in pursuit of the financial objective to realize aggregation cost synergies. A challenge that strengthens the merit of the approaches taken, at least from the Vodafone side, was that there were differing equity holdings among the entities that positively engaged in and contributed to the success of what has now been documented. From a cultural or corporate heritage perspective companies (or Vodafone equity interests) that engaged in the globalization initiative had simultaneously dealt with being heralded under the Vodafone corporate umbrella and, for many, the brand. This dimension combined with all other aspects of culture suggested elsewhere contributed a period of turbulence in individual and company cultural identity; however, the espoused globalization paradigm transformation forged ahead and was not unduly encumbered by such turbulence, perhaps attesting to the strength of that emergent and developing collective culture and its motivation. Daft (2001, p. 501) states that "each part of the (transnational) organisation can serve as an independent catalyst, bringing together unique elements with synergistic potential, perhaps other firms (for example, suppliers) or subsidiaries (and/or affiliates) from different countries to improve performance".

The objective was never, at least as discussed in Chapters 3 and 4, to invoke a center-controlled organizational paradigm; it may have been suicidal to have pursued that approach. What was clear, however, was the need to converge activities hitherto local to a homogeneous global level and polarized interorganizational level—the sense of transformation. Having recognized that operational matters should be local, with consideration of any aggregation imperatives of the cultural diversity, the meta-influence or "pull" was to be focused on the strategy and, from an interorganizational perspective, accept the asymmetry and timing of benefits arising.

It is important to emphasize that we are not discussing here solely the "home" culture, be it corporate or country, but also that of the organization with whom business was to be conducted globally in this new and initially undefined paradigm. Paramount therefore was to focus on the "what" and be flexible in the first instance with the "how," recognizing that there may an opportunity for future convergence by agreement of the parties; the interorganizational relationship and conduct or strategic level was the primary focus. Engagement in this way with a clear vision and supporting strategy, taking input and guidance from the affected parties toward the strategy and not interfering in local operational matters, effectively created a cultural bridge that transcended all engaged cultures.

Again, this was seated in experiential learning toward a paradigm for the telecom industry mobile network infrastructure supply for which there was no evident precedence. It ran counter to intuition, yet organizationally it was effective in operation and financial performance for Vodafone. This virtual organization, although invisible in existence, extent, and operation, developed through practice its own collective and performing culture. The journey paradigm approach that was taken, an informally structured grouping of overlapping and cross-interested clusters of common interest, did not conform to any precedent stereotype and is therefore posited as one that should be added to the portfolio of executive choices. With the IOS we bridged the differences of time and distance through which open disclosure with minimal content confidentiality, borne in trust and mutual confidence within and between organizations, was embedded into the collective culture.

Then came the change, or even reversal, as documented in Chapter 5, and a default to a classical stereotype, center control. It was as though individuals and teams detached and void of currency in operating experience somehow were better able to lead than those already in role. As discussed, this approach did not meet with favor among informed and engaged key stakeholders, whose goodwill had been vested in the extant informal organization. This move could not be considered strategic; it ignored or did not seek to understand what existed and was financially performing beyond expectation. It instead deferred to preemptive stereotype absent of fit-for-purpose considerations beyond ego and culture, equating somewhat to a controlling paradigm, which was ill advised.

The overall organizational change under the One Vodafone initiative involved more than this hitherto global stream of activity, yet the successful history over many years was discounted or, dare I say, ignored in preference to the mandated organizational stereotype. My role was developed toward the same aggregation synergy objective yet evolved and developed around seats of control, which in some cultures is the norm, even though those same cultures, albeit with different people, were functioning well under the extant regime. We were not moving from a standing start but had traction and momentum combined with results. Although prior attempts were made, and failed, to formalize the extant organization, the key stakeholders, albeit to no avail with the dissenting majority, preferred now to pursue such formalization.

The resetting of the accrued social capital was easy to do with such a central move, and the ensuing organizational changes developed in the classical and independent way with directed third parties. I doubt that the social capital can be regained quickly, if at all. History, of course, will be the judge, although further changes to centralization have taken place since April 2005. The purpose of this book is not to sit in judgment but through this disclosure to share the counterintuitive outcomes of this experiential (organization)al learning for the benefit of the scholars and business practitioners of the future who may be faced with the challenges of true globalization—*experiential* here meaning the combination of a journey, experiment, and experience.

7 Conclusions

Going Global Is a Transformational Journey

Amid the onset of the forthcoming and formative complexities that were to beset Vodafone in 1998 and with firm economic aspirations to be realized, what was to be the way forward? How would you have delivered the aggregation cost synergies required and structured the organization to deliver them? Hindsight is wonderful; however, learning from success and failure remains vital.

There was in the beginning no extant and obvious organization within Vodafone to take on the leadership of the endeavor. The assignment, for the aggregation cost synergies from the mobile network infrastructure investments, came to me at the end of 1998 as an adjunct to my primary role (IT and program management director in Vodafone Limited) because the UK had critical mass with Ericsson in what was to become the pathfinder supplier cluster engaging in-country operating companies with that same supplier interest. Although there were relationships locally with Ericsson, there had been no attempted global business aggregation, as also true at the beginning for Nokia, Nortel, and Siemens. There was a multiplicity of cultural divisions, in part because many of the later engaging Vodafone entities originated outside the company (AirTouch and Mannesmann), which for them was a new collective identity.

To contemplate a preemptive plan to navigate one's way through this maze to a successful outcome may perhaps have been like living in cloud cuckoo land, and we did not pursue that path. Whatever was to be the emergent paradigm to which or through which we would transition, transformational change was inevitable. Given the absence of precedence within the industry, a lack of transformational process, and no extant transition management, no amount of planning would have enhanced the prospect of a sustainable and successful outcome, as documented to be the case. This book has sought to present the experiential learning from such an endeavor as input for those so challenged in the future.

We were to embark on and adapt to an experiential or process-oriented journey.[1] It is difficult now to envisage that such an industry-leading action with incumbent complexities could be approached any other way. Or perhaps it may be seen as a metaphor, to quote Morgan, "a way of thinking and a way of seeing."[2] To exemplify, Orlikowski and Hofman contrast the European and Trukese journey approaches.[3] The European begins with a plan whose effort throughout the "voyage" is to remain "on course." Dealing with the unexpected would require first to alter the plan and to then respond accordingly as envisaged by Lewin's three-stage change model of "unfreezing," "change," and "refreezing."[4] Bevan makes reference to the interpretation of this characterization as a destination-oriented journey metaphor,[5] this process being viewed as a "rational, structured and linear journey."[6] On the other hand, the Trukese begin with an objective rather than a plan, set off toward said objective, and respond to conditions in an ad hoc fashion through utilization of information provided by the wind, the waves, the tide, etc. They steer accordingly with all effort directed toward whatever is necessary to reach the objective of the process-oriented journey.

Bevan, expanding further on the work of Inns, states that the "process-oriented" journey is essentially an explorative process where clear outcomes are not known in advance and that change is cyclical, with no arrival or final "homecoming," namely:

> *Change is not as programmable and predictable as Lewin-type models imply, since repercussions on different parts cannot always be accurately forecast. The development of the journey metaphor in relation to organisational change from a destination-oriented model allows important, but previously hidden elements of the journey to come to the fore: uncertainty, circularity, exploration, and unpredictability.[7]*

Change cannot and should not be "frozen," nor should it be viewed as a linear sequence of events within a linear time period; instead, it should be viewed as a continuous process.[8] Macredie and Sandom indicate that different supporters of this perspective include the view that change is a continuous process aimed at aligning an organization with its environment and is best achieved through many small-scale incremental changes that, over time, can amount to a major organizational transformation.[9]

Orlikowski discusses another interesting dimension of change—"situated change"—that is, "organisational transformation is seen here [in the situated change context] to be an ongoing improvisation enacted by organisational actors [individuals or teams] trying to make sense of and act coherently in the world"; such circumstances exactly parallel this program, in that the organizational changes to effected here are [or were] not planned, a point also challenged by Orlikowski in the same reference.[10]

Bevan discusses the work of Bridges, who asserts that a major reason why change projects do not succeed is the failure to take account of the impact of transition.[11] Bridges distinguishes between *change*, which is situational, and *transition*, which is the psychological process people go through to come to terms with the new situation. He defines three phases to the transition process: an *ending*, which leaves the old situation behind; a *neutral zone* between the old and new reality; and a new *beginning* if people have first made an ending and spent some time in the neutral zone. Change will not succeed unless transition takes place. Transformational change is not about espousing a new organization and a migration will somehow emerge from the status quo; the adaptive nature of the process described in this book demonstrates the focus on the in-between state through encouraging those affected to immerse in and embrace themselves in the propositions (neutral zone) of sustainable outcomes (ending)—a form of self-navigation rather than imposed ending.

Nutt and Backoff propose that a vision can provoke uncertainty that leads people to resist; and to cope with change, a leader initiates the change process by calling on a development team to uncover barriers that can block the vision.[12] Although not clarified, the contextual assumption drawn is limited to that of a single organization and does not appear to anticipate the interorganizational or virtual contexts discussed in this book. Nutt and Backoff conclude by declaring that four aspects of organizational (not interorganizational) transformation have been neglected in the literature: the role of a vision, uncovering barriers and issue tensions, ways to fashion win-win actions for a core issue tension, and uncovering and aligning actions for related issue tensions. They assert that a vision provides the trigger and should offer "a strategic and inspiring picture of what the organisation can become, indicating whom the organisation wants to serve, how this will be done, and the regard and image these actions can produce."[13]

Finally, they comment that a transformation is more likely (to be success-ful) when leaders empower (or delegate to) key people and trust them to find ways to realize a vision through development team activities (or virtual workstreams, in my case study); specifically, with respect to leaders, they say that in their approach leaders should be "on tap, but not on top." The experimental approaches that were taken toward the globalization of the intra- and interorganizational business relationships, together with experiential organizational learning outcomes discussed in this book, have demonstrated in practice successful new paradigms in environments of far greater com-plexity than Nutt and Backoff appear to have anticipated or considered.[14] Embedding matters of rationale and progressive thoughts and, through the leadership, delegated actions, set in the context of the vision and strategy of those affected by the strategy and who responsible for its operationalization, we emerged more productive, progressive, and counterintuitive to effect a positive outcome.

To change an organization's culture, you must first change people's behavior. Charismatic leadership may grab headlines, but steady and consis-tent leadership actually results in changes to the bottom line.[15] Further, Daft posits that transformation leaders are "characterised by the ability to bring about change, innovation, and entrepreneurship" and that "transformation leaders motivate followers not just to follow them personally but (also) to believe in the vision of corporate transformation, to recognise the need for revitalisation, to sign on for the new vision, and help institutionalise the new organisation process." He also states that transformational leaders build a coalition to guide the transformation process and work to develop a sense of teamwork among the participating group. Such a coalition should include people from all levels of the organization who can engage the commitment of others (within their company and/or organization) and successfully guide the transformation process (to the achievement of the realization of the business objectives).[16]

In the recount in this book I was the leader through the formative stages of this journey, who, together with my cross-cultural direct team, was supported by and worked with and through a virtual management team drawn from the key stakeholders in the Vodafone operating companies. This was shown to create a strong leadership forum that assured consistency with strategic direction, executable and sustainable economic outcomes in the fulfillment of and contribution to the stated Vodafone Group aspirations.

Given that the extent of the emergent nonhierarchical virtual and horizontal organization, which effectively bridged the cultural and local hierarchical company complexities, was invisible save the economic delivery to Vodafone, the organization can certainly be claimed to have aspired to the teachings of Trahant et al. and Daft. It reflected, in fact, a constructive yet collaborative approach with a strong leadership, with an effective social network to guide the transformational transition journey continuum. The outcomes were demonstrably sustainable over the longitudinal period and in aspiring to the requisite organization satisfied the opportunities for innovation and the adaptation of the invisible, informal virtual network organization to achieve the Vodafone aggregation cost synergies.

Successful outcomes often appear to have been easily attained through an obvious process, yet to those engaged in the experience they are anything but. Management tend to sit in judgment of the "what" and, perhaps to their peril, discount, take credit for, or ignore or fail to understand the basis upon which such success was realized. The case here espouses the need for leadership for such complex and transformational endeavors seated in the context of a process-oriented journey metaphor. A leader delegates to and engages key stakeholders and incumbent but hitherto invisible talent in the organization and accepts and adapts to the ideas of others concerning execution, subject only to compliance with the agreed vision and strategy; in this case, the strategy is globalization, and the outcome being sought by Vodafone and the chosen partners is aggregation cost synergies.

Regarding management style, one should differentiate between "being a driving force" (leader: setting vision and strategy) and "being a driven force" (manager: immersed in tasks, objectives, and control). The objective outlined here was not primarily to achieve cost reduction but to stimulate and motivate leverage in the extant Vodafone globally dispersed organization in its new collective context (the changes after merger and acquisition being the principal but not only changes) moving toward the aggregation cost synergies as a sustainable outcome through means not understood or predetermined. Through experiential practice the roles of many individuals in the Vodafone operating interests engaged in an unwritten adjunct to their roles and responsibilities that extended their local tasks into the global domain, often without true recognition; yet they were all positive catalysts to a significant transformational change without whom what is written could not have happened. All of this was seated in individual goodwill and that of individuals in the Ericsson, Nokia, Nortel, and Siemens organizations.

What is reported in this book was unique, counterintuitive, and successful; the formalization of the economic agenda was fixed, but the organizational means of achieving the economic goals was flexible and adaptive through the process-oriented journey. The particular contextual circumstances included the following:

▶ The uncertainty of being an industry leader
▶ An amalgam of cultural (in the broadest sense) complexities
▶ A focus on positively leveraging the organization (in contrast to a focus on cost reduction)
▶ Virtual dynamic formation of a community of boundary-crossing individuals both within and between organizations
▶ The emergence of a community culture seated in the social network leading to the accrual of social capital
▶ The existence of situated change or disruptive events

Given the experimental and experiential learning agenda, the transformations being sought were realized through a transition continuum. The transformational organizational changes were incremental but nevertheless progressive, an informal invisible organization save the economic results (within and between several organizations with a global footprint, all aspiring to a shared global business relationship with Vodafone)—in all a leadership pull, not a management push.

The concept of "going global is a journey" and this new stereotype will bring abundant joy to the true leaders out there and all who work with them; however, it will bring serious discomfort to those hierarchically oriented managers placed in such circumstances seeking to aspire to the full potential of the organization. Chapter 5 portrays the resetting of social capital through the termination of the experiential journey, as perhaps a lesson in which knowledge can be extracted in the differences between leadership and management. Perhaps (entrepreneurial) leaders are born and managers are trained, leading to the notion of innovative performance in the former circumstances and compliant execution in the latter. Do not be locked in to third-party, set-piece stereotypes; consider the journey approach, and be prepared to experiment and aspire to the requisite outcome. Surprise yourself, and engage with your team directly for the organizational development in fulfillment of the agreed strategies. Delegate to the team in preference to third parties who may disengage and demotivate your team.

Going Global Means Going Beyond International

At the commencement of this journey Vodafone and those organizations with whom they engaged were all international companies—they were geographically dispersed but did not operate as a homogeneous whole. Such established operations are more likely to operate in the image and under the control of the home company (HQ). The transnational model, on the other hand, is an organization extended to the international arena and is used by large multinational companies with subsidiaries (and/or equity interests, in this case study) to exploit both global and local advantages; it represents the most current thinking about the kind of structure needed by complex global organizations.[17]

Daft clarifies that achieving coordination, a sense of participation and involvement by subsidiaries (or equity interests), and a sharing of information, new technologies, and customers requires a multidimensional form of structure. The transnational model therefore is more than just an organizational chart but a state of mind, a set of values, and a shared desire to make a worldwide learning system (or, perhaps, global objective) work. In such organizations, "each part of the [transnational] organisation can serve as an independent catalyst, bringing together unique elements with synergistic potential, perhaps other firms [for example, suppliers] or subsidiaries [or equity interests] from different countries to improve performance."[18]

Although these points address the model, they do not define the organizational structure approach or the transition approach from the present multi-organization international state to such a transnational model. However, the experiential journey in this case, aimed at globalization strategy in the supply chain stream for mobile network infrastructure to achieve global aggregation cost synergies, did aspire to the aforesaid characteristics. Interestingly, the end point in this discussion was not just a transnational outcome within the Vodafone organization, at one stage addressing over twenty equity operating interests, but it also impacted the business organization within and between Ericsson, Nokia, Nortel, and Siemens as they all aligned globally. I suspect that the outcome demonstrated in this book both confirms and extends the thinking espoused by Daft.

Global boundaries between companies, markets, and people have become irrevocably blurred.[19] A multinational structure is one that creates a federation of national entities stemming from a single parent. A global organization is one in which the world is treated as an integrated whole organized around a strong headquarters that focuses on efficiencies at the global scale. A transnational organization is neither centralized nor decentralized but contains aspects of each of the other two strategies.[20] In a transnational structure, the parent organization may centralize certain core processes and/or activities. Henry Wendt, when he was CEO of SmithKline Beecham, offered this explanation:[21]

The difference in outlook between transnationals and multinationals [international] is the difference between a globe and a map. The surface of a globe has neither a beginning nor an end, neither a centre nor a periphery; it is a continued integrated whole. A map has a definite centre, peripheral places, and remote corners; it is a discontinuous, hierarchical fragment. And for the traditional multinational, the home market and the headquarters stand at the centre of the map and send out expectations to progressively less important provinces. In sum, the transnational corporations view the world as one vast, essentially seamless market in which all decisions are grounded solely in the desire to gain a global competitive advantage.

The evolving boundaryless solution, founded in the transnational format, might best be described as glocal, because it aims to merge a global strategy with respect for local presence.[22] The glocal company utilizes local control but also calls for central integration and economies of scale; at least, that is the theory. What has been demonstrated in this book conforms to what has been stated in the literature, although, as discussed, the intra- and interorganizational outcomes were the product of an experiential journey in pursuit of economic goals and not a preemptive organizational design exercise. The presumption, therefore, is that the inclusive journey approach in pursuing, in this case a shared and multi-organizational strategy of globalization, did respect through its engagement the local presence, to the point of the resetting of the social capital (discussed in Chapter 5). Having characterized elsewhere the mobile telecom business as an in-country service business and transactions and operations aimed to the target aggregate cost synergies, entity clusters within Vodafone impacted by a decision were consulted in advance of confirmation, and in the Lead OpCo extended model center or global operational intra- and interorganizational business responsibilities, were assigned on behalf of their cluster and the center function.

There is an underlying presumption in the discussion of organizational models of an absoluteness of control, meaning 100% owned subsidiaries or entities; as discussed, this was not the case for the Vodafone equity interests, the percentages of which varied throughout the longitudinal period, yet the journey approach taken and structure was such as to continue to motivate their engagement and contributions in the collective. Additionally, the aforesaid organizational model notions appear to assume center control and stimulation of activities throughout the network of companies, which was not the case here. Although there was a mutual recognition and agreement to leverage the economies of scale through the alignment globally to a homogeneous interorganizational whole, the center role (undertaken by me and my direct team) took the position of a center-led paradigm in preference to center control. That is, vision, strategy, and governance were at the center, and all operational aspects of the interorganizational relationships were at the periphery toward the end-customer, meaning the operating companies were all "bounded" by the strategy.

The outcome was the emergence of a virtual and nonhierarchical informal organization that bridged the vertical hierarchies of the in-country operations. I was the assigned Vodafone leader working with my cross-cultural center team together with and through the Lead OpCos, the various vendor-specific operator clusters, and the global leaders and teams of Ericsson, Nokia, Nortel, and Siemens. There was no sense of control, which established conditions akin to those of the requisite organization as anticipated by Jaques. My center team initially included individuals joining on a secondment basis from the Vodafone operating companies; some individuals joined an MBA program in addition to the demands of their global roles. The Lead OpCos and selected others, critical to this model, formed part of the center-led virtual leadership team. Why pay attention to Jaques at all? According to Kleiner, Jaques's ideas may be useful in predicting not only which companies will be profitable but which midlevel managers in any company will make the best CEOs twenty years hence.[23] Kleiner also notes that

Jaques's theory is probably invaluable for anyone trying to drive profitable transformation at the business-unit level.

The fact is that in the transnational (or global) informal and virtual organizational structure that emerged, the notion of control over said resources was nonexistent. There was no center control in the period leading to the resetting of social capital, yet the Vodafone organization worked as a homogeneous whole in the interorganizational business relationships. This virtual organization, on the other hand, was to exercise a meta-influence in its mode of operation to assure executable outcomes for those activities and tasks leading to collective aggregation cost synergies that leveraged the sum of the group. Any local in-country requirements that had or may have applicability to others in the future were also acceded to a global level in the interests of group leverage.

This was another counterintuitive characteristic of the Vodafone community or social network, wherein locally the goal was not to compete with what had been established globally but to work in support of it. This characteristic likely was the reason for success because the Vodafone community collectively built the global organizational structure within which trust emerged; the way of working was not externally imposed. A definition of trust posited by Ring and Van de Ven is an individual's confidence in the goodwill of the others in a given group (the virtual social network) and the belief that the others will make efforts consistent with the group's goals.[24] Volkoff et al. state that boundary-spanning roles (within and between organizations) must be filled with entrepreneurial risk takers whose willingness to try something new can provide the necessary flexibility.[25]

According to Faucheux, collaboration is implicit in the practice of meta-management, or the management of management.[26] The dynamics of virtual organizing are closely tied to self-organizing, in making sense of one's action through elucidation of the experience of the actors (individuals) themselves—who are those best situated for doing so. Faucheux then states that the very logic of virtual organizing drives toward the longer term and toward more responsible relations with the environment. Of interest too is Mowshowitz's theory of a virtual organization (as the informal and virtual social network) expressed as a set of principles for meta-managing (the influence of the horizontal virtual organization spanning the local in-country hierarchies) goal-oriented activity (realization for Vodafone of aggregation cost synergies) based on a categorical split between task requirements and their satisfiers.[27] In this view the essence of virtual organization is the systematic ability to switch satisfiers in a decision environment of bounded rationality; the management of such switching in this book was the established supplier-specific global forums. The notion of reassigning virtual workstreams was an accepted and positive practice always done in the cluster interest.

Lipparini and Fratocchi note an emergence of transnational organizational architectures (TOA) in which value-generating activities are distributed among different countries and actors (individuals), then recomposed at the corporate level without losing efficiency.[28] They discuss the concept of a central individual of high relational intensity and with interfirm architecture management (or boundary crossing) and leveraging functions; this would broadly equate to my own role. The strategic roles they propose are those of global scanner, relationship builder, competencies combiner, functional coordinator, system integrator, and strategic orchestrator. Finally, they point out that TOAs are characterized as metastructures that embrace the fabric of the external relationship; they have organizational and geographic boundaries, which can rapidly be redefined, as can focal points and centers of excellence (Lead OpCos).

Wiesenfeld et al. have said that organizational identification may be the critical glue linking virtual workers and organizations.[29] Through its impact on employee's motivations, organizational identification facilitates coordination and control. The strength of identification determines some critical beliefs and behaviors: interpersonal trust, desire to remain with the organization, willingness to cooperate with others accept organizational goals as their own, willingness to perform extra-role behaviors. It is, therefore, important to identify factors that create and sustain identification of virtual employees, recognizing that the determinants of identification may differ from those of nonvirtual employees.

What has been demonstrated with support from the extant literature is that the complexities of the experiential intra- and interorganizational structures that emerged experientially during the journey transition continuum are new and yet requisite for the situational context. Although there was complexity in narrative, this was not so in practice, given the delegative nature of its operation in preference to control. Through the delegation the complexities were distilled to simplicity from a leadership perspective, as the leaders to whom the tasks were assigned were obliged together with their virtual team to the complexities and dynamics for those tasks and responsibilities they accepted. The differentiation of these virtual and informal organizational structures as either transnational (or global) or international has been shown with the supporting rationale for the outcome rather than the design.

The success through the social network and the accrued social capital in this motivated, center-led model that bridged an amalgam of cultures to form a collective culture was clear; the internal financial aggregation cost synergy objectives were surpassed and delivered by and through Vodafone's in-country operating interests. I certainly did not assert direct control over the applied resources in this globalization endeavor nor did I seek to, yet the individual and collective interest within Vodafone and between Ericsson, Nokia, Nortel, and Siemens achieved the desired outcome. Control, therefore, is not always essential to performance in transnational stand-alone and linked organizational structures; in fact, perhaps to the contrary. Collective and distributed or delegated virtual leadership and the ensuing flexible structures provided for a motivated engagement and sustainable outcomes and deliveries. The virtual organization formed was an outcome, not a design, and was informal and a significant benefactor of the goodwill of all concerned. This is a case example of a new organizational stereotype for the consideration of academics and business leaders alike in *going beyond international*.

Going Global Means Working Together

There are three critical factors of a company's IT (and IS) infrastructure that management should assess. "Connecting" is the degree to which IT platforms link information sources, media, locations, and users (globally). "Sharing" (within and between organizations) makes possible coordinated effort and therefore the benefits associated with teamwork, integration, and extended scope. And, finally, "structuring" holds the most potential for the strategic exploitation of information (eRelationship), meaning structure is created by information about information.[30]

In the "informed" organization, all individuals have access to all the necessary information to perform their jobs and are empowered to perform tasks previously done by their supervisors. Management (or aspiring leaders) therefore must shift their orientation from controlling to providing counsel, a potentially perceived "power shift."[31] It has been argued that substantial economic waste occurs arising from information systems that are (independently) developed and either unused or unused by the very people for whom they were designed to assist.[32] The interests of the application developers and the line managers who must implement the IS must be aligned; perhaps, stating this point differently, the developers must align their work product to the perceived needs of the line managers and users to facilitate team success.

In the Vodafone-Ericsson situation the interorganizational IS, eRelationship, needed by objective to aspire primarily to the strategic interorganizational requirements while leaving open the option to localize the in-country interorganizational use. In their case study Yetton et al. report an organizational change in which there was a particular interaction of organizational, individual, and technological factors for which IT was an initial catalyst for that change.[33] At each stage of the evolution of the change, a solution to the next problem was found or the next opportunity taken. This is a dynamic that aligns with the notion that "it is what managers do, not what they plan, that explains their success." Yetton et al. conclude that the continual adaptation of technology through individual mastery and organizational learning and the management of risk were central to achieving a strategic fit (or outcome) in which IT became embedded in the firm's core business processes, all of which was realized through an incremental change process.

Burn and Barnett (p. 216) define virtual organizations as electronically networked organizations that transcend conventional organizational boundaries with linkages that may exist within and between organizations.[34] According to Schein, the concept of virtual organizational culture is the degree to which members of a (virtual) community have common shared values and beliefs.[35] Tushman and O'Reilly note that organizational cultures that are accepting of technology, highly decentralized, and change oriented are more likely to embrace virtuality and proactively seek these opportunities within and without the organization.[36] Burn and Barnett (p. 216) also note that virtual culture is hence a perception of the entire virtual organization held by its stakeholder community and operationalized in choices and actions that result in a feeling of *globalness* with respect to value (and information) sharing and time-space arrangement. Sieber and Griese state that the virtual organization is recognized as a dynamic system, and hence one wherein traditional hierarchical forms of management control may not apply, about which little is written.[37]

Dyer et al. outline the difference between the traditional *arm's-length model* of sourcing, one in which any form of commitment is avoided, with the *partner-model* of supplier management, or Japanese-style partnerships. The conclusion is that the latter model results in superior performance because partnering firms do the following:[38]

▶ *Share more information* and are better at coordinating interdependent tasks
▶ Invest in *dedicated or relationship-specific assets* that lower costs, improve quality, and speed product development
▶ Rely on *trust to govern the relationship*, a highly efficient governance mechanism that minimizes transaction costs

Research indicates that rather than employ a "one-size-fits-all" strategy for sourcing, firms should think strategically about supply chain management; in this context the chosen partner-model was appropriate, given the Vodafone business relationship with Ericsson and subsequent such global partners. The combination of these partners represented significant collective global expenditure, prohibitive switching costs, and a level of risk in moving to alternative suppliers.

A lateral (or horizontal) organization is a mechanism for decentralizing general management decisions and creates an ability to be multidimensional and flexible.[39] Only when it develops the ability to transfer, share, and leverage such fragmented knowledge and expertise will the company be able to exploit the benefits of organizational learning.[40] The proposition here is that the logical extension of these views to the intra- and interorganizational relationships discussed in this book hold true. A further finding is that the vertical information flows framed by the hierarchical reporting relationships would swamp the less well-established horizontal links, unless these cross-unit relationships were also formalized to give them life. What has in fact been shown here is that the cross-unit, in this case extended to mean within and between organizations with a global footprint, was an informal information flow, the system for which, eRelationship, co-evolved over the longitudinal period to meet the collaborative needs of the users irrespective of organization.

For data and knowledge to have been shared, particularly tacit knowledge, trust was an essential prerequisite, which in fact allowed the journey approach and the ensuing experiential learning to prevail; in effect, the level of trust directly influences the need for control.[41] Development of an IOS benefits from strong social capital, and successful development produces social capital. Although the journey co-evolution approach of eRelationship (the Vodafone-Ericsson IOS system), absent of the normal formalities of specifications, plans, and budgets did work, it nevertheless has been shown that it required clear leadership.[42]

It was important, however, not to create an information overload, the content in this instance being structured, determined, and managed by the various user groups in the virtual global community, all using a common "tool set." In this way there was an assurance that the information and knowledge would be consistent with the operational focus of the relevant user cluster. To the extent there may have been a knowledge gap, it was between this system and that used by the Vodafone finance organization. There was a certain reluctance of said teams at that time to incorporate synergy reporting into their management reporting protocols for the ease of report creation and generation. The latter was a time-consuming (two- to three-month) manual process over which certain finance teams nevertheless still wanted to audit their in-country output for consolidation, a banal position for them to have taken. The only assurance, as a result, was that the timing of relevant information was already dated and did not contribute to business management.

Another industry first for Vodafone in the pursuit to leverage its global scale for the generation of collective aggregation cost synergies in the acquisition, deployment, and operation of mobile network infrastructure was the progression to reverse electronic auctions (eAuctions); this included online eRFI and eRFQ, all using the Emptoris application suite. This also became an accelerating Vodafone virtual supply chain management community pursuit, to good effect, in many sourcing applications, with synergies of significance.[43] The mobile network infrastructure eAuctions were, of course, preceded by a protracted manual process for the 3G network in Greece to be installed and in operation in advance of the 2004 Olympics, the supplier decision for which was taken in January 2003.

The first live Web-based eAuction was for a UK second 3G supplier "Buy-decision" in October 2003. For the period covered in this book through October 2005, such a simplified approach to an otherwise complex topic of mobile network infrastructure generated interest and focus in the multisupplier clusters in Vodafone. The experience was to demonstrate an accelerated convergence to the pricing floor at a rate and in a time scale not realizable through conventional negotiations, and despite the constraints of the market and game. That is, in practice the granularity of the network equipment interchangeability and interoperability was constrained by the suppliers' chosen implementation of the industry standards.

Nevertheless, through one particular "rule" in the eAuction protocol—any supplier RFQ bid affecting its GPBs was automatically to become the new global price, regardless of a win or lose outcome in the supplier's favor. Such events were examples of how to leverage at the global level all in-country requirements that had a multi-operator relevance. This experience forms part of a broader topic in the context of the application of game theory to strategic business applications for both "negotiations" and the organizational development dynamic, to which I will turn my attention in a later publication.[44]

What has been shown through this experience is the benefit of sharing data and knowledge within and between global organizations in mutual business relationships. This sharing takes place through the collaboration seated in the virtual social network and the depth of mutual trust contributing to the accrual of collective social capital and an emerging collective culture—the unstructured, yet progressive approach to the co-evolution of the IOS through the experiential transformational journey toward true globalization in the interorganizational relationships between Vodafone and one of its principal suppliers. The ensuing progression to the eAuctions created yet another catalyst for Vodafone's realization of collective aggregation cost synergies, albeit again with an accepted asymmetry in the synergy realization—the quid pro quo for the successful suppliers was market share and for the less successful, an understanding of the prevailing market albeit at some cost.

Going Global Involves Getting People Going

In the context of a transnational solution Bartlett and Ghoshal contrast "the traditional change process" with "the emerging change process."[45] The traditional change process is the sequence of a change in formal structure and responsibilities (anatomy), followed by a change in interpersonal relationships and processes (physiology), and then a change in individual attitudes and mentalities (psychology). The emerging change process commences with a change in individual attitudes and mentalities, then a change in interpersonal relationships and processes, and finally a change in formal structure and responsibilities; these views are attributed to approaches taken by Japanese and European companies. Important to note is that transformation is as much a function of the individual's behavior within the organization as it is of the strategies, structures, and systems that top management introduces.[46]

The people on whom the focus was set were both simultaneously within and between the organizations of Vodafone and those of its globalizing international partners. The scope of the cultural complexity, across more than twenty Vodafone operating interests and the international partners, with each of whom a homogeneous global interorganizational business relationship was being sought, was diverse and multilevel.[47] The consequence of seeking to resolve a preemptive organizational design in isolation with an all-embracing plan toward the global synergy objectives was an untenable thought, not to mention the plan for transition. To mitigate this challenge, in fact, the eventual experiential outcome was initiated in a small embryonic Vodafone-Ericsson cluster, forming the inaugural forum in which the strategy was first disclosed. Although everything from that point forward is history and recorded in this book, the experience of the journey formed the basis of the motivating catalyst and the organizational development thereafter. It was not so much an exercise in organizational design but a case of the informal and virtual organization iteratively adapting collectively to deliver for Vodafone the required aggregation cost synergies. That journey concluded with Vodafone having embraced a global (or transnational) paradigm, initially with Ericsson and later expanding to include Nokia, Nortel, and Siemens and more than twenty Vodafone in-country operating interests.

One may reflect on the pace at which such radical change should be implemented. For the record, the pace of the transition of this combination of intra- and interorganizational relationships, hitherto perceived radical, being an outcome of the process-oriented journey approach to leverage the scale of global synergies, was not preordained, as the end point was not known. Radical change in this context means that "radical change replaces the status quo with a new order of things and as a result may create serious disruptions in structures, processes, operations, knowledge, and morale."[48] Although based on a single field study, it was nevertheless shown that gradual implementation of radical change may be feasible and effective in some situations. The conclusion was that the pace of implementing change (rapid versus gradual) should be distinguished, at least conceptually, from the nature of change intended (radical versus incremental), and that the two be considered separate choices for the change agent. The evidence outlined in this book conforms to and supports these views within which the balance between the pace of implementation in consideration of the magnitude of the endeavor was correct, albeit set and delivered by the emergent, various organizational business relationships with the focus on the synergies for Vodafone.

Two relevant concepts advanced by Watson and discussed by Bevan in the context of organizational change that had the potential to give rise to unexpected outcomes in organizational change programs are the "paradox of consequences":

Human actions often have unintended consequences which may be quite different from or even in direct opposition to what was intended. This is because their fulfilment typically depends on the action of others who will have their own interests, interpretations and priorities.[49]

Watson develops these ideas into his own "basic paradox of organizations":

The means that are used by the controlling management of the organisation to achieve whatever goals they choose or are required to pursue do not necessarily facilitate the effective achievement of these goals since these "means" involve human beings who have goals of their own, which may not be congruent with those of the managers.[50]

For the endeavors discussed in this book, the paradox of consequences was accommodated through the delegation of objectives to those individuals and team clusters impacted, cross-country and cross-organization, which assured sustainable outcomes in line with the Vodafone financial ambitions. The organization or social network with its emergent social capital and emergent but aggregated culture managed to good effect the various interdependencies; that was their opportunity. For the basic paradox of organizations, again the delegative leadership approach and the informality therein stimulated and motivated the individuals to overcome "antibodies," as they were self-managed and not subject to direction. Bevan also references Vince and Broussine for a definition of another paradox, described as the tensions between clarity and uncertainty and the "self contradictory" nature of individual emotions that are a constant characteristic of any change process.[51] Uncertainty, of course, is a characteristic of the process-oriented journey paradigm on which the community appeared to thrive.

Bevan references O'Connor, who suggested that organizational change itself can also be viewed as a paradox:

Change and change processes run counter to fundamental interests of management such as control, stability, predictability, rationality and economic results.[52]

This observation is valid for this discussion, at least for the dimension of the experiential approach of the transition toward globalization and its related rationale. For example, conventional thinking would see the request to accede "power" commercially to an external global function of which management is a part runs "counter to fundamental interests of (local in-country) management." The evidence reported shows that even though this may have been a counterintuitive proposition, it was voluntarily accepted and worked, thereby leveraging the sum of the parts to be greater than the whole in the collective group interest. Again, from a managed perspective, the paradox may be valid; however, from a leadership and delegative perspective, although the stated attributes may have been present, they neither became a concern nor a disruption to the collective Vodafone ambitions.

Notwithstanding the "hurdles" expressed in the extant literature and the specific approach and complex situational circumstances, the conditions for a requisite organization in the period extending to April 2005 were such as to facilitate overcoming such prior and espoused observations. Perhaps the leadership, (my) style, and maturity (extensive international and cross-cultural experience) played their role along with my vast social network and the social and intellectual capital accrued therein. This developing agenda functioned unabated from late 1998 until April 2005 (the point of resetting social capital) and delivered substantive aggregation cost synergies in accordance with Vodafone's objectives. Despite the differing opinions of certain Vodafone key stakeholders concerning the ensuing center-controlled organizational option for this mobile network infrastructure sourcing endeavor, that same social network collaborated fully with me in effecting the organization changes requested by management. This clearly attests to the accrued social capital in my social network, even with the disappointment at the lack of recognition for the financial achievements over the years of our informal and (perhaps unfortunately) invisible virtual organization. In April 2005 we moved from an adaptive, motivated, and requisite organization within which there scope for innovation and personal development to a structured, center-controlled design.

The successes (and failures) recorded in this book demonstrate that through a common strategy, albeit with the accepted recognition of the asymmetry of benefits and the timing, there were demonstrable trust and integrity of both the leadership and each other for the voluntary accession of power locally in favor of group leverage. Although the extant literature demonstrates that a number of pitfalls existed, the resolve of the geographically dispersed organizations of Vodafone and Ericsson, Nokia, Nortel, and Siemens had sufficient resolve and momentum to neutralize them, but at times inner tensions had to be resolved.

To lead the strategy forward and nurture the ensuing supporting organizational developments, to delegate from the center and empower, to populate the center team with secondees from the Vodafone operating companies, and to take a mentoring role in focusing on individual personal development, the migration to Lead OpCos all placed the power to perform into the social network and at the point of interface to the end-customer. With the axis of rotation and momentum in virtual clusters of common interest led by the Lead OpCos, the meta-influence was strengthened through control by a combination of boundary-crossing individuals, and the social and intellectual capital accrued therein led to a resilient and motivated social network up to April 2005.

Perhaps my training as a mediator for conflict resolution also played its role, at least in recognizing and accepting that there is always more than one approach to issues and opportunities, the relevant experiential learning being that to accede to the team in the absence of any overriding reason or objection to pursue its recommendation leads to sustainable outcomes and timely deliveries—leadership versus management. The experiential process-oriented journey approach taken, although counterintuitive, did embrace all parties, released human imagination, conquered adversities or the potential thereof, and aspired to being a requisite organization. It did *get people going* and consistently delivered greater than the declared internal aggregation cost synergy targets for Vodafone.

Inception of a Requisite Organization

If I were to repeat such an assignment today, how might I approach the opportunity? The short answer is "who knows?" Transformational change with its embedded and varied complexities, as has been demonstrated, is not a set-piece play. Although a renewed objective may be the same in name, assuredly the situational context will not be so, even if others perceive it as similar or indeed the same, perhaps under the banner of "globalization." It would commence at a new point in time, under different market (demand) conditions, new competitive landscape and dynamic, various states of global transparency and politics, different composition of the engaged parties and complexities of the cultural blend (as discussed herein), all collectively contributing to a new game.

Although perhaps not thought of this way in the application of game theory (seated in economics), business in the broadest sense is a game that also transcends to consideration and matters of organization. The (virtual) organization forms part of an organizational system that embraces the people and the dynamics of the environment within which they are seated or by which they are influenced or impacted; this includes their own minds and motivation, for example. Each time, therefore, the issue becomes, what is the business game of the day?—a relevant and interesting matter to return to in greater depth perhaps on another occasion, so too might be the anatomy of organizational and business change.

Recall that the endeavor discussed in this book commenced as an interorganizational (1:1) relationship and business transformation within and between two globally dispersed organizations, Vodafone and Ericsson. What is posited herein is that this formed the foundation of the requisite organizational model that was the transitional stimulus proving the aggregation cost synergy yield objectives for the acquisition and deployment of model network infrastructure sought by Vodafone (a matter of public record). This model was then experientially varied or adapted to encompass a 1:N relationship (Vodafone:Ericsson, Nokia, Nortel, Siemens, etc.) or several intra- and interorganizational relationships for transformation. In summary, the virtual organization in discussion transcended the boundaries of the organizations and their in-country operating companies therein, noting that on the Vodafone side all engaged companies had different and evolving equity interests. I would posit, nevertheless, that the experience, knowledge, and wisdom of this experiential journey is not bounded by the context of this case and therefore has applicable merit for more general consideration.

However, from the acquired experiential learning espoused in this account and by way of supplemental contribution to that written by others, I would posit that there is no rule base that assures a successful transformational outcome. To the contrary, there are perhaps a basic number of recurring and relevant considerations that must be taken into account, seated in the context of the timing and objectives of the new business and organizational challenge. It is likely that there may be additional or new situational considerations latent in those discussed. My sense would tell me that even to repeat this exact objective would necessarily call for an interesting debate, if for no other reasons than the continuing consolidation and dynamic of the formation of the mobile operators, the maturing of certain markets, and the ensuing business challenges therein.

The mobile network infrastructure supplier consolidation was afoot in 2006, with the Chinese emerging as challenging global competitors (principally Huawei and ZTE). Hitherto China had a dominant growth from which the non-Chinese infrastructure suppliers (Ericsson, Nokia, Nortel Siemens, as they then were) contributing substantively to their business performance. Hence, the approach to be taken or mandated to repeat such a globalization challenge in this new and continuing business game is uncertain.

Reflecting on this unique experience I outline in Figure 7.1 considerations for practice in transformational change, all leading to a generalized illustrative

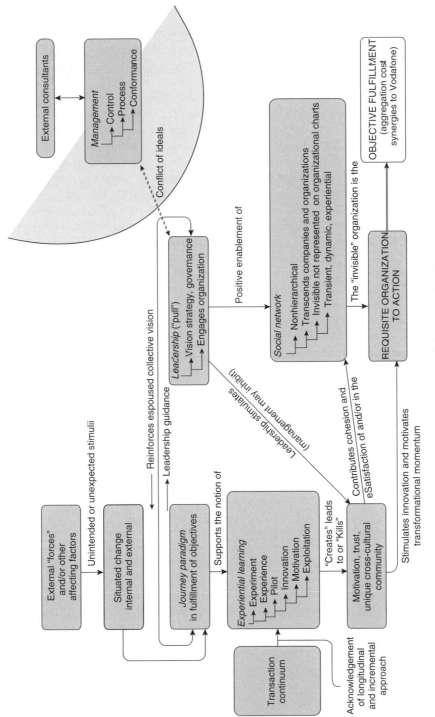

Figure 7.1 **Global networks: journey to globalization and a requisite organization**

model of the network discussed. The following discussion of considerations should now be read in conjunction with reference to the model shown in the figure.

Consideration 1: *Planned versus journey approach.* The nature of the transformation implies a move to a structure not previously experienced either within or, in this case, and between, the engaged organizations and the industry. The journey paradigm taken provides for flexible capability of dynamically absorbing and adjusting in direction and resources for the situated change without being distracted from the vision, strategy, and immediacy of the near-term objectives. The stimulus for those engaged parties is the espoused collective vision and strategy of the leadership, be that singular or plural. Such in-built flexibility moderates or allows for the impact of the unintended or unexpected stimuli, be they positive or negative, arising from unanticipated factors external to or within the engaged community.

Although the leadership is within and therefore part of the community, it nevertheless has a role of guidance in the event the individuals or teams are unable to make sense of such situated changes. Such an organizational construct supports an experiential approach when engaged in a pathfinder program that has global significance or that affects a broad community, as in evidence in this case. A predetermined, planned approach, wherein there are attempts to anticipate the unexpected, may have the characteristic of being more focused on the plans and compliance thereto, which is more akin to management, and be less flexible or timely in responding to situated change.

Consideration 2: *An experiential approach.* Such an approach acknowledges at the outset that the business outcome or organizational approach of a transformational journey is not a foregone conclusion. Given no established industry forerunner or experience that can be applied to the requisite organizational and relationship paradigm, the notion of experimentation in such circumstances is not inappropriate to create an environment within which experimentation is blended with collective experience to enable experiential learning. This has, or in this case had, the potential to set the basis for innovative outcomes and nonnormative or constrained thinking, all leading to counterintuitive initiatives with engaged virtual organization clusters and structures. This extended to convergent practice, which enhanced the intra- and cross-organizational economic synergy yields, none more so than the move to eCommerce practices and the industry-leading introduction of reverse electronic auctions (eAuctions) applied to the complexities of mobile network infrastructure.

I would posit that absence of an experiential approach to globalization, combined with the emergence of the informal and nonhierarchical virtual horizontal organization that transcended company and organizational boundaries, the recorded financial aggregation cost synergies successes for Vodafone might have eluded us. Such an approach acknowledges the incremental approach toward transformational change. Delegated leadership, objectively facilitated and encouraged by the collective leadership, stimulates an inner community culture of motivation, trust, and mutual satisfaction resulting in

positive collective outcomes, which in this case led to a unique and economically successful cross-cultural virtual community or invisible organization.
Management wherein control, process, and compliance prevails is more likely
to inhibit such a successful, sustainable outcome.

Consideration 3: *Leadership versus management.* Throughout this book
the word *manager* has been used, both by me and in quotations from the
literature; however, I have concluded that there are serious differences or
conflicts of ideals between management and (strategic) individual and collective leadership. I have characterized the former as being somewhat confirma-
tive and perhaps operating "in the box"; the latter is selectively conformant
but does not act with disregard to the "house rules" and would tend to
operate and encourage operation in innovative, or "out of the box" behavior
to attain the desired business objectives. I posit that management tend to
direct control as leaders tend to influence; the former commands a following,
and the latter motivates a following who act on their own accord toward the
espoused collective vision and strategy.

Manager is a role appointment that may enjoy hierarchical authority,
analogous to command and control. Although a leader tends to be person-
able, is considered natural in the role, and may not conform to the espoused
hierarchy, absent of such organizational roles, the desired business performance may not be achieved. Managers tend to discourage the informal or what
is outside their control; leaders positively encourage the informality or the
values vested in the social network and its key stakeholders. The resulting
social capital, although intangible, can add significant accrued goodwill value
to the engaged businesses. Leadership is about accepting that there is more
than one approach to opportunities or problem resolution, perhaps the most
powerful leadership coming from those tasked with execution, leading to the
reinforcement of true empowerment and multiple bosses focused on the
delivery of outcomes in support of the community objectives. Leadership in
my experience embraces delegation to management; it is perhaps synonymous with the doing being done and not about the doing; I would posit that
leaders do not make good or effective managers.

I was fortunate that my lead role in the business, albeit informal in the
Vodafone community generally, was often reinforced in supplier meetings by
the executive of Vodafone; at least in the period through April 1, 2005, that
an implied reinforcement of authority in practice. Communication by the
leadership aimed to inspire has to be open and honest, treating those being
addressed with respect rather than carefully crafting communication that says
much but tells little or nothing; the fact is that the informal network all too
often preempts events anyway. It is counterproductive to keep people
guessing. An analogy in life might be an earthquake. If one is at the epicenter of an earthquake, damage is significant; the farther away one is, the less
the discomfort and damage. If one, figuratively speaking, is at the epicenter
of communications, the proximity creates an awareness of events; however, as
in the virtual world, as one becomes more distant, the immediacy of knowledge is poor and concerns are aroused that defocus the business.

Transparency, save truly commercially sensitive information, should where possible be encouraged to enhance the level of trust and knowledge of those on whom the organization is relying for success, and from which others may also learn and enhance the business performance, eRelationship being one such example.[53] Ultimately, business is a game, and the issue or question becomes, what is the game your business or organization is seeking to play? In this case it was resolved to be a transformation transition that later experientially emerged in several dimensions from the current position in 1998. The application of game theory is as relevant between as within businesses and organizations, a discussion to which I may return on another day. The core theme is the requirement to move from being egocentric to allocentric for game (or organizational outcome) success.

Consideration 4: *Motivation, trust, and culture.* People are not pawns in a management game; to the contrary, whatever the espoused organizational construct (or in this particular case, multi-organizational) and assignment of roles and responsibilities, there remain individual nodes in a complex social network or system in which there are visible and, no doubt, invisible individual and clustered interconnections. The role of the individuals singularly or collectively is dynamic, and the performance of such networks results from their interaction and is most likely driven by their inner culture and motivation. In transformational change (and perhaps in the steady state) and the transition thereof, the dynamics of this network may not be predictable or assured. A clear determinant, however, is the ability of the business to define the level and clearly stated objectives role, perhaps in the language of Jaques: the maturation and level of the leadership assignee is the limiting determinant of the success of the business.[54] One should also perhaps consider tenure; the role of leading the transition is not the same as that required to operate in the steady state, yet once assigned, people often do not get moved on.

Daft is clear about the requirements of a leader, which may require investigating and reviewing track records, giving due consideration to changes in the situational context, which may be something to which the business itself is unable to adapt.[55] Rooke and Torbert also provide interesting guidance in their discussion that "leaders are made, not born, and how they develop is critical for organization change."[56] There must be an organizational structural dynamic if the market in which the businesses (or organizations) function is itself a competitive variable, yet organizations all too often are driven by structure and not market.

The notion of combining experiential learning with inspirational, stimulating, and inclusive individual and collective leadership (in contrast to potentially inhibitive management) has been shown to engender mutual trust in the social networks that functioned within and across global organizations. Through alignment with the collective vision and strategy, individuals in the leadership enabled a social network motivated to contribute to and deliver through their goodwill the collective goal, which led to a unique virtual cross-community organizational culture.[57] Such "managed" informality may also stimulate innovation and motivate transformational momentum. The inclusive, nonhierarchical horizontal organizational approach recognized that ideas, whether or not correct, and innovation are not derived from appointment or position in an organizational hierarchy but result from experience.

Consideration 5: *The social network.* An informal, interconnected, complex network of individuals that have the power to determine outcomes, both positive and negative, exists in all organizations. Perhaps key influencing factors on outcomes include recognition and motivation. The idea that there is a difference between the espoused organization and that in practice is, of course, not new. What may be new is to promote and support such a nonhierarchical network for which there is no organizational chart against which to benchmark the operation, as in the case of the invisible organization discussed in this book; yet the economic performance of this organization was recognized (at least in Vodafone) and had a multi-organization business dependency.

Until superseded, the host venue for global meetings in the formative Vodafone-Ericsson days was rotated among the participating countries; when this rotation was superseded, the meetings were held either in the UK, Germany, or Italy. The social network, inclusive of several key stakeholders, although self-governing within Vodafone, was nevertheless compliant with the limited formal governance structure of the organization, which necessitated balancing resolutions and agreement from within. Presence in this social network was not by appointment or hierarchical position but by initiation of those from within on the merits of anticipated contribution or relevance. Although Vodafone was the anchor or common organization, the social network in operation transcended organizational boundaries globally to include at least Ericsson, Nokia, Nortel, and Siemens, all operating in the form of the founding model adapted as discussed in Chapter 4.

I would encourage future leaders engaged in such complex and multicultural global transformational endeavors to positively engage and leverage the power of the informal social network; let it work for you by enabling it to work effectively for itself. The sources of greatest input for mediated decisions are seated within the organization, but when functioning hierarchically, such talent and innovation may be inhibited from surfacing; management often prefers to seek external guidance, input, and transformational execution. The power and collective performance of the nonhierarchical social network linking vertical hierarchies was certainly in evidence in Vodafone until April 1, 2005.

Consideration 6: *The inception of a requisite organization.* All of the foregoing leads to the formation of a requisite organization. In this case the requisite organization was informal, but not all such examples lack structural formality. It is posited that the organizational outcome to which we aspired was conformant in practice to that anticipated by Jaques, namely, "The pattern of connections which ought to exist between roles if the system is both to work efficiently and to operate as required by the nature of human nature and the enhancement of mutual trust." Jaques adds that the term *requisite organization* means "doing business with efficiency and competitiveness, and the release of human imagination, trust, and satisfaction in work."[58]

I posit therefore that by result and for the period it was permitted to function, this organizational model effectively captured in practice, through the connections in the social network and the collective leadership, the network imagination, trust, satisfaction, and, above all, the economic results being sought by Vodafone. It was as though in agreeing to the vision, strategy, and asymmetry of yield between the parties, the organizations formed in the social network were dynamic, self-forming, accommodating to situated change (external or internal), and consistent in action toward the realization and sustainability of the common aggregation cost synergy objectives—a sign of leadership? Management, in contrast, is more likely to seek to mandate and plan such realization with, from my experience, questionable outcomes. Such a paradigm represents a true challenge for those who embrace stereotypical thinking and preemptive organizational designs.

Consideration 7: *Situational context.* We now come full circle. This reflective experiential presentation and analysis relates to an endeavor that took place over a seven-year period; when and how it happened sit in its contextual past. Recognition of the varied situational circumstances is key to the interpretation of this work that concludes in seven "considerations," as it should be for that of others representing "rules" as an outcome. So many situational factors dynamically combine and vary to affect outcomes that make repeating the actions in other circumstances of transformational change impossible. A key factor is combined complex interactions between the choice of leadership, the people in the organizations, the teaming, the engaged organizations, the extant organization and company structures therein, equity structures, politics (both national and organizational), the market customer and supplier competitive cycles, timing, the continuing and emergent impact of global transparency, cultures, technology, and governance.

Faced with what has the appearance of being a replay of former experiences is not de facto an encore for a former team or the alumni from a former company. My proposition, and preference, is therefore to recommend the consideration of forming a requisite organization rather than a stereotypical set piece seated in the former experiences of one or several individuals as undoubtedly the situational circumstances will not be the same. One should not acquiesce to comfort or mainstream thinking if it does not evidence sustainable competitive progress or, ultimately, advantage. Be sure the theories of Jaques are upheld or, if ignored, done so on a qualified basis!

Postscript

Finally, the social network or invisible organization as I have described it was perhaps a performing and truly (if not only) global "crown jewel" within Vodafone, having contributed value in the globalization and transformation of interorganizational business relationships commencing with Ericsson and later including those with Nokia, Nortel, and Siemens, not to mention the intraorganizational relationships within Vodafone.

It became important to accept that the derivation of the aggregation cost synergies had at times to be constructed around the doctrine of equivalence, not mandated in exact replication, given the cross-supplier mix and the legacy of the extant Vodafone in-country mobile operator networks. The old adage of "half the price and double the volume" was not applicable in a market absent of RRPs or price lists, thereby leading to nonlinear price-cost relationships.

It is perhaps too bad that the first example of the meritorious intentions of One Vodafone was in an emergent and economically performing mobile network infrastructure that had existed since the end of 1998 and not something still in discussion at the time of the broader One Vodafone dialogue. This virtual organization had inadequate visibility to the executive of the company who may have been unaware of the value of what became a requisite organization and may therefore not have been understood fully by them or their external advisers.

It was a pleasure and privilege to have had the opportunity of the experiential learning espoused in this book. I have closed with a number of relevant considerations to open the transformational globalization debate for others in practice or academia. It remains a case of horses for courses, with the merits of the chosen approach being in the outcome and the motivated sustainability thereof. Enjoy your leadership journey of the future in a requisite organization. Bon voyage!

Notes

1 Introduction

1. Jaques, E. (1996). *Requisite Organization*. 2nd Edition. Arlington, VA. Cason Hall & Co.
2. Ashkenas, R., Ulrich, D., Jich, T., and Herr, S. (1998). *The Boundaryless Organization*. San Francisco, CA. Jossey-Bass, Inc.
3. Bartlett, C. A., and Ghoshal, S. (1998). *Managing Across Borders; The Transnational Solution*. Boston, MA. Harvard Business School Press.
4. Ashkenas, R., Ulrich, D., Jich, T. and Herr, S. (1998). *The Boundaryless Organization*. San Francisco, California, U.S.A., Jossey-Bass, Inc.: pp. 275–276.
5. Ashkenas, R., Ulrich, D., Jich, T. and Herr, S. (1998). *The Boundaryless Organization*. San Francisco, California, U.S.A., Jossey-Bass, Inc.
6. Daft, R. L. (2001). *Organization Theory and Design*. 7th Edition. Cincinnati, OH. South-Western Publication.
7. Inns, D. (1996). *Organisation Development as a Journey*. London. Pitman.
8. Morgan, G. (1986). Images of Organization. Beverly Hills, CA: Sage Publications: p. 12.
9. Grant, D., and Oswick, C. (1996). *Introduction: Getting the Measure of Metaphors*. London. Sage Publications Limited.
10. Orlikowski, W. J., and Hofman, J. D. (1997). "An Improvisational Model for Change Management: The Case of Groupware Technologies." *Sloan Management Review* 38(2): 11–21.
11. Lewin, K. (1951). *Field Theory in Social Science*, New York, Harper Collins.
12. Bevan, H. (1997). *Managing Today While Creating Tomorrow: Actionable Knowledge for Organisational Change in an NHS Hospital*. Doctor of Business Administration (DBA). Henley Management College, Henley, UK.
13. Macredie, R. D., and Sandom, C. (1999). "IT-Enabled Change: Evaluating an Improvisational Perspective." *European Journal of Information Systems* 8(4): 247–259.
14. For example, Dawson, P. (1994). *Organizational Change: A Processual Approach*. Paul Chapman Publishing; Pettigrew, A. and Whipp, R. (1993). "Understanding the environment." In *Managing Change* (Mabey, C. and Mayon-White, B., Eds)., Open University/Paul Chapman Publishing, London, pp. 5–19; Wilson, D.C. (1992). *A Strategy of Change*. Routledge, London.
15. Rockart, J. F. (1998). "Towards Survivability of Communication-Intensive New Organization Forms." *Journal of Management Studies* 35(4): 417–420.
16. Galbraith, J. R. (1994). *Competing with Flexible Lateral Organizations*. Reading, MA. Addison-Wesley Publishing Company, Inc.
17. Ghoshal, S., and Bartlett, C. A. (1998). *The Individualized Corporation: A Fundamentally New Approach to Management*. London. William Heinemann.

18. Galbraith, J. R. (1993). *The Business Unit of the Future*. San Francisco, CA. Jossey-Bass, Inc.

19. Burn, J., and Barnett, M. (1999). "Communicating for Advantage in the Virtual Organization." *IEEE Transactions on Professional Communication* 42(4): 215–222.

20. Schein, E. (1990). Organizational Culture. *Amer. Psychol.*, 45(2): pp 109–119

21. Tushman, M. L., O'Reilly III, C. A. (1996). "Ambidextrous Organizations: Managing Evolutionary and Revolutionary Change." *California Management Review*, 38(4): pp. 8–29.

22. Sieber, P. and Griese, J. (1998). "Organization Virtualness" in Proc. VoNet-Workshop. Bern, Switzerland: Simowa, April.

23. Mowshowitz, A. (1997). "Virtual Organization." *Communications of the ACM* 40(9): 30–37.

24. Faucheux, C. (1997). "How Virtual Organizing Is Transforming Management Science." *Communications of the ACM* 40(9): 50–55.

25. Lipnack, J., and Stamps, J. (1993). *The TeamNet Factor: Bringing the Power of Boundary Crossing into the Heart of Your Business*. Essex Junction, VT. Oliver Wright Publications, Inc.

26. Brown, C. V. (1999). "Horizontal Mechanisms Under Differing IS Organization Contexts." *MIS Quarterly* 23(3): 421–454; Mohrman, S. A. (1993). "Integrating Roles and Structure in the Lateral Organization," in *Organizing for the Future: The New Logic of Managing Complex Organizations*, J. R. Galbraith, E. E. Lawler III and Associates (eds.), Josey-Bass, San Francisco, pp. 109–141; Porter, M. E. (1985). *Competitive Advantage: Creating and Sustaining Superior Performance*, Free Press, New York.

27. Bultje, R., and van Wijk, J. (1998). "Taxonomy of Virtual Organisations, Based on Definitions, Characteristics and Typology." *virtual-organization.net Newsletter* 2(3), September 1: pp. 7–20. http://www.virtual-organization.net/files/articles/nl2-3.pdf.

28. *Social Capital Building Toolkit* [Version 1.0] January 2003 [Thomas Sander, Kathleen Lowney].

29. Lipnack, J., and Stamps, J. (1997). *Virtual Teams: Reaching Across Space, Time, and Organizations with Technology*. New York. John Wiley & Sons, Inc.

30. Lipnack and Stamps (1997), p. 228; Case, J. (1996). *Open Book Management*. Harper Collins, New York; Schuster, J. (1996). *The Power of Open Book Management*. John Wiley & Sons, New York; Coleman, J. S. (1988). "Social Capital is the Creation of Human Capital." *American Journal of Sociology* (1988 Supplement), S98.

31. De Meyer, A. (1991). "Tech Talk: How Managers Are Stimulating Global R&D Communication." *Sloan Management Review* 32(3): 49–58.

32. Lipparini, A., and Fratocchi, L. (1999). "The Capabilities of the Transnational Firm: Accessing Knowledge and Leveraging Inter-firm Relationships." *European Management Journal* 17(6): 655–667.

33. Lewis, J. D. (1999). *Trusted Partners: How Companies Build Mutual Trust and Win Together*. New York. The Free Press.

34. Inns (1996). "Organisation development as a journey," Oswick, C. and Grant, D. (eds), *Organisation development, metaphorical explorations*, London, Pitman, p. 28.

35. Olk, P. (1998). "A Knowledge-Based Perspective on the Transformation of Individual-Level Relationships into Inter-organizational Structures: The Case of R&D Consortia." *European Management Journal* 16(1): 39–49.

36. Larsen, K. R. T. (1999). "Virtual Organization as an Interorganizational Concept: Ties to Previous Research." *virtual-organization.net Newsletter* 3(1): 18–33.
37. Steinfeld, C., Kraut, R., and Plummer, A. (1998). "The Impact of Interorganizational Networks on Buyer-Seller Relationships." *JCMC.* http://jdmc.huji.ac.il/vol1/issue3/steinfld.html.
38. Chisholm, R. F. (1998). *Developing Network Organizations: Learning from Practice and Theory.* Reading, MA. Addison-Wesley Publishing Company, Inc.
39. Trist, E. L. (1983). "Referent Organizations and the Development of Interorganizational Domains." *Human Relations,* 36(3), pp. 369–284; Trist, E. L. (1985). "Intervention Strategies for Interorganizational Domains" in R. Tannenbaum and F. Massarik, eds. *Human Systems Development: New Perspectives on People and Organizations.* Josey-Bass, San Francisco.
40. Kanter, R. M. (1991). "Transcending Business Boundaries: 12,000 World Managers View Change." *Harvard Business Review* 69(3): 151–164.
41. Handy, C. (1995). "Trust and the Virtual Organization." *Harvard Business Review* 73(3): 40–50.
42. Daft (2000); Bass, M. B. (1990). *Bass & Stogdill's Handbook of Leadership: Theory, Research, and Managerial Applications,* 3d ed. Free Press, New York; Seltzer, J. and Bass, M. B. (1990). "Transformational Leadership: Beyond Initiation and Consideration", *Journal of Management,* 16, pp. 693–703; Tracey, J. B. and Hinkin, T. R. (1996). "How Transformational Leaders Lead in the Hospitality Industry," *International Journal of Hospitality Management,* 15(2): 175–176.
43. Katzenbach, J. R. (1997). "The Myth of the Top Management Team." *Harvard Business Review* 75(6): 83–91.
44. Lewis, J. D. (1999). *Trusted Partners: How Companies Build Mutual Trust and Win Together.* New York. The Free Press.
45. Ibbott, C. J. (2001). *An IS-Enabled Model for the Transformation and Globalisation of Interorganisational and Intercompany Relationships.* Doctor of Business Administration (DBA). Brunel University, UK, p. 222.
46. Schein, E. H. (2004). *Organization Culture and Leadership.* 3rd Edition. San Francisco, CA. The Jossey-Bass Business & Management Series.
47. Schein (2004).
48. Robinowitz, C. J., and Carr, L. W. (2001). *Modern-Day Vikings: A Practical Guide to Interacting with the Swedes.* Yarmouth, ME. Intercultural Press, Inc.
49. Jaques (1996).

2 The Birth and Growth of Vodafone and Wireless Telecoms

1. Meurling, J. and Jeans, R. (1997). *The Ugly Duckling: mobile phones from Ericsson—putting people on speaking terms.* Stockholm, Sweden. Ericsson Mobile Communications AB, p. 21.
2. Meurling, J. and Jeans, R. (1994). *The Mobile Phone Book: The invention of the mobile phone industry.* London, England. Communications Week International, p. 57.
3. Meurling and Jeans (1997), p. 30.
4. Ibid., p. 21.
5. Meurling and Jeans (1994), pp. 59–61.

6. Ibid., p. 78.
7. Ibid., pp. 93–94.
8. Merriden, Trevor (1993).
9. http://news.bbc.co.uk/1/hi/business/4813534.stm. March 16, 2006.
10. Beer, J. (2005). "Tremors Along the Value Chain." *Efficient Purchasing*, premier issue, no.1 (Fall): 18–21, quote from p. 18.
11. Ibid., p. 21.
12. Ibid., p. 21.
13. Ibid., p. 18.

3 The Journey to a Global Network Starting Positions: How It All Began

1. Inns, D. (1996). *Organisation Development as a Journey*. London. Pitman.
2. Orlikowski, W. J. (1996). "Improvising Organisational Transformation over Time: A Situate Change Perspective." *Information Systems Research* 7(1): 63–92.
3. Orlikowski, W. J., and Hofman (1997). "An improvisational Model for Change Management: The case of Groupware Technologies." *Sloan Management Review* 38(2): 11–22.
4. We are discussing here the open and transparent interorganisational information system to (using the words of Orlikowski and Hofman, p. 12) provide "electronic networks that support communications, coordination, and collaboration through facilities such as information exchange, shared repositories, discussion forums and messaging."
5. Set out in page 9 of the Vodafone AirTouch Plc "Listing Particulars Relating to the Issue of Ordinary Shares in Vodafone AirTouch Plc in Connection with the Offer for Mannesmann AG," which was put to the Mannesmann shareholders on November 19, 1999.
6. Bultje, R., and van Wijk, J. (1998). "Taxonomy of Virtual Organisations, Based on Definitions, Characteristics and Typology." *virtual-organization.net Newsletter*. http://www.virtual-organization.net/files/articles/nl2-3.pdf.
7. Ibbott, C. J., and O'Keefe, R. M. (2004). "Trust, Planning and Benefits in a Global Interorganizational System." *Information Systems Journal* 14(2): 131–152.
8. Bultje and van Wijk (1998).
9. Ibid.
10. Ibbott, C. J., and O'Keefe, R. M. (2004). "Transforming the Vodafone/Ericsson Relationship." *Long Range Planning* 37(3): 219–237.
11. Orlikowski (1996).
12. Trahant, B., Burke, W. W., and Koonce, R. (1997). "12 Principles of Organizational Transformation." *Management Review* 86(8): 17–21.
13. E-mail dated October 5, 2000.
14. Jarvenpaa, S. L., and Stoddard, D. B. (1998). "Business Process Redesign: Radical and Evolutionary Change." *Journal of Business Research* 41(1): 15–27.
15. Davidson, W. H. (1993). "Beyond Re-engineering: The Three Phases of Business Transformation." *IBM Systems Journal* 32(1): 65–79.
16. Bultje, R. and van Wijk, J. (1998). Taxonomy of Virtual Organisations, based on definitions, characteristics and typology, *virtual-organization.net Newsletter*. http://www.virtual-organization.net/files/articles/nl2-3.pdf.

17. Lipparini, A. and Fratocchi, L. (1999). "The Capabilities of the Transnational Firm: Accessing Knowledge and Leveraging Inter-firm Relationships." *European Management Journal* 17(6): 655–667.

18. Faucheux, C. (1997). "How Virtual Organizing is Transforming Management Science." *Communications of the ACM* 40(9): 50–55.

19. Mowshowitz, A. (1997). "Virtual Organization." *Communications of the ACM* 40(9): 30–37.

20. Kanter, R. M. (1994). "Collaborative Advantage: The Art of Alliances." *Harvard Business Review* 72(4): 96–108.

21. Regarding joint supply chain, see Corbett, C. J., Blackburn, J. D., and Van Wassenhove, L. N. (1999). "Case Study—Partnerships to Improve Supply Chains." *Sloan Management Review* 40(4): 71–82. Regarding the leadership role, see Franke, U. (1998). "The Evolution from a Static Virtual Corporation to a Virtual Web—What Implications Does This Evolution Have on 'Supply Chain Management'"? *virtual-organization.net Newsletter.* http://www0.virtual-organization.net/news/nl_2.2/nl_2-2a4.pdf. Regarding global interorganizational structures and relationships, see Hughes, J., Ralf, M., and Michels, B. (1998). *Transform Your Supply Chain: Releasing Value in Business.* London. International Thomson Business Press.

22. Lipnack, J. and Stamps, J. (1993). *The TeamNet Factor: Bringing the Power of Boundary Crossing Into the Heart of Your Business.* Essex Junction, Vermont, U.S.A., Oliver Wright Publications, Inc.

23. Brown, C. V. (1999). "Horizontal Mechanisms Under Differing IS Organization Contexts." *MIS Quarterly* 23(3): 421–454; Mohrman, S. A. and Mohrman, A. M., Jr. (1993). *Organizational Change and Learning.* San Francisco, California, U.S.A., Jossey-Bass, Inc.; Porter, M. E. and Millar, V. E. (1985). "How Information Gives You Competitive Advantage." *Harvard Business Review* 63(4): 149–160.

24. Venkatraman, N., and Henderson, J. C. (1998). "Real Strategies for Virtual Organizing." *Sloan Management Review* 40(1): 33–48.

25. Ring, P. S., and Van de Ven, A. H. (1994). "Developmental Processes of Cooperative Interorganizational Relationships." *Academy of Management Review* 19(1): 90–118; Handy, C. (1995). "Trust and the Virtual Organization." *Harvard Business Review* 73(3): 40–50; Hughes, J., Ralf, M. and Michels, B. (1998). *Transform Your Supply Chain: Releasing Value in Business.* London, UK, International Thomson Business Press.

26. Regarding sharing and trust being crucial, see Ishaya and Macaulay (1998). Regarding multilevels, see Kanter (1994). Regarding horizontal engagement, see Cohen, S. (1997). "On Becoming Virtual." *Training and Development* 51(5): 30–37 and Jarvenpaa, S. L., Knoll, K., and Leidner, D. E. (1998). "Is Anybody Out There? Antecedents of Trust in Global Virtual Teams." *Journal of Management Information Systems* 14(4): 29–64.

27. Ashkenas, R., Ulrich, D., Jich, T. and Herr, S. (1998). *The Boundaryless Organization.* San Francisco, California, U.S.A., Jossey-Bass, Inc.

28. De Meyer, A. (1991). "Tech Talk: How Managers are Stimulating Global R&D Communication." *Sloan Management Review* 32(3): 49–58.

29. Sveiby, K. -E., and Simons, R. (2002). "Collaborative Climate and Effectiveness of Knowledge Work—an Empirical Study." *Journal of Knowledge Management* 6(5): 420–433.

30. Urch Druskat, V., and Wolff, B. S. (2001). "Building the Emotional Intelligence of Groups", *Harvard Business Review*, March.

31. Huener, L., von Krogh, G., and Roos, J. (1988). "Knowledge and Concept of Trust", in Krogh, G., Roos, J., and Kleine, D. (Eds), *Knowing Firms, Understanding, Managing and Measuring Knowledge*, London, Sage.

32. Tschannen-Moran, M. (2001). "Collaboration and the Need for Trust", *Journal of Education Administration*, 39(4): 308–331.

33. Ibid.; Tschannen-Moran (2001).

34. Cule, P. E., and Robey, D. (2004). "A Dual-Motor, Constructive Process Model of Organization Transition." *Organizational Studies* 25(2): 229–260.

35. Van de Ven, A. H. and Poole, M. S. (1995). "Explaining development and changes in organizations", *Academy of Management Review* 20(3); 510–540.

36. Cule and Robey (2004).

37. Kotter, J. P. (1996). *Leading Change*. Boston, MA. Harvard Business School Press.

38. The steps are adapted from Kotter (1996).

39. Lipnack and Stamps (1993).

40. Ibid.

41. Kanter, R. M. (1994). "Collaborative advantage: the art of alliances." *Harvard Business Review* 72(4): 96–108.

42. Schein, E. H. (2004). Organizational Culture and Leadership 3rd Edition, San Francisco, Josey-Bass.

43. Olk, P. (1998). "A Knowledge-Based Perspective on the Transformation of Individual-Level Relationships Into Inter-organizational Structures: The Case of R&D Consortia." *European Management Journal* 16(1): 39–49.

44. Williams, H., and Borman, M. (1996). "Collaboration: More Than the Exchange of Information." *EM—Interorganizational Systems*. http://www.electronicmarkets.org/netacademy/publications.nsf/all_pk/75.

45. Lipnack and Stamps (1993); Faucheux (1997).

46. Byrne, J. A. (1993). "The Virtual Corporation." *Business Week*, 98–103.

47. Wiesenfeld, B. M., Raghuram, S., and Garud, R. (1998). "Communication Patterns as Determinants of Organizational Identification in a Virtual Organization." *Journal of Computer Mediated Communications*. http://www.ascusc.org/jcmc/vol1/issue3/steinfld.html.

48. Gristock, J. J. (1998). "Organisational Virtuality: A Conceptual Framework for Communication in Shared Virtual Environments." First International Conference on Presence, BT Laboratories, Martlesham Heath, Ipswich, UK.

49. Galbraith, J. R. (1994). *Competing with Flexible Lateral Organizations*. Reading, Massachusetts, U.S.A., Addison-Wesley Publishing Company, Inc.

50. Katzenbach, J. R. (1997). "The Myth of the Top Management Team." *Harvard Business Review* 75(6): 83–91.

51. Eisenhardt, K. M., Kahwajy, J. L., and Bourgeois, L. J., III. (1997). "How Management Teams Can Have a Good Fight." *Harvard Business Review* 75(4): 77–85.

52. Lengel, R. H., and Daft, R. L. (1988). "The Selection of Communication Media as an Executive Skill." *The Academy of Management Executive* 2(3): 225–232.

53. Bevan, H. (1997). Managing Today While Creating Tomorrow: Actionable Knowledge for Organisational Change in an NHS Hospital. Doctor of Business Administration. *Henley Management College*, Henley, UK.; Carr, D. and Johansson, H. (1995). *Best practices in re-engineering*, New York, McGraw-Hill.

54. Hammer, M. and Stanton, S. (1995). *The re-engineering revolution: A handbook*, New York, Harper Collins: 160.

55. Ibid., 158.

56. Bevan (1997); Oblensky, N. (1994). *Practical business re-engineering—Tools and techniques for achieving change*, London, Kogan Page.
57. Mohrman, S. A., and Mohrman, A. M., Jr. (1993). *Organizational Change and Learning*. San Francisco, CA. Jossey-Bass.
58. Mowshowitz (1997).
59. Jaques, E. (1996). *Requisite Organization*. 2nd ed. Arlington, VA. Cason Hall & Co.
60. Bultje and van Wijk (1998).
61. Ibbott, C. J. (2001). *An IS-Enabled Model for the Transformation and Globalisation of Interorganisational and Intercompany Relationships*. Doctor of Business Administration (DBA). Brunel University, UK.

4 Adapting the Requisite Organizational Model

1. The term *requisite organization* means "doing business with efficiency and competitiveness, and the release of human imagination, trust, and satisfaction in work" (Jaques, E. [1996]. *Requisite Organization*. 2nd Edition. Arlington, VA. Cason Hall & Co.).
2. Vodafone AirTouch Listing Particulars Relating to the Issue of Ordinary Shares in Vodafone AirTouch Plc in Connection with the Offer for Mannesmann AG of December 20, 1999. To quote, "The Board expects the benefits of this transaction to generate synergies of approximately £500m on a proportionate after tax cash flow basis in 2003 (with approximately 20 per cent of such synergies coming from increased revenues, 40 per cent from cost savings and 40 per cent from capital expenditure savings) and approximately £600m on a proportionate after tax cash flow basis in 2004 (with approximately 25 per cent of such synergies coming from increased revenues, 40 per cent from cost savings and 35 per cent from capital expenditure savings)."
3. Vodafone Group Press Release, 12 May 2000 "Vodafone AirTouch announces Board Appointments."
4. Investor Relations—Business Review—Global Services for the year ended March 31, 2004.
5. Sander, T., and Lowney, K. (2003) *Social Capital Building Toolkit* (Version 1.0). Saguaro Seminar: Civic Engagement in America, John F. Kennedy School of Government, Harvard University, January 2003.
6. Orlikowski, W. J. (1996). "Improvising Organisational Transformation over Time: A Situated Change Perspective." *Information Systems Research* 7(1): 63–92.
7. Sander and Lowney (2003).
8. Ibid.
9. Ibid.
10. Jaques (1996).
11. Beer, J. (2005). "Tremors Along the Value Chain." *Efficient Purchasing*, premier issue, no.1 (Fall 2005): 18–21.

5 Resetting the Social Capital

1. Schein, E. H. (2004). Organizational Culture and Leadership 3rd Edition, San Francisco, Josey-Bass: p. 93
2. Jaques, E. (1996). *Requisite Organization*. 2nd Edition. Arlington, VA. Cason Hall & Co.

3. http://www.ybmarkets.co.uk/downloads/public/11291_0.pdf.
4. http://www.vodafone.com/start/media_relations/news/group_press_releases/2003/press_release23_06.html.
5. http://www.forbes.com/finance/mktguideapps/personinfo/FromPersonIdPersonTearsheet.jhtml?passedPersonId=865114; emphasis added.
6. http://www.vodafone.com/article_wide/0,3041,CATEGORY_ID%253D403%2526LANGUAGE_ID%253D0%2526CONTENT_ID%253D233998,00.html.
7. http://www.vodafone.com/article_with_thumbnail/0,3038,OPCO%253D40000%2526CATEGORY_ID%253D200%2526MT_ID%253Dpr%2526LANGUAGE_ID%253D0%2526CONTENT_ID%253D244923,00.html.
8. http://www.vodafone.com/assets/files/en/analyst_2004_hydon.pdf.
9. http://www.vodafone.com/assets/files/en/One_Vodafone_Andy_Halford.pdf.
10. Part of Vivendi SA, France's No. 2 mobile telecommunications operator, in which Vodafone has a 44% equity interest (p33). SFR also owns 40.5% of Neuf Cegetel, France's No. 2 fixed-line telecommunications operator. http://www.apropos.sfr.fr/data/master/webfile/170800926846292E4BD872B.pdf.
11. Schein (2004).
12. Jaques (1996).
13. Ibid, p. 18.
14. Based on Sveiby, K. -E., and Simons, R. (2002). "Collaborative Climate and Effectiveness of Knowledge Work—an Empirical Study." *Journal of Knowledge Management* 6(5): 420433.
15. Jaques (1996).
16. Nalebuff, B. J., and Brandenburger, A. M. (1996). *Co-opetition*. London. Profile Books Limited.
17. http://www.vodafone.com/article_with_thumbnail/0,3038,OPCO%253D40000%2526CATEGORY_ID%253D200%2526MT_ID%253Dpr%2526LANGUAGE_ID%253D0%2526CONTENT_ID%253D276178,00.html.
18. http://www.vodafone.com/assets/files/en/vod1245gmprl.pdf.
19. http://business.timesonline.co.uk/article/0,9076–2283260,00.html.
20. http://www.vodafone.com/article_with_thumbnail/0,3038,OPCO%253D40000%2526CATEGORY_ID%253D200%2526MT_ID%253Dpr%2526LANGUAGE_ID%253D0%2526CONTENT_ID%253D285633,00.html.
21. http://www.vodafone.com/article_with_thumbnail/0,3038,OPCO%253D40000%2526CATEGORY_ID%253D200%2526MT_ID%253Dpr%2526LANGUAGE_ID%253D0%2526CONTENT_ID%253D286595,00.html.
22. http://www.vodafone.com/article_with_thumbnail/0,3038,OPCO%253D40000%2526CATEGORY_ID%253D200%2526MT_ID%253Dpr%2526LANGUAGE_ID%253D0%2526CONTENT_ID%253D238960,00.html.
23. http://www.vodafone.com/article_with_thumbnail/0,3038,OPCO%253D40000%2526CATEGORY_ID%253D201%2526MT_ID%253Dpr%2526LANGUAGE_ID%253D0%2526CONTENT_ID%253D290349,00.html.

6   Building Global Relationships

1. Jaques, E. (1996). *Requisite Organization*. 2nd Edition. Arlington, VA. Cason Hall & Co.
2. Orlikowski, W. J. (1996). "Improvising Organisational Transformation over Time: A Situated Change Perspective." *Information Systems Research* 7(1): 63–92.

3. Jaques (1996).
4. Daft, R. L. (2001). *Organisation Theory and Design.* 7th Edition. Cincinnati, OH. South-Western College Publishing: 507; Bass, B. M. (1990). *Bass & Stogdill's Handbook of Leadership: Theory, Research and Manegerial Applications,* 3ʳᵈ ed., New York, New York Free Press; Seltzer, J., and Bass, B. M. (1990) "Transformational Leaderhsip: Beyond Initiation and Consideration", International Journal of Hospitaltiy Management 15, No. 2: p165–176. *Journal of Management,* 16: 693–703; Tracey, J. B. and Hinkin, T. R. (1996). "How Transfornational Leaders Lead in the Hospitaltiy Industry", *International Journal of Hospitality Management,* 15, No. 2: 165–76.
5. Daft (2001).
6. Jaques (1996).
7. Rooke, D., and Torbert, W. R. (2005). "Seven Transformations of Leadership." *Harvard Business Review Reprint* 0504D (April).
8. Nalebuff, B. J., and Brandenburger, A. M. (1996). *Co-opetition.* London. Profile Books Limited.
9. Senge, P., Scharmer, C. O., Jaworski, J., and Flowers, B. S. (2006). *Presence: Exploring Profound Change in People, Society, Organizations, and Society.* London. Nicholas Brealey Publishing.
10. Ibid.
11. Jaques (1996).
12. Faucheux, C. (1997). "How Virtual Organizing Is Transforming Management Science." *Communications of the ACM* 40(9): 50–55.
13. Daft (2001).
14. Nortier F. (1995). "A New Angle on Coping with Change: Managing Transition!" *Journal of Management Development* 11(4): 32–46; Bridges, W. (1986). "Managing organizational transitions", *Organization Dynamics,* Summer 1986: 24–33.
15. Jaques (1996); Rooke and Torbert (2005).
16. Senge et al. (2006).
17. Ibid.
18. Mattias Forsbäck (email: January 11, 2007).

7 Conclusions

1. Inns, D. (1996). *Organisation Development as a Journey.* London. Pitman.
2. Morgan (1996); Grant, D., and Oswick, C. (1996). *Introduction: Getting the Measure of Metaphors.* London. Sage Publications Limited.
3. Orlikowski, W. J., and Hofman, J. D. (1997). "An Improvisational Model for Change Management: The Case of Groupware Technologies." *Sloan Management Review* 38(2): 11–21.
4. Lewin (1951).
5. Bevan, H. (1997). Managing Today While Creating Tomorrow: Actionable Knowledge for Organisational Change in an NHS Hospital. Doctor of Business Administration (DBA). Henley Management College, Henley, UK.
6. Inns (1996).
7. Bevan (1997).
8. Macredie, R. D., and Sandom, C. (1999). "IT-Enabled Change: Evaluating an Improvisational Perspective." *European Journal of Information Systems* 8(4): 247–259.

9. Ibid.; Dawson (1994); Pettigrew and Whipp (1993); Wilson (1992).

10. Orlikowski, W. J. (1996). "Improvising Organisational Transformation over Time: A Situated Change Perspective." *Information Systems Research* 7(1): 63–92.

11. Bevan (1997); Bridges (1995).

12. Nutt, P. C., and Backoff, R. W. (1997). "Facilitating Transformational Change." *Journal of Applied Behavioral Science* 33(4): 490–508.

13. Ibid.

14. Ibid.

15. Trahant, B., Burke, W. W., and Koonce, R. (1997). "12 Principals of Organizational Transformation." *Management Review* 86(8): 17–21.

16. Daft, R. L. (2001). *Organisation Theory and Design*. 7th Edition. Cincinnati, OH. South-Western College Publishing.

17. Ibid.

18. Ibid.

19. Ashkenas, R., Ulrich, D., Jich, T., and Herr, S. (1998). *The Boundaryless Organization*. San Francisco, CA. Jossey-Bass.

20. Ghoshal, S., and Bartlett, C. A. (1998). *The Individualized Corporation: A Fundamentally New Approach to Management*. London. William Heinemann.

21. Ashkenas et al. (1998).

22. Ibid.

23. Kleiner, A. (2001). Elliott Jaques Levels with You. *strategy + business* 22(1st Quarter), Reprint 01109, pp. 1–10.

24. Ring, P. S., and Van de Ven, A. H. (1994). "Developmental Processes of Cooperative Interorganizational Relationships." *Academy of Management Review* 19(1): 90–118.

25. Volkoff, O., Chan, Y. E., and Newson, E. F. P. (1999). "Leading the Development and Implementation of Collaborative Interorganizational Systems." *Information & Management* 35(2): 63–75.

26. Faucheux, C. (1997). "How Virtual Organizing Is Transforming Management Science." *Communications of the ACM* 40(9): 50–55.

27. Mowshowitz, A. (1997). "Virtual Organization." *Communications of the ACM* 40(9): 30–37.

28. Lipparini, A., and Fratocchi, L. (1999). "The Capabilities of the Transnational Firm: Accessing Knowledge and Leveraging Inter-firm Relationships." *European Management Journal* 17(6): 655–667.

29. Wiesenfeld, B. M., Raghuram, S., and Garud, R. (1998). Communication Patterns as Determinants of Organizational Identification in a Virtual Organization. *Journal of Computer Mediated Communications*. http://www. ascusc.org/jcmc/vol1/issue3/steinfld.html

30. Haeckel, S. H., and Nolan, R. L. (1993). "Managing by Wire." *Harvard Business Review* 71(5): 122–132.

31. Benjamin, R. I., and Levinson, E. (1993). "A Framework for Managing IT-Enabled Change." *Sloan Management Review* 34(4): 23–33.

32. Markus, M. L., and Keil, M. (1994). "If We Build It, They Will Come: Designing Information Systems That People Want to Use." *Sloan Management Review* 35(4): 11–25.

33. Yetton et al. (1994).

34. Burn, J., and Barnett, M. (1999). "Communicating for Advantage in the Virtual Organization." *IEEE Transactions on Professional Communication* 42(4): 215–222.

35. Schein, E. (1990). "Organization Culture" *American Psychol.*, Vol. 45 No. 2: 109–119.

36. Tushman, M. L. and O'Reilly III, C. A. (1996). "Ambidextrous Organization: Managing evolutionary and revolutionary change," *California Management Review*, Vol. 38 No. 4: 8–29.

37. Sieber, P., and Griese, J. (1998). "Organizaion virtualness," *Proc. VoNet-Workshop*. Bern, Switzerland: Simowa Verlag

38. Dyer, J. H., Cho, D. S., Chu, W. (1998). "Strategic Supplier Segmentation: The Next 'Best Practice' in Supply Chain Management," *California Management Review*, Vol. 40 No. 2: 37–77.

39. Galbraith, J. R. (1994). *Competing with Flexible Lateral Organizations*. Reading, MA. Addison-Wesley Publishing Company.

40. Ghoshal, S., and Bartlett, C. A. (1996). "Rebuilding Behavioral Context: A Blueprint for Corporate Renewal." *Sloan Management Review* 37(2): 23–36.

41. Ibbott, C. J., and O'Keefe, R. M. (2004). "Trust, Planning and Benefits in a Global Interorganizational System." *Information Systems Journal* 14(2): 131–152.

42. Ibbott, C. J., and O'Keefe, R. M. (2004). "Transforming the Vodafone/Ericsson Relationship." *Long Range Planning* 37(3): 219–237.

43. Beer, J. (2005). "Tremors Along the Value Chain." *Efficient Purchasing* 1(Fall): 18–21.

44. Regarding game theory, see Nalebuff, B. J., and Brandenburger, A. M. (1996). *Co-opetition*. London. Profile Books Ltd.

45. Bartlett and Ghoshal (1998).

46. Ghoshal and Bartlett (1996).

47. An example of just a narrow dimension of national culture and practices is shown in Morrison, T., Conaway, W. A., and Borden, G. A. (1994). *Kiss, Bow, or Shake Hands*. Avon, MA. Adams Media Corporation.

48. Gallivan, M. J., Hofman, J. D., and Orlikowski, W. J. (1994). Implementing Radical Change: Gradual Versus Rapid Pace. *Proceedings of the International Conference on Information Systems 1994* Edit 15: 325–339.

49. Bevan (1997), p. 51; Watson, T. (1995). *Sociology, work and industry*, London, Routledge, p. 65.

50. Bevan (1997), p. 52; Watson (1995), p. 247.

51. Bevan (1997), p. 52; Vince, R., and Broussine, M. (1996). "Paradox, defence and attachment: Accessing and working with emotions and relations underlying organizational change." *Organisational Studies* 17(1): 1–21.

52. Bevan (1997), p. 52; O'Connor, E. (1995). "Paradoxes of participation: textual analysis and organisational change." *Organisational Studies* 16(5): 769–803.

53. Ibbott and O'Keefe (2004). "Trust, Planning and Benefits", pp. 131–152.

54. Jaques (1996).

55. Daft (2001).

56. Rooke and Torbert (2005).

57. Schein (2004).

58. Jaques (1996).

Index

Introductory Note

References such as "178–179" indicate continuous discussion of a topic, whilst "66 ... 69" indicates scattered references to a topic throughout a range of pages. Wherever possible in the case of topics with many references, these have either been divided into sub-topics or the most significant discussion of the topic is indicated by page numbers in bold. Only a small number of key references have been given (indicated by "*(key ref(s). only)*") for topics that are mentioned dozens or hundreds of times without ready breakdown into subheadings.